FDR's Utopian
Arthur Morgan of the TVA

Twentieth-Century America Series
Dewey W. Grantham, General Editor

FDR's Utopian
Arthur Morgan of the TVA

Roy Talbert, Jr.

UNIVERSITY PRESS OF MISSISSIPPI
Jackson & London

Library of Congress Cataloging-in-Publication Data

Talbert, Roy.
  FDR's utopian.

  (Twentieth-century America series)
  Bibliography: p.
  Includes index.
  1. Morgan, Arthur Ernest, 1878-1975.
2. Tennessee Valley Authority.   3. Hydraulic
engineers—United States—Biography.   I. Title.
II. Title: Franklin Delano Roosevelt's utopian.
II. Series.
TC140.M67T35   1987   363.6'092'4   [B]   87-4990
ISBN 0-87805-301-8 (alk. paper)

British Library Cataloguing in Publication data is available.

The paper in this book meets the guidelines for permanence
and durability of the Committee on Production Guidelines
for Book Longevity of the Council on Library Resources.

Photograph of Arthur Morgan courtesy of Antioch College
All other illustrations courtesy of TVA

For my parents,
Roy and Betty Talbert

Contents

Acknowledgments

Beginning in 1966 I had the opportunity to interview Arthur Morgan, and in the years remaining before his death I talked with him extensively. If the following pages show that I have seldom relied solely on his frequently selective memory, knowing him firsthand was a fascinating experience, and I very much appreciate his willingness to be interrogated. Initially my appraisal of him was colored too favorably by the reform tradition that was erupting at about the time we met. In that respect it is fortunate that the vicissitudes of life delayed completion of my study of Morgan for another twenty years. If I still seem in some way biased in my tale, it is not for want of viewing Morgan from different perspectives.

I read Arthur Morgan's biography of the famous Utopian Edward Bellamy at Furman University, and to that institution I am grateful, especially to Francis W. Bonner, Delbert H. Gilpatrick, William E. Leverette, Jr., and John H. Crabtree, Jr. At Vanderbilt University, Henry Lee Swint suggested the topic to me, and Dewey W. Grantham directed my first research paper on Morgan. To them, and to V. Jacque Voegeli and Paul K. Conkin, also of Vanderbilt, I am profoundly thankful. John Thomas of Brown University and Otis L. Graham, Jr., of the University of North Carolina in Chapel Hill read early versions of the manuscript. Their comments were not only extremely helpful, but shamelessly plagiarized. I am also indebted to a cadre of twentieth-century scholars who, with their own fine studies, encouraged me with their growing interest in Arthur Morgan. Richard O. Collin and Glenda Sweet, colleagues at Coastal Carolina, tried valiantly to help me tell this story with some grace. These friends deserve credit for any merit this work may have, and I am responsible for its shortcomings.

The staff at the several libraries consulted were critically important and long suffering. As a professional calling, I hold librarianship among the noblest. Over the years, Ruth Bent of the Olive Kettering Library at Antioch College in Yellow Springs, Ohio, has been a major aid and friend. Similarly, Mary Bull and her reference staff in Kimbel Library at my own institution have proved invaluable.

At the University of South Carolina, President James B. Holderman,

Provost Francis T. Borkowski, Vice-President John J. Duffy, and my own deans, John F. Vrooman and Elizabeth K. Puskar, provided critical financial support from the university's several faculty development programs, without which this work could not have been concluded. I am also particularly thankful for the assistance of my wife, Jane, who is not only a world-class word processor and an excellent analyst of Franklin D. Roosevelt's difficult handwriting, but an uncommon source of inspiration and support.

Introduction

In 1966 I found Arthur Morgan in Yellow Springs, Ohio, in a plain, aging white frame house. He and his wife were quite old, and the house smelled of age, of medicine and mildew. He had given the front over to his nonprofit corporation, Community Service, Inc., for at the age of eighty-eight Morgan was still actively promoting his view of simple, ethical living in small, self-sufficient communities. The tall, slim, and only slightly stooped octogenarian introduced me to his world through a four-mile hike down a beautiful glen. He talked philosophy all the way.

I had come to see him because I knew that he had led a remarkable adventure at Antioch College in the 1920s and that in 1944 Columbia University Press had published his sound, but distinctly admiring, biography of Edward Bellamy, the great Utopian of the Gilded Age. I knew, too, that between Antioch and his series of works on Utopia, Morgan was from 1933 to 1938 the chairman of the board of directors of the Tennessee Valley Authority, reporting directly to that man in the White House, Franklin D. Roosevelt. I was interested in Utopia, and for a graduate degree I aimed to learn if Morgan's role in an important New Deal experiment was in any way related to the idealism he had expressed at Antioch and in his writings on human improvement.

Morgan had at that time been mostly ignored by New Deal historians. For the most part they rejoiced in the New Deal, and it was almost as if they were afraid to look at the bizarre episode involving Morgan, the TVA, and Roosevelt. After World War II they had a New Deal success story in the Authority that had become an international wonder, an absolutely superb demonstration of what the free world was all about. Why tempt fate by focusing on its Utopian midwife? Morgan was thus generally overlooked, except for occasional mention of the extraordinary climax when Roosevelt intervened personally, just before turning to face the archdemon Hitler. The TVA emerged from World War II as one of the best-loved aspects of the New Deal. The popular press never got over being dazzled by it, and for a considerable time the historical establishment was equally awestruck.

This volume pretends to be no technical history of the TVA, and it is difficult to imagine one ever needing to be written. The Authority, with

its numerous missions in electricity production, flood control, navigation, forestry, recreation, economic development, and so forth, is quite
overwhelming. To this day nobody agrees on just what the TVA really
is. It is big and it has a way of coming up with what, if they are not always
new ideas, are at least institutional missions. I accept the agency for what
it has been since 1938: a mammoth federal undertaking with surprising
power, flexibility, and survivability. It kept its magical reputation for at
least as long as Social Security, but eventually both came under criticism, as did the entire liberal edifice begun back in the 1930s.

By the 1980s something had clearly happened. The TVA was under
attack as just another heartless bureaucracy by thousands of consumer
advocates, environmentalists, and the entire antinuclear movement. The
Authority slipped badly in the polls, and with a downward shift in
public opinion regarding this sacrosanct monument to the best of the
New Deal came an upward swing in scholarly attitudes toward Morgan.
No longer dismissing him, historical circles seemed inclined to suggest,
in the privacy of professional discussions, that an analysis of Morgan and
his contributions could offer some new avenue of interpretation, that
Morgan might have represented another approach that somehow could
have avoided the present troubles of the TVA. In focusing on Morgan,
his world view, and the early TVA, I hope to provide some answers to
these questions that have only fairly recently developed regarding Morgan's part of the experiment in the Tennessee Valley. New Deal historiography, to the limited extent it has dealt with Morgan, has pegged him
as a visionary. In the slow process that eventually demanded a reappraisal
of his significance, historical interest in him has always revolved around
the question of his vision. This work attempts to illuminate how Morgan
saw the TVA, the origins of his ideas, and his relationship to Roosevelt,
and in general to respond to requests for a fuller story of Morgan than has
heretofore been available. The Utopian's basic historical importance
rests on the fact that Roosevelt appointed such a man to such a post and
that their connection lasted for as long as it did.

Some explanation is required of the manner in which the term *Utopian*
is used in these pages. I use it loosely. To limit its application only to the
relatively few "Utopian" novels or to the slightly greater number of
"Utopian" communities of the past two hundred years or so would be to
omit unfairly those who, like Morgan, were always on the verge of
coming out. Morgan contemplated Utopia, and he regarded such an
endeavor as the proper function of an enlightened person. I believe that
there is a little Utopianism in all of us, and Morgan's generation frequently had more than its share. He and a surprisingly large group of his

contemporaries embraced the possibility of perfection. They did this in a manner and with an attitude unique to their times, as they had to, and if they seem quite strange to us, they were nevertheless serious about moral reform. They shared a general view of the world that allowed for fantastic optimism in the face of cultural and economic disintegration. Roosevelt himself could sound Utopian, especially when he spoke of the Tennessee Valley.

In this work, I call Morgan both a progressive and a Utopian. I do not believe the terms to be contradictory or exclusive of each other. For all their practical reforms and their serious intent, most progressives had inherited an overweening belief in their ability to change, fundamentally, scientifically, and morally, their world and its people. I call this persistent view Utopian. The progressives were vague and deliberately expansive in their thinking. Caught in the transition from nineteenth-century America to a new and confusing age, part of the energy of Morgan's generation was based on the moral certainty of the old world and part of it was rooted in the scientific sentiments of the new. I suggest in the following pages that in many ways Morgan was an archetypal progressive, and I do believe him to have been such. Still, the term *progressive* is so amorphous that another apology is required. In matters of morality, methodology, prejudice, professionalism, love of efficiency, localism, and conservation, to mention some of the characteristics of progressivism, Morgan represents both its best and its worst. That grand and vague movement was also political, however, and there Morgan fails to qualify. While he recognized the utility of the legislative investigation as a tool for exposing evil, educating the public, and producing desirable social change, Morgan was essentially antipolitical. Not only does this curious position, clearly part of his Utopianism, separate him from most other progressives, but it was also a critical factor in determining his fate. No one has ever claimed that progressivism was monolithic, and with Morgan we have an especially intriguing example of not only most of its aspects but of its slow and painful demise.

Morgan's is a fascinating story that begins before the turn of the century, and his enormously varied life has a number of intriguing aspects to it. When Roosevelt called him to the White House in 1933, Morgan was an important engineer, educator, and moral reformer. His biography is a complex one, and if I ask the reader to delay viewing the historic 1930s until we have freely roamed through Morgan's world, it is only because in all his reform efforts he worked with a unique singleness of purpose, and it is impossible to understand the Arthur Morgan of 1933 without knowing the Morgan of 1913. His pre-TVA years are, moreover, too unusual and interesting to omit, and there is a certain consistency in the broader elements of his thought that can be captivating for those inclined to meditate with him.

It is not my intent to reveal in this introduction the story of what happened to Morgan when he met his historic fate back in the Great Depression. Specialists of the period already know the general plot. To them I offer what I trust are worthy details and a reasonable handling of the evidence. For the general reader, whom I hope to interest and edify, I have attempted to tell Morgan's story in relation to the larger American experience and to present something of the drama that called him to center stage. Having been fascinated by Morgan for so long, I have tried to think of my students as I wrote and to make reading this book as interesting and informative as I could. I trust my academic colleagues will forgive me for moments of informality and that my students will be equally sympathetic with the requirements of scholarship.

FDR's Utopian
Arthur Morgan of the TVA

CHAPTER 1

The Electric City

The story begins in 1893, forty years before the New Deal, at a time when the principal characters have not yet reached manhood. Franklin D. Roosevelt is eleven, well-traveled in Europe, on his way to a first-class education at Groton, Harvard, and Columbia Law School. David E. Lilienthal, the youngest member of the cast, has yet to be conceived; he will not appear until 1899 to begin his brilliant climb to the chairmanship of the Atomic Energy Commission and, with his *TVA: Democracy on the March* to become a great spokesman for modern liberalism. Arthur E. Morgan, the focus of this study, is a lonely, confused, melancholy lad of fifteen. He has no idea where he is going.

The year 1893 serves as a starting point because it is then that Morgan begins a diary, leaving a fairly distinct historical trail.[1] It is also the year we find him in Chicago, come to see its World's Fair, the Columbian Exposition. The young Franklin Roosevelt is there as well. His wealthy and well-connected father was an alternate fair commissioner from the state of New York. The Roosevelt family visited the exposition twice, once to view its construction in 1892 and again after its opening in 1893. For Franklin, it was probably just another trip to another great sight. For Morgan, however, Chicago was to be an opportunity for a face-to-face encounter with the force that will affect his life so greatly and so adversely when his historic moment comes.

Chicago's White City, as the fair came to be called, was the grandest of the American celebrations of the wonders of modern civilization, the show of the 1890s. What a chance for a young man! How dazzled he must have been by it all, the monstrous buildings so Victorian, the tremendous technical marvels, the Grand Canal with its statues and fountains bathed in electric color. Ostensibly the exposition celebrated the four hundred years since Christopher Columbus came to the New World. In a larger sense, however, it signaled the advent of a new age, and if one looks for a particular event to symbolize the emergence of America into

1. Morgan's diaries are in the Arthur E. Morgan Papers, Olive Kettering Library, Antioch College, Yellow Springs, Ohio; subsequently referred to as Morgan Papers. Unless otherwise indicated, the quotations and materials on Morgan's early life come from these diaries.

the twentieth century, the Chicago fair serves mightily well. That, at least, was the meaning of Chicago to Henry Adams, grandson and great-grandson of presidents, whose visit to the White City spurred him to a new interpretation of modern history.

It was Adams who saw at Chicago in 1893 the meaning of the new age, who found the single unifying force that would dominate the next century. Electricity. Not the static electricity that Thales of Miletus knew about in classical Greece six hundred years before Christ, and not the atmospheric electricity that Benjamin Franklin experimented with before the American Revolution. What Adams saw in Chicago was harnessed electricity, harnessed under the control of man, and possessed of unbelievable power. This was the new electricity, inaugurating the electrical age, and it is appropriate to pause a moment and contemplate with Adams the meaning of Chicago in 1893 and those huge, new engines that he, Roosevelt, and Morgan, along with millions of others, saw at the exposition.

In a world that has come to expect electricity as a natural right, one cannot appreciate how startling this thing called electrical power really was. Thomas A. Edison had only just invented the incandescent light-bulb back in 1879, followed by his perfection of the dynamo, the generator that could take mechanical energy and translate it into electrical power. By 1882 the first electric utility, the Edison Electric Illuminating Company, had begun service to all of eighty-five customers in New York City.

Edison started with direct current, which limited severely the range of electrical transmission, but after 1886 when George Westinghouse produced an alternating-current system, the path opened for large-scale production and long-range transmission of electrical power. While steam, gas, or oil could power these dynamos, the best drive by far proved to be water, and it would be powerful water turbines that motored the great hydroelectric plants of the age just dawning.

Chicago vied successfully to host the exposition largely out of a desire to prove that the city had outgrown its rough-and-ready reputation, and its sponsors outdid themselves in building the splendid White City on the southside lakeshore. Because the fair officials had failed to agree on a color scheme, they compromised with various shades of white; hence, White City. Indeed, it must have seemed truly luminous at night when the roving beams of the giant searchlights, to universal amazement, transformed it into a phantasmagoria. It was, in actual fact, the alabaster city of "America the Beautiful."

The first modern world's fair had been Queen Victoria's Crystal Palace back in 1851, and electricity had become an important theme in the numerous fairs that followed. These electrical exhibits grew more sophisticated as the telegraph, the telephone, and the phonograph, in turn, astounded visitors as examples of the power of electricity. International fairs were enormously important in the Victorian period, and each subsequent show offered more fantastic lighting displays. Chicago, however, was the culmination, the great triumph for electricity. For the first time an international exposition gave a separate building to electricity, and in fact all of the exhibits displayed the most glorious of lighting effects. The White City was "all an electrical exhibit," noted one observer. It was the Electric City.

Edison was the natural hero at Chicago, and to him was given center stage in the Electricity Building. There he put his masterpiece, the exhibit that caught everyone's eye: an athenaeum spouting a cylindrical shaft seventy-eight feet high, studded with eighteen thousand incandescent lights. As a whole, one reporter noted, the building rivaled the sun itself in brilliancy. In Paris a few years earlier, the maximum horsepower of any of the electrical engines had been a measly thirty-five hundred, while at Chicago the minimum was twenty-eight thousand. Also at Chicago, Edison unveiled his prototype of a device that recorded both pictures and sound, the forerunner of the moving camera and further evidence of the amazing promise of electricity.

The first really credible electrical exhibit had come two years earlier in Frankfurt, Germany, but by 1893 gigantic advances had been made both in dynamos to generate great power and in sophisticated transmission lines. Overall, the effect of the lighting in the White City was so great as to allow it to be seen miles away, with the claim that under proper conditions the effect could be viewed for a distance of one hundred miles.

And the impact of electricity was everywhere. Those of a more practical nature were surely impressed with the hundreds of electrical gadgets, household appliances of every description operating through the wonder of this new power, including electric cigar lighters, washing and drying machines, irons, dish washers, air conditioners, hair curlers, and even a system to turn off the lights automatically by merely climbing into bed. What demonstrative wonders of the arrival of electricity![2]

2. The *New York Times* gave extensive coverage to the Chicago Columbian Exposition. For electricity, see especially May 9 and 13, and June 2 and 10, 1893. A substantial amount of contemporary material from the fair is extant. Excellent images are in photographic collections such as *Martin's World's Fair Album-Atlas and Family Souvenir* (Chicago: C. Ropp and Sons, 1892); *Official Views of the World's Columbian Exposition* (Chicago: Photo-Gravure Co., 1893); and a reprint of the 1894 J. W. Buel, *The Magic City: A Massive Portfolio of Original*

Henry Adams saw all of these electric marvels in Chicago, and for him the great new generators, the dynamos, became the critical symbol for the new age. Containing huge and mysterious electromagnets, wrapped in glistening copper wire, these machines were the size of a house, and they completely captivated Adams. "One lingered long among the dynamos," he noted, "for they were new, and they gave to history a new phase." Eventually Adams found himself praying to the Dynamo as medieval man had prayed to the Virgin, for he could see "only an absolute *fiat* in electricity as in faith."[3]

Morgan spent ten days at the fair with his father and sister, and, as so often is the case in history, his diary entries contain no wonderful revelations that his teenage eye had caught the staggering implications of what Adams later described. Morgan was nothing more than an average tourist, complaining about how tiring he found all the walking and gawking. Still, one can read into his chronic testimony about poor health (in Chicago it was headaches and a throbbing wisdom tooth) somewhat more than the average aches and pains of a world's fair visitor, for the diary already has suggested Morgan's hypochondria.

One cannot, however, expect this teenager from a small town in Minnesota to be as skilled a cultural analyst as the erudite Adams. He was no different from other visitors, who could be simply ecstatic over an eleven-ton cheese from Ontario and a ton-and-a-half chocolate Venus de Milo from New York. People murmured among themselves about the fair being open on Sunday, and they were downright scandalized by the Middle Eastern exhibits. What sights to electrify an audience! If Little Egypt's belly dance was not as daring as others at the fair, she has survived in American folklore. For those interested in more serious matters, such as the making of American history, the fair was also the site for the World's Congress of Historians, held in conjunction with the American Historical Association. There in Chicago, Frederick Jackson Turner gave his famous Frontier Speech. For his part, Morgan found

---

Photographic Views of the Great World's Fair and Its Treasures of Art, Including a Vivid Representation of the Famous Midway Plaissance (New York: Arno Press, 1974). See also the reprint of Benjamin C. Truman's 1893 *History of the World's Fair: Being a Complete and Authentic Description of the Columbian Exposition from its Inception* (New York: Arno Press, 1976). For recent accounts, see David F. Burg, *Chicago's White City of 1893* (Lexington: University Press of Kentucky, 1976), and Reid Badger, *The Great American Fair: The World's Columbian Exposition and American Culture* (Chicago: Nelson Hall, 1979). For the Roosevelt connection to the fair, see Geoffrey C. Ward, *Before the Trumpet: Young Franklin Roosevelt, 1882–1905* (New York: Harper & Row, Publs., 1985), p. 123.

3. Henry Adams, *The Education of Henry Adams* (New York: Modern Library, 1918), pp. 342, 381.

himself most impressed by the huge telescopes on display, and he was equally thrilled, if one can believe his diary, by viewing the largest load of grain ever to come into Chicago. Apparently his only purchase at the fair was that of a small gold nugget, which Morgan calmly records without giving any indication of where he stood on the greatest issue of the day— the fight between the gold bugs and the silverites over national monetary policy. Already it looks as if he is not overly interested in politics.

This view of Morgan in Chicago provides not the slightest hint that the White City touched him in any profound way. And yet, the entire backdrop for Morgan's historical moment will be painted in the images of electrical power. Perhaps Morgan was so caught up in the agony of adolescence that he simply missed the countless indicators of the nature of the new century that was about to open. The fact that Morgan came to Chicago and failed to see as Adams saw is only of minor interest, to be noted here simply for the fascinating historic nexus that brought the young Morgan before the new electrical god. Electricity, and Morgan's handling of it as a matter of public policy, is the key to his fate. Had Morgan been set afire, as was Adams, by the vision of an electric future, his story might very well have been a different one.

The truth of the matter may be that Morgan never cared much for electricity, and in this regard his apparent lack of interest in 1893 may be suggestive of a frame of mind that would serve him ill in the 1930s. On the other hand, it is also true that Morgan always maintained that his greatest hero was the venerable Edison. At one and the same time, Morgan loved the inventor and missed the salient implications of his discoveries.

Of course, few people were as absorbed as Henry Adams with the dynamo as the proper symbol for the new age. For most, that symbol continued to be the railroad, and one can hardly find a more powerful image in the mind of the nineteenth century. It was the locomotive that took the steam engine to its logical extreme, that annihilated time and space, and that produced the railroad engineer as a hero for the plain folk. It was the train in whose honor huge cathedrals, complete with stained glass and towering spires, were constructed, and that with astonishing ease demonstrated its immense authority by dictating the very way civilized man told time. In 1883 the railroads of the United States and Canada adopted a plan to standardize time based on zones, and without any legal coercion we stopped establishing noon by the overhead position of the sun and switched to consulting the railroad schedule. A technological innovation produced, as it almost always does, a social change. So powerful was the force behind the railroad's need for standard time that no legal basis was considered necessary until 1918, when Congress mandated a time system that had already been accepted for thirty-five years.

But, as Adams saw in 1893, the era of the railroad was approaching its peak, and it was merely a matter of laying a bit more track. The old symbol of progress and power would be replaced by a new one— electricity, not only to power the trains themselves, but to deliver personal energy directly to the people. Even the positive side of the nuclear genie would be discussed in terms of its ability to produce electricity, while the computer age would be essentially electrical in nature. And what a wonderful symbol electricity was, once man domesticated it! Electricity literally gave power to the people, and the age of darkness finally and completely ended.

When the Tennessee Valley Authority and the Rural Electrification Administration brought power to the farms and small towns of an impoverished South in the 1930s, people spoke in terms, not of power, but of light. And when they boasted about "gittin' lites," they meant more than their magical ability to hit a switch and flood a room with brilliance, although in terms of an overarching symbol one need look no further than "light" for the key. They also meant their new electric pumps for indoor plumbing, electric washing machines, electric ranges, electric home freezers, all of the conveniences promised at the White City, and more. They meant an absolute change in their standard of living, a remarkably fundamental revolution in status and thinking. Not only was electricity scientific and industrial, it was democratic. Not only was it a matter of engineering, of rivers, dams, and turbines, but as its impact created an insatiable demand it would become, in addition to very big business, a critically important political issue. Who was to control this vast power, and how was the interest of the people to be protected?

By 1896 most of the White City had been sold to surplus dealers, but Henry Adams continued to visit and study the remains. Morgan, on the other hand, took his gold and went back home to Minnesota. It was to St. Cloud, north of Minneapolis on the Mississippi River, that his family had moved from Ohio shortly after Morgan's birth on June 20, 1878. His father, John Morgan, came from Indiana, and his mother, Anna, from Massachusetts. Together they produced three children, of whom Arthur was the second, between two sisters, and what seems to have been a rather unhappy marriage, even by nineteenth-century standards.

The small town of St. Cloud, not so many years removed from the frontier, had little of which to boast. Its most famous character had been the radical feminist and abolitionist editor Jane Grey Swisshelm, whose subversive activities led the respectable townspeople to dump, unceremoniously no doubt, her printing press into the Mississippi River. A quarrying industry provided jobs for a population that was largely immigrant and Catholic. St. Cloud did have a small normal institute for the training of teachers, which along with the land itself offered what little outlet Morgan could find for his growing curiosity about nature and the nature of right living.[4]

If a case can be made that Morgan's development was affected by the nineteenth-century conflict between religion and science, perhaps it is not too much to suggest that this crisis found expression within Morgan's immediate family. His father was the scientific one. John Morgan called himself an engineer, operated a small business in that field, and won election a number of times as city and county surveyor. If the Morgans were middle class, as the vacation to Chicago suggests, they were not wealthy—partly because John appears to have cared more for tramps in the woods or work in his makeshift chemical laboratory than for tending to his business. Apart from his lack of economic success, John also liked tobacco and alcohol, both characteristics for which neither his wife nor his son ever forgave him. Worst of all, John did not go to church, and when called upon he could make a good case for religious skepticism. The young Arthur viewed his father through the eyes of his mother: as a lazy, drinking, carousing ne'er-do-well.

From his mother, the religious one, Arthur received at least a full measure, and maybe more, of New England Puritanism, which she had translated into the Baptist faith in the hinterland of Minnesota. She was the steady influence in the family, teaching school and taking in boarders to sustain the household. There is little doubt that his mother's influence molded Morgan into a most pious young man, and he drove himself unmercifully to please her.[5]

His youthful diaries reveal an intense effort at self-discipline and a

---

4. The best information on St. Cloud can be found in the Federal Writers' Project, *Minnesota: A State Guide* (New York: Viking Press, 1938), pp. 255–61. See also Theodore C. Blegen, *Minnesota: A History of the State* (Minneapolis: University of Minnesota Press, 1963). Jane Grey Swisshelm's newspaper letters, and an excellent biographical introduction, are in Arthur J. Larsen (ed.), *Crusader and Feminist: Letters of Jane Grey Swisshelm, 1858–1865* (St. Paul: Minnesota Historical Society, 1934). The destruction of her press shifted popular opinion behind Swisshelm, and she was soon back in business. In 1863 she moved to Washington, D.C., where she volunteered as a nurse, worked as a clerk in the war department, and founded another paper, *Reconstructionist*. With the end of the war she retired from public life, living until 1884.

5. This picture of the Morgan family emerges from the diaries of John D. Morgan in the Morgan Papers. See also Lucy Griscom Morgan, *Finding His World: The Story of Arthur E. Morgan* (2nd ed.; Yellow Springs, Ohio: Kahoe and Co., 1928).

constant striving for improvement. In this there was always a hint, often pretty broad, of martyrdom, a feeling that he deserved more for his efforts than he received. More kindness? More attention? More of whatever it was he so desperately missed. He worried frequently about his health, and this concern seems to have been so acute as to suggest some basic emotional problem. Whenever he did poorly at school, for example, he invariably explained it away by noting in his diary: "Am not feeling well."

Years later a psychologist at Antioch College reviewed these diaries and concluded that Morgan's insomnia, general sickliness, and weariness may have been unconsciously magnified "to excuse himself at times from having to meet his mother's perfectionist standards."[6] Physical limitations may very well have been the only alibi his demanding mother would accept. At any rate, for the rest of his life he resorted to this familiar defense mechanism whenever he ran into difficulty. The greater his problem, the poorer his health.

Having few friends, Morgan spent much of his adolescence alone, either reading or out in the woods collecting botanical samples. A knack for finding unusual specimens was the one extraordinary achievement of his youth. He became recognized as something of a local expert who could identify all sorts of plants and flowers. His efforts as a naturalist won him further reward when he began sending articles to *Popular Science News*. The diary entry for January 29, 1896, notes that he had received a copy of that magazine with two of his contributions in it. His pieces must have been very short, for the issue contains nothing with his name on it. But he kept sending articles, and a year later the editors gave him a by-line—making him a published author at age eighteen. One of his most revealing pieces came in 1901, when he was twenty-three, with a theme about nature's search for equilibrium, which he termed "a great co-operative commonwealth where every plant and animal shall be helpful to the whole and none shall be necessarily destructive."[7]

Each year, in the back of his diary, Morgan faithfully recorded his self-directed reading. In 1893 he read, besides works on botany and some children's stories, a biography of Emanuel Swedenborg, William Rounseville Alger's *The Genius of Solitude*, John William Draper's *A History of the*

6. Clarence Leuba, *A Road to Creativity, Arthur Morgan: Engineer, Educator, Administrator* (North Quincy, Mass.: Christopher Publishing House, 1971). Very helpful on the psychological point of view.

7. Arthur E. Morgan, "The Smallest Flowering Plant," *Popular Science News* 31 (December 1897), 271; "Why Few Harmful Animals and Plants," *ibid.*, 35 (December 1901), 283.

Conflict between Religion and Science, and Edward Bellamy's *Looking Backward*.[8] These books represent heavy reading for a boy of fifteen, and it is impossible to know precisely what influence they had on the young Morgan, although an introduction to Swedenborg's brand of spiritualism might be strange at any age. Alger's work probably reinforced Morgan's natural inclination toward solitude, and it also may have aided him in his determination to be "dead to the world." The work by Draper, while not as famous as Andrew White's on the same subject, dealt with a problem with which Morgan grappled on a personal, family level. It would be several years before he found his own answer to the conflict between religion and science, when he forced a curious combination of the two.

The diary reveals no immediate impact made by *Looking Backward*, but that Utopian novel about a man who wakes up in the year 2000 certainly had some influence on Morgan, because one of the first things he did after his TVA experience was to write a biography of Bellamy, and a fairly sympathetic one at that. The reading for 1893 is typical of the sort of material into which Morgan immersed himself, though he later drifted into the ancient classics as well as the great English and American works of the nineteenth century, while continuing his scientific study.

When Morgan was graduated from the St. Cloud high school, which went only to the eleventh grade, he had achieved a modicum of personal development as well as the beginnings of a personal philosophy. Committed to the scientific inquiry of his father as well as to the moralism of his mother, he was attempting to combine the search for truth with the honest, hard-working, pious, and successful life his mother demanded for him. "And taking the natural law as my guide," he said as he concluded his 1896 diary, "I will try to advance during the coming year, or during such part of it as I am here."

Despite that characteristic fatalism, Morgan was in fact physically and mentally energetic, and he had become a sensitive observer of nature and society. He already recognized himself as a daydreamer, though that was one habit he never tried to change; indeed, his favorite pastime when not collecting lichens and other specimens was speculating about how to improve the world, both physically and socially. He also developed a remarkably intense sense of mission, for his own self-improvement and

8. William Rounseville Alger, *The Solitudes of Nature and of Man: or, The Loneliness of Human Life* (Boston: Roberts Brothers, 1869); the title on the cover is *The Genius of Solitude*; John William Draper, *A History of the Conflict between Religion and Science* (New York: D. Appleton and Co., 1874); Edward Bellamy, *Looking Backward, 2000–1887* (Boston: Ticknor and Co., 1888). Morgan's diaries from 1893 to 1897 have a list of books read by him. The Morgan Papers also contain a handmade booklet entitled "Books I Have Read," compiled about 1897.

for the rest of society. But he still had no idea of just what he was going to do with his life.

So he went west. With a few dollars in his pocket and his worldly possessions in a small bundle, he struck out on foot to work his way to Colorado, where he had relatives. When he reached Denver in the late fall of 1897, much of the feverish excitement was over and the Wild West had become more civilized. Butch Cassidy and his Hole-in-the-Wall Gang had only a few more years to operate in this country, and the last of the old-style outlaws would be gone. The era of the great gold and silver rushes had ended with the big fields at Cripple Creek in the early 1890s. By the time Morgan reached Central City, it boasted a concert hall and the Teller House, one of the great frontier hotels, and when his curiosity overcame his rigid morality long enough for him to enter one of the town's casinos, he found it "quiet and orderly."[9]

Earning money primarily as a logger, Morgan decided to enter college. Apparently the officials at the University of Colorado in Boulder found his St. Cloud credentials not to their liking and required him to enroll in preparatory school. He never completed the semester, offering his now well-worn excuse of poor health . . . this from a young man who claimed to have cut seventy-five logs in one day. His indecision continued after he quit school in December. He complained that he was sick, that his brain was confused, and that he missed having close friends.

What seems significant here, especially in light of the remarkable career that follows, is that Morgan had very little formal schooling. Except for another and equally futile attempt at college the next year, Morgan never received any advanced training. If one can fairly easily dismiss, as the University of Colorado did, the public school system of St. Cloud in the 1890s, Morgan was to a very large extent self-educated.

But what of romance? Surely not even the most unusual teenager can develop without at least once being smitten. Morgan met Lois Foster at a Colorado mission school on a Sunday afternoon, and from the beginning his relationship with her was tied to a new emphasis on piety. He went to Lois's church, fundamental and enthusiastic, and soon he found himself at the altar, after which he wrote, "I believe that I have given up any selfish motive that I have had. . . ." He began teaching Sunday School, and shortly thereafter he and Lois became engaged.

This youth's problems were not to be ended with the love of a good

9. Muriel Sibell Wolle, *Stampede to Timberlane: The Ghost Towns and Mining Camps of Colorado* (Boulder: Muriel S. Wolle, 1949), conveys the flavor of Central City and other mining towns in an era just ending when Morgan reached Colorado. The Morgan diaries for 1898 and 1899 cover his experiences in Colorado.

woman, for such Lois can be presumed to have been. The old feelings
.hat he was ill, that he could not bear the demands of work, that his mind
could not handle his problems, continued to haunt him. "Oh, for the
ability to stand apart," he wrote, "and look at myself so that I might
judge the path that is best." Uncertainty plagued him: "My head gets
muddled and my ideals and ambitions get all covered up under the stress
of present work." Soon after the engagement, Morgan developed a
common condition known as cold feet. Maybe Lois was not the woman
for him. She seemed terribly dependent on her mother, Morgan projected, and she lacked what he called "sound judgment," a failing that he
could by now easily identify in others.

Fortunately, a man came to Boulder whose advice Morgan trusted—
Dr. John B. DeMotte, author of *The Secret of Character Building*.[10] Apparently Demotte, of whom history seems to remember little, was in town
on a lecture tour. His book, the only hard evidence available on him,
maintained that character had a physical basis, that repeated actions,
good or evil, actually created channels in the brain. After a period of time
these channels became fixed and thus determined behavior. Morgan
loved this combination of morality and biophysics, and so enthusiastic
was he that he secured an appointment with the good doctor for advice
on Lois, education, and career prospects. However absurd DeMotte's
theories may have been, Morgan genuinely liked him: "Never met a man
whose face showed a purer life or a truer." DeMotte, for his part, seems
to have offered warm encouragement to the troubled young man, including advising him to carry through with the marriage to Lois.

Despite his appreciation of the doctor's advice, Morgan decided
against marriage, and with summer's end he broke it off. The relationship
with Lois, however, was responsible for a renewal of Morgan's dedication
to lead a Christian life. He resumed his pious search for purity: "tried to
act like a Christian today and to keep my health in the best condition and
to look at people charitably [*sic*]. . . . My endeavor to make progress has
. . . consisted in an instinctive attempt to be a Christian and a gentleman. . . . Tried to be a nobleman and a Christian, but nearly failed in
both."

Back in March 1898, he and Lois had read together *The Christian's Secret
of a Happy Life*.[11] This book, by Hannah Whitall Smith, attempted to
combine the doctrine of salvation by faith with that of salvation by

10. John B. DeMotte, *The Secret of Character Building* (Chicago: S. C. Griggs and Co.,
1893).
11. Hannah Whitall Smith, *The Christian's Secret of a Happy Life* (Chicago: F. H. Revell,
1883), p. 24.

works—with a strong touch of perfectionism. Smith had the idea that total faith in God removed the inclination to sin and guaranteed good works, thereby allowing the Christian to fulfill his duty to be holy as Jesus was holy. "We are to be delivered from the power of sin," she wrote, "and are to be made perfect in every good work to do the will of God."

Morgan wanted to believe this; he wanted to be holy, but he was so aware of his own deficiencies that he knew he could never achieve perfection. He created a sort of Benjamin Franklin checklist for himself to see if each day he had acted as a Christian gentleman should. Although his efforts at self-discipline were far more successful than Franklin's, he never stopped condemning himself for his failures. In maintaining such standards, Morgan also had high expectations of others, and he developed a hair-trigger judgment based on firm stereotypes.

Hannah Smith portrayed the Christian's constant battle with Satan, the eternal Tempter and enemy of the Christian. Morgan, however, in his search for purity, was fighting his own weakness, not the temptations of Satan. This put his piety on a personal level, and made it easy for him to move from a concentration on religion to ethics, but before he finally broke with the church and embraced philosophy he made this last effort to believe.

The year before, Morgan had read a book that seems to have had a great influence on his life—or perhaps it expressed ideas he had formulated independently. Charles M. Sheldon's *In His Steps*, published in 1896 and read by Morgan in 1898, became one of the standard works of the Social Gospel, and its popularity continued well into the twentieth century.[12] *In His Steps*, loaded with the heavy sentimentality of the Gilded Age, confused Jesus with Paul (a mistake common to many Christians) and saw the world and this life as evil. The meaning of the ministry was nearly lost among strictures against tobacco and alcohol, but the book did oppose the institutional church in that it placed the responsibility for a Christian life on the individual, not on the acceptance of a creed. Sheldon wrote of a group of church members who agreed to make every decision of their lives based on "what would Christ do?" Such an idea doubtless appealed to Morgan, who told himself that he had made the same decision with his own life—he was willing to make a personal commitment, even if it involved great hardship, to live on a higher plane.

Despite his comparative isolation in the West, Morgan shared much of the prevailing national climate of opinion. As an essentially self-educated man, he enthusiastically read the works of Charles Darwin and Herbert

12. Charles M. Sheldon, *In His Steps* (Chicago: Advance Publishing Co., 1896).

Spencer and accepted the theory of evolution and much of Social Darwinism. Biological analogies abound in his diaries and journals. He thought Thomas H. Huxley a genius, and survival of the fittest became a byword for him. He believed that the race was improved by physical hardships and necessity. He used the term *race* as loosely as most people of his time to mean whatever is implied by Nordic, Teutonic, Anglo-Saxon, or Anglo-American, and he believed this group to be the standard-bearers of civilization. Most educated Americans, of course, quite agreed with Morgan on this point.

The idea of a racial heritage and evolution led Morgan to a deep concern, which remained with him, about heredity. He bemoaned what he saw as the declining birthrate of the educated, warning that they had a responsibility to have children because "we are leaving all the scum and trash of the country to be parents of the next generation."[13] Such statements appear frequently in his private writings, and they clearly reflect his elitism. Morgan also accepted the theory of the inheritability of acquired characteristics—even blaming his nervousness on his father's use of tobacco. This subject was of major concern to Morgan, related as it was to his fears about his health. Because his failures were physical, and because he had inherited that condition, his lack of success was not his fault. "I find limitations in me," he complained, "that I have not caused and that must be because of the sins of others."[14]

Morgan's feelings were part of the hereditarian attitude finding increased expression by the turn of the century. Like many others, he had growing fears about the racial quality of immigrants, and he felt that criminals, paupers, and the insane should not be imposed upon posterity. In his mind he carried a picture of the United States declining because the proper people were outnumbered. When Morgan developed these thoughts, which would stay with him for the next quarter of a century, the term *eugenics* had only recently been coined by Francis Galton in 1883. Morgan probably was not acquainted with it then, but he would be a charter member of the American Eugenics Society, and while he was chairman of the board of TVA he would be asked to serve as president of that group.[15]

In Colorado, Morgan made one personal decision that would have great bearing on his future. Just like the characters of *In His Steps*, he

13. This quotation comes from one of two notebooks that Morgan began in Colorado and wrote in occasionally for the next several years. The entry above is dated April 30, 1900. Hereinafter cited as Morgan Journal. Morgan Papers.

14. *Ibid.*

15. Chapter three contains additional material and references on eugenics.

vowed not to take any job that did not contribute to the general good: "Unless my work results somehow in a conservation or increase of life—in its broadest sense—I am a beggar."[16] He noted, for example, that it would be impossible for him to work in a store that sold alcohol. He wrote his mother, "No job is important enough to hold at the cost of any sacrifice of Christian principle."[17] Such a decision severely limited the kinds of employment opportunities Morgan might find, and indeed he never did locate a permanent position in Colorado, though he tried his hand at a number of enterprises, including selling fresh vegetables and good books to miners, both noble and abject failures.

There was little reason for Morgan to believe that his sojourn in Colorado had been worthwhile. He had not been able to get a formal education, nor had he found a career. In many ways he knew as little about what he wanted to do as when he left Minnesota. On the other hand, he had formulated some principles by which he would lead his life, and he had developed an optimistic feeling about the natural harmony of the universe and the possibility for human progress.

The Arthur Morgan who returned to St. Cloud in the summer of 1900 was not the same tortured boy who had departed three years earlier. He was now twenty-two years old, six feet two and quite slim, and the photographs of him show a healthy vitality. One in particular, taken shortly after his return in 1900, when he had a temporary job as a timber cruiser, depicts him decked out in a heavy-weather outfit, the closest he ever came to looking handsome and dashing. While he continued, most of the time, to look as somber as Calvin Coolidge, he felt stronger and more confident, no longer spending an inordinate amount of time worrying about his health. He had also outgrown that oversized concern for living a pious and holy life, although his acute self-awareness about what he would do with that life continued. While he still lapsed into occasional spells of depression, by and large he had come to believe in the existence of the answers he sought and even in the possibility of their discovery.

The Colorado experience also seemed to have crystallized for Morgan a commitment against religious ideology, and he finally came to recognize that dogmatism was shared by both the fundamentalist and the atheist. With this conviction his religious habits changed, and the impact of the church lessened. After Colorado he lost his faith in a clearly defined supernatural, but he replaced it with an equally firm belief in the

16. Morgan Journal, June 18, 1900.
17. Morgan to Mother, March 17, 1900, Morgan Papers. In *Finding His World*, p. 39, his wife says Morgan once quit a job in a sawmill because the lumber was to be used for a gambling house.

existence of perfection and purity. "I am waiting for revelation—if revelation is real," he wrote in 1901, "but I am waiting to know that I may deny revelation if revelation is not real. I am waiting for that to happen to me which will happen to the man who waits for the eternal."[18]

Morgan developed a kind of transcendental identification with eternity, with whatever was real and pure. When he rejected traditional religious dogma, he created one of his own: he believed in purity, or, rather, he intuited the possibility of purity. Like any good dogmatist, Morgan never understood that his reliance on intuition was just as irrational as any other faith. Right out of the nineteenth century, straight from antebellum New England, that faith was drastically out of step with the scientific approach of the young century that he and the country faced. In other ways, however, he was as scientific as any man of his time; it was not for nothing that he climbed the glaciers of Colorado to find a rare lichen for shipment to eastern universities, and in his later life as the country's premier hydraulic engineer, the gathering of data became something of a fetish for him.

Morgan always continued, however, to use intuition as his basis for the appraisal of the nature of men, and perhaps that habit was his greatest weakness. If he intuited that someone was unworthy, he became incapable of reaching any compromise at all; he simply rejected that individual. When he did that with his fellow members on the TVA board, he created a dramatic situation—for himself, politically.

Although Morgan came out of this religious jumble with a position of agnosticism about the supernatural, he always maintained that the life of Jesus provided a proper model for right-thinking people. The teachings of Jesus, he felt, were not to be accepted on faith, but because they withstood critical examination; those were perfect principles for life, in fact, the only sane and really practical way of living. "Christ," he said, "is the far off point to be reached by human evolution—the use of the divine that is in us."[19]

Religion and science combined in Morgan, a child of the Social Gospel, to produce a moral reformism, a kind of perfectionism buttressed by the scientific method, Christian Socialism for a technological society. By this time he prided himself on having a scientific attitude: "My life has been lived in possession of the scientific temperament," he wrote in his journal in 1901. Possessing that, he convinced himself that he accepted nothing on faith, that he perceived a "general system of the

18. Morgan Journal, May 13, 1901.
19. *Ibid.*, February 16, 1901.

universe" into which every fact and principle must fit in order to be held valid. This appreciation of unity and the whole came, he wrote, through his study of biology. "Since then, all studies are branches of biology."[20]

The neatness and efficiency of socialism probably appealed to Morgan's sense of balance and unity. By early 1901 he had come to see socialism as the most logical economic system: "I have been finding myself for the last two years more and more inclining toward socialism. It seems right to me that cooperation of production should succeed the present system of competition. It seems devilish for competition to live *much* longer." He clipped from a newspaper a socialist platform calling for the outrageous ideas of nationalization of industry, social security, women's rights, and peace, commenting: "As a whole, and as far as it goes, I think it is good, and most of these demands will doubtless be granted. . . ." After reading *Equality*, Edward Bellamy's sequel to *Looking Backward*, he called it "a great book—great in its dreams. Let all the people read it."[21]

As the twentieth century opened, Arthur Morgan was a young man with a large social conscience coupled with missionary zeal. His years of self-criticism and castigation had developed a sound personal character, but he tended to be as demanding of others as he was of himself. He had decided opinions, particularly about morality, right and wrong, the ethical and the unethical. He had built considerable confidence in himself and felt that in time he would find his place. Viewing Morgan as a perfectionist of the nineteeth century brings to mind earlier reformers: Theodore Weld, abolitionist; Brigham Young, Mormon leader; Sylvester Graham, health food enthusiast; John Humphrey Noyes, Christian communist of Oneida. The influence of these men was ending when Morgan was born; they, and scores of others, were involved in the social upheaval of the mid-nineteenth century. That time had ended, but Morgan stood in its tradition and that tradition was a part of him, even as the country moved into the twentieth century.

This look at Morgan's youth cannot be complete without some attempt to place him in the perspective of his times. His generation was roughly that of 1880 to 1920, and when one delves into the intellectual history and biography of that period, in order to put Morgan into some context, he no longer looks unique. A hundred years later Morgan's soul-searching concern for purity, his moralism, somehow combined with a genuinely scientific bent, make him seem quite bizarre. However, the forces that

20. *Ibid.*

21. *Ibid.*, no date, probably the winter of 1901–1902. Edward Bellamy, *Equality* (New York: D. Appleton and Co., 1897).

affected him were at work on others, and when he is viewed with them he seems more understandable. In our time of triumphant moral relativism, one can easily fall into the trap of judging Morgan by current standards. His world was chockfull of moral absolutes. As Henry F. May has noted, the national credo might very well have been "the reality, certainty, and eternity of moral values"—until World War I, not to mention Freud and Einstein, blasted them into meaninglessness.[22] For all their talk about science, most people of Morgan's time were strict moralists, and a value-free world view would have seemed not only impossible but unthinkable.

Lest it be considered odd that Morgan fought so hard for his physical development or that he made the sternest of judgments about what he would and would not do with his life, Otis L. Graham, Jr., reminds us of any number of people from this generation who took on personal adventures, often alone as did Morgan, and who had a firm vision of their life purpose.[23] This turn-of-the-century crowd could be as mystical and as broadly reformist as any of their antebellum forebears. It is simply a fact that when they embraced science with a naïve nineteenth-century enthusiasm, they never relinquished their moralism.

What a great turbulent decade was the 1890s, particularly after the Panic of '93 and the ensuing depression. The socialists were organizing, and the term Christian Socialism had a specific, and not particularly terrifying or contradictory, meaning. The farmers were profoundly mad at the world, and at the eastern establishment in particular. Turmoil characterized the political scene. While the return of prosperity after 1896 forestalled disaster and put a Republican back in the White House, the decade spawned many like Morgan: self-educated half-geniuses driven by their attempts to reconcile religion with science. They moved easily into the just emerging professions, which then allowed virtually unchallenged entry, dreaming of universal reform through the force of their moral will and technical skill.

One thinks of Theodore Roosevelt, who put himself to physical trials similar to Morgan's. Or of Henry A. Wallace (1888–1965), a general reformer, usually regarded as something of a mystic, who triumphed in the New Deal, becoming Franklin D. Roosevelt's vice-president in the third term and for many his logical successor as liberal leader. This generation also had its share of fascinating and strange women. Consider Mary "Yellin' " Lease (1853–1933), that outrageous Populist orator who

22. Henry F. May, *The End of American Innocence: A Study of the First Years of Our Own Times, 1912–1917* (Chicago: Quadrangle Paperbacks, 1959), p. 9.

23. Otis L. Graham, Jr., *An Encore for Reform: The Old Progressives and the New Deal* (New York: Oxford University Press, 1967), pp. 47–48.

is alleged to have advised Kansas farmers to raise less corn and more hell.[24]

Her other causes are just as interesting: her hatred for the British as well as for the gold standard, her break with orthodox religion and conversion to theosophy, her work for woman's suffrage, prohibition, evolution, birth control, and the first Roosevelt. Her conflicts and her contradictions are just as fascinating as Morgan's, and it is delightful to learn that she too was at the Chicago Exposition in 1893, representing the state of Kansas, which had just fallen to her Populists. Most striking, however, is the book she produced in 1895 with the classic nineteenth-century title: *The Problem of Civilization Solved.* Here she proposed, among other things, that white planters should take over what we now call the Third World and somehow use black and yellow "tillers of the soil" to solve the problems of food producton, overpopulation, war, and it goes without saying, the abolition of poverty on this terrestrial globe.

Or take Raymond Robins (1873–1954), a veritable gold mine of comparisons with Morgan. He too went to Colorado as a youth, where his work in the mines made him a Populist and a "single-tax" man. He took a law degree, had a profound religious experience, sojourned in Alaska, where he made a fortune in gold, only to use much of his treasure as a settlement worker in the slums of Chicago. Active in reform politics, he was sent to Russia in 1917 by President Woodrow Wilson as part of our effort to keep the Kerensky government in power and in the war just before the Bolsheviks took over. He also organized cooperatives among citrus growers in Florida, fought for recognition of the Soviet Union, and urged Herbert Hoover to deal forcefully with the depression. His internal conflicts, which seem somewhat similar to Morgan's, led to a nervous breakdown in the 1930s. Before his death he became a socialist, and he gave his large Florida estate over to conservation and scientific experimentation.[25]

The list could go on, but this brief one serves to demonstrate that Morgan can be comfortably placed in the context of *fin de siècle* and early twentieth-century reform. Moralists all, they abound in the next chap-

24. The latest statement on the study of Wallace is Richard S. Kirkendall's essay on him in Otis L. Graham, Jr., and Megan Robinson Wander (eds.), *Franklin D. Roosevelt: His Life and Times, An Encyclopedic View* (Boston: G. K. Hall and Co., 1985), pp. 441–43. Lacking a biography of Mary Elizabeth Lease, see the articles on her in the *Dictionary of American Biography*, Supplement One (New York: Charles Scribner's Sons, 1944), pp. 488–89, and *Notable American Women, 1607–1950: A Biographical Dictionary* (Cambridge: Belkap Press, 1971), II, 380–81.

25. Raymond Robins is also described in the *Dictionary of American Biography*, sup. five (1977), pp. 578–80.

ter, occupying even the White House. Some, like Morgan, lingered well into the twentieth century, but the fundamental impulse of their generation was stopped dead in its tracks by the dual blows of the Great War and the reaction against Bolshevism.

If such a widening of focus makes Morgan appear less bizarre, it is nevertheless true that one of the strangest things about him was that he continued the methods and vocabulary of this ended era of moral reform, continued them all the way to the New Deal. That he was a generation behind the times seems never to have occurred to him, and he judged the New Deal and the Tennessee Valley Authority as he had learned to do in the 1890s. One suspects, therefore, that adaptation to changing world views, to use a biological analogy he would have appreciated, was emotionally and philosophically impossible for Morgan.

CHAPTER 2

Progressive Success

S hortly after the opening of the new century Morgan settled
down and began a career. Starting as a ditch-digger for his
father, within little more than a decade he became this
country's most prominent hydraulic engineer. More than that, he
achieved substantial recognition in a number of areas, all aspects of an age
that has come to be called the Progressive Era. Upon reviewing the
several dimensions of his life from 1900 to 1920, it may very well be that
Morgan can be called a model progressive, for he demonstrated a great
many of the era's characteristics.

John Morgan taught his son to shoot elevations with a transit and to lay
lines for ditches and levees, and that was about all the training Arthur
Morgan got when he made the fortuitous decision to become a hydraulic
engineer—one who controls the movement of water. Later he was to
claim that he analyzed the job market and discovered that the drainage of
wetlands was a new field in which a young man without any formal
credentials might get established. It may be that he simply found nothing better to do with his life than to go to work for his father.

Morgan always did have a knack for looking back and assigning
purpose to what may have been the luck of the draw, and it is interesting
that he never gave his father any credit for his later success. One of his
better books, fifty years away, was entitled *Search for Purpose*. In terms of
his avowed purpose to go about doing good, one must agree that his
engineering profession was clearly morally acceptable. He was a man
who made poor land productive, a wonderful thing for a progressive.

However he came to his career, Morgan certainly entered the market at
the right time. The drainage business had been developing since the late
1880s, and after the turn of the century it fairly boomed as the progressives stressed both conservation and land reclamation. From 1900 to 1904
there were some seven million acres in organized drainage enterprises in
the United States, and in the next four years that figure jumped to more
than eighteen million. Morgan was right in the middle of that dramatic
growth.[1]

---

1. George W. Pickels, *Drainage and Flood-Control Engineering* (New York: McGraw-Hill
Book Co., Inc., 1941), p. 7.

Now that the western frontier was no longer boundless, the need for land required that areas once considered unsuitable, land bypassed in the country's development because it was low and wet, be drained and rendered useful through reclamation. The efficient progressives set about draining wetlands in such places as the vast Mississippi Valley and the low country of the southeastern coast. To the progressive mind, such activities were part and parcel of the conservation mentality. While certain natural areas were to be preserved in their pristine beauty, particularly under Theodore Roosevelt, other "wastelands" were to be "improved."

Here a major difference must be noted between reclamation and latter-day environmentalism. The modern environmentalist opposes destruction of natural habitats, while drainage enthusiasts meant to correct nature's "flaws." Bays, swamps, bogs, and marshes by the thousands perished, and numerous species were doubtlessly endangered, as a result of the progressives' love of productivity and their concomitant hatred of waste.

In his early work as an engineer, Morgan constructed ditches for drainage and levees for flood control in eastern Minnesota, making investigations and preparing engineering plans for the reclamation of large peat marshes. He got his training on the job, and in 1905 his father's retirement gave him control of the family business, small though it was. With drive and ambition, Morgan established himself in St. Cloud as a young professional with good prospects, and his business began to grow. He stopped writing in his diary, making only intermittent journal entries, and while the record we have of him is fairly faint during these years, the business correspondence and newspaper reports of his projects all reflect early success.

In 1904 he celebrated his new stability by marrying the young, intelligent, and beautiful Urania Jones, who had come to town with her family two years earlier. She was a physician of osteopathic persuasion, having studied under Dr. Andrew Taylor Still, the founder of an approach to medicine that stressed disturbances in the musculoskeletal system. Her historical image is barely perceptible, but she seems to have had a great calming effect on Morgan, and her osteopathic principles must have appealed to him. No doubt he appreciated the concept that the body had an inherent capacity for disease resistance and repair. He similarly approved of her reluctance to prescribe drugs as well as her belief that the body's organs enjoyed a kind of reciprocal relationship. Osteopathy fit nicely with his concern for wholeness and unity, and it probably made wonderful sense to him. A son, Ernest, was born in 1905, and judging by the absence of expressions of pain in his skimpy journal, this was a satisfying, perhaps even happy, time for Morgan and his young family.

Meanwhile, Morgan continued to advance his career. In 1905 his father's professional association, the Minnesota Engineers and Surveyors Society, placed the older Morgan on a statewide committee to recommend revisions in Minnesota's drainage laws. Arthur Morgan had already scrutinized these antiquated statutes and felt that they needed considerable changing to enable modern drainage efforts to move apace. The basic legal problem involved standardizing various codes and requirements to allow a drainage program to cut through multiple jurisdictions. One could not drain a swamp, for example, if it straddled two or more counties or edged into the poor side of an incoprorated area—not when the several legal entities had inconsistent and contradictory construction codes and ordinances. Rivers and their systems, Morgan understood in his holistic fashion, must be treated as a unit, and the political process had to be realigned and brought in tune with nature. It did not work any other way.

Morgan, precisely because of his concern for what he called the whole, found it relatively easy to accomplish this mental reorientation. Seeing the big picture was almost a natural ability for him, and he also became skilled at suggesting legislative revisions. He did all the work for his father on the Minnesota committee, handled a large correspondence, and he lobbied for political support for his proposals. He got the endorsement of the Engineers Society and the following year pushed his bill through the state legislature. Soon he was secretary-treasurer of the society and editor of its annual publication.[2]

In the midst of this early success, a tragedy: his wife died, perishing of typhoid fever in the late fall of 1905, leaving Morgan with an infant son. Now the agony returned, his lonely thoughts once more appearing in long journal entries addressed to his son.

After the death of Urania he threw himself into his work with even greater intensity. In 1906 various pressure groups scheduled a National Drainage Congress in Oklahoma City for purposes of creating political unity and gaining federal dollars. Like so many other lobbies, the drainage proponents wanted government subsidies based on receipts from the sale of federal lands. Morgan used his new influence to secure an appointment as Minnesota's representative to the Oklahoma meeting, and he had high hopes for the future of drainage. The conclave bogged down in political intrigue and soon collapsed, to be replaced by a better-

2. *Saint Paul Pioneer Press*, Jan. 26, 1905, and Jan. 19, 1906.

organized group in the southern Mississippi Valley. This area presently became the focus of the drainage movement, and later Morgan would locate there himself.

Before moving his business to Tennessee, however, Morgan accepted a job with the United States Department of Agriculture. As early as 1901, in response to demands from the drainage industry, Congress had created an Office of Drainage Investigations within the Department of Agriculture as a means of providing direct technical aid on large drainage programs. Local money had to pay for the actual construction of the drainage systems, but the government provided free analysis and planning. Morgan, a bright young engineer making the proper contacts, seems to have been recruited by Drainage Investigations, and his appointment shows no hint of patronage or favoritism.

Leaving his son with Morgan's own parents, the widower moved to Washington, D.C., in 1907. The capital was then the intellectual center of the broadly defined conservation movement, reaching its peak under Theodore Roosevelt and his faithful adviser, Gifford Pinchot. An important group of people, much like Morgan, in the Department of Agriculture, the Smithsonian Institution, and the Geological Survey, was not only busy analyzing the fantastic amount of natural and anthropological data on the continent so recently conquered, but its members were doing so from a moral and religious base very similar to his. That group set the tone for conservation, and it was the first to note the importance of seeing the country's river basins as unified systems.[3]

Morgan would have found a congenial home with these fellow scientific moralists, but the truth of the matter is that he was in Washington only for brief periods. Most of the time he was out in the boondocks, riding through swamps on horseback, living in the field, running crews, and drafting drainage plans. Morgan and his colleagues in Drainage Investigations responded to requests for assistance, either from state governments or from what appear to have been informal, self-appointed committees of local boosters. Part of Drainage Investigations' work

3. Samuel P. Hays, *Conservation and the Gospel of Efficiency: The Progressive Conservation Movement, 1890–1920* (Cambridge, Mass.: Harvard University Press, 1959). Michael James Lacey has examined the intellectual framework of the most important conservationists in his "The Mysteries of Earth-Making Dissolve: A Study of Washington's Intellectual Community and the Origins of American Environmentalism in the late Nineteenth Century" (Ph.D. diss., George Washington University, 1979). Lacey's conservationists seem remarkably like Morgan. Not only did they stray widely from their technical fields in their analyses, but they stressed creativity, social engineering, and character development in writings filled with Utopian images. Lacey also spotted the "moral and religious impulses which . . . underpin their . . . science of humanity" (p. 349).

involved encouraging economic development through land reclamation, and their reports were official documents carrying the imprint of the federal government regarding the drainage prospects for a given area. As such, the reports heavily influenced local financing for a project and could make or break the real estate market, depending on the nature of the official evaluation. If one were attempting to sell land under water, nothing was more to be desired than to have the U.S. government approve one's plans to drain the property.

Morgan became one of the government's top field engineers, and during the winter of 1908 he directed in eastern Missouri and Arkansas a very large design project for the St. Francis River basin, which he conducted with his headquarters in Jonesboro, Arkansas.[4] Given this level of success for someone with absolutely no formal training in engineering, a word on Morgan's preparation, style, and methodology may be worthwhile. Morgan appears to have been a genuine example of practical education, and this must be remembered when he later organizes his own college under the cardinal principle that real-world experience is esssential for proper education. He knew his success had not come from the classroom.

Addicted to reading, he seems to have consumed engineering texts, but there is no evidence of any great aptitude in mathematics. It may be that Morgan moved so quickly to the managerial ranks that he was never required to demonstrate strong technical skills, and he may not have had many. Almost certainly his staff handled the detailed work, and Morgan habitually went to great pains to seek out and hire exceptional people. While it is certainly true that his holier-than-thou attitude alienated some, it is more impressive that he could inspire a high level of confidence—almost devotion—from the people who stayed with him. After about 1912, he was always surrounded by disciples.

Having had his ticket punched at the federal level, with the professional credentials thus implied, and with substantial contacts in private business, Morgan made the obvious move—he left government service and entered the market, which was eager to implement just the sort of

---

4. Arthur E. Morgan, assisted by O. G. Baxter, *Report on the St. Francis Valley Drainage Project in Northeastern Arkansas* (Washington: U.S. Government Printing Office, 1911). Other engineering works by Morgan include *A Preliminary Report on the St. Francis Valley Drainage Project in Northeastern Arkansas* (Washington: GPO, 1909); Morgan and S. H. McCrory, *Preliminary Report upon the Drainage of the Lands Overflowed by the North and Middle Forks of the Forked Deer River and the Rutherford Fork of the Obion Riber in Gibson County, Tennessee* (Nashville: no pub., 1910); Morgan, McCrory, and L. L. Hidinger, *A Preliminary Report on the Drainage of the Fifth Louisiana Levee District* (Washington: GPO, 1911). All available in the Morgan Papers.

drainage schemes he had been promoting. The money was in the contracts to construct the drainage systems, and from his government work
he knew precisely where the action was. In 1910 he opened his own
engineering firm in Memphis, Tennessee, as the senior partner with
another former government engineer. Shortly thereafter he received
admission into the American Society of Civil Engineers as an associate
member, "realizing what began as a very faint hope years ago and has
become a serious desire." Professional certification was now his, and the
Morgan Engineering Company, with Morgan as president, became a
financial success. His projects ran from Tennessee to Louisiana, along
the Mississippi River; they involved constructing miles of canals for
drainage and lengthy levees for flood control, as well as dams and
bridges.[5]

Not surprisingly, his years in the field had begun to tell on him. The
malaria he contracted in the swamps could be easily diagnosed by his
physician, but there remained that old malaise that seemed to defy
treatment. The doctor suggested that he remarry, and there was something almost methodical about his courtship of Lucy Griscom.

He found Lucy teaching chemistry and home economics at Wellesley
College in Massachusetts. Although she was as plain as Urania had been
beautiful, she was to have a tremendous influence on his life and its
direction. Not much over five feet tall, she was given to wearing frumpy
frocks, wide-brimmed hats, and plain black pumps, and it was the simple
and wholesome life that she loved.

(More than fifty years later this writer will join the Morgans at their
table for lunch, and conversation will progress as if Lucy, now near
death, is not present. She will be hunched over a bowl of honest vegetable
stew, slurping from a large spoon grasped in a childlike fist. I will
compliment the housekeeper on the delicious wheat rolls, mentioning
that Miss Lucy had toiled vigorously to demonstrate the utility of whole
grains to the mountaineers of Tennessee. "And why did she do that?" the
housekeeper will ask in an innocent attempt to keep the conversation
going. "She said it was good for you," I will reply equally innocently, not
looking at Lucy, who seems almost comatose except for the steady
movement of her spoon. "It is, you know!" she will suddenly gasp from
somewhere behind that spoon. Those are the only words I will ever hear

5. Arthur Morgan diary, May 7, 1910. For a concise statement of Morgan's work while in
Memphis, see "Statement of Engineering Practice of Arthur E. Morgan," and "Arthur E.
Morgan, Record of Experience," Morgan Papers. Information on Morgan's partner in
Memphis can be found in *Leroy Lemayne Hidinger, M. ASCE, 1879–1951,* a memoir prepared
by Garver W. Miller, printed privately, Morgan Papers.

from her, for she slumps back over her bowl, and in a year she will be dead. Still, in that one simple statement will be revealed something of the force of her life, something of the dedication, the determination she brought to her marriage with the often uncertain Arthur.)

Women graduates in home economics back in the Progressive Era, and especially those from Wellesley, were taking the lead in settlement work and other reforms, and Lucy might very well have wound up in a similar line had her reforming impulse not found expression in her husband's career. She was a Quaker to boot, connected to the famous Biddles of Philadelphia, and as a nutrition expert she could be righteous in her assertion of the necessity of a proper diet and efficient, moral living. Morgan's own righteousness, dormant while he drained his swamps, received a shot in the arm from Lucy's staunch Quaker Godliness and Wellesley superiority.

The Morgans took up residence in Memphis, a fascinating city blending the progressivism of Mayor Edward H. Crump with a reputation as one of the most wicked places in the country. Apparently uninvolved in any of the civic reforms, and certainly without dabbling in the sin, Morgan became a respected member of the business establishment, having come so far from his youthful socialism as to find his commerical colleagues "a remarkably fine set of men."[6]

He seems to have regained happiness in Memphis, where he formed associations that kept his mind tuned to intellectual and social problems. For discussions of such matters he met regularly with "The Egyptians," a group of prominent business and professional men. Bolton Smith, founder of the group and Morgan's close friend, a Memphis banker though not a native Southerner, was something of a liberal in Memphis, particularly in race relations. Liberalism on race in that time and place meant primarily opposition to lynching. Political and social equality were matters best left unaddressed.[7]

In Memphis, Morgan joined, for a brief time, the Unitarian Church, whose intellectualism made loose demands on him in terms of super-

---

6. Arthur Morgan diary, April 6, 1914. For a description of Memphis during Morgan's stay there, see William D. Miller, *Memphis During the Progressive Era, 1900–1917* (Memphis: Memphis State University Press and the American History Research Center, 1957). In 1909 Morgan, in Memphis as a government engineer, recorded: "Went to vaudeville show in the eve. Which fact I am ashamed to record." Morgan diary, Feb. 21, 1909.

7. See Bolton Smith's letter to the editor, "Memphis Lynching," *New Republic* 12 (Aug. 11, 1917), 51. In the Morgan Papers there are two privately printed pamphlets by Smith: *Some Mississippi Valley Problems* (Memphis, 1918) and *The Importance of a Philosophy Dealing with the Relations of the Negroes and Whites in the Country* (Memphis, 1919). A speech by him,

natural commitments. He never could make a public profession of faith, however, and eventually he drifted into an unofficial, but close, relationship with Lucy's liberal branch of the Society of Friends.

We face now the question of what it meant, in a year like 1912, to be a progressive. Important as it is to understanding Morgan, this task is formidable indeed because of the amorphous nature of progressivism. The term *progressive* here is used in its American sense, different from the more leftist European meaning. Furthermore, progressivism cannot be limited to the Progressive party, which Theodore Roosevelt formed in 1912 in an ill-fated attempt to regain the presidency. He bolted the GOP to lead his own party, and by splitting the vote he threw the election to the Democrat Woodrow Wilson, forever confounding history students required to define progressivism.

Here, progressivism also means more than Wilson and his administration. It means Roosevelt, and Wilson, and their time. Progressivism refers to nothing less general than the dominant charcteristics of the American scene from Roosevelt's ascension to the presidency upon William McKinley's assassination in September 1901, until the outbreak of World War I. Progressivism is used to mean the climate of opinion that enveloped that period. All the crusades of the progressives were moral, one way or another, and it is in his moralism, as well as his engineering, that Morgan seems an archetypal progressive. Moral reform goes back at least to the seventeenth century, with peaks now and again, and the Progressive Era is a respectable high point on that historical curve.

The emphasis on moralism and ethical considerations that pervades Morgan's writings, even his business letters, makes him seem stilted, stern, and colorless, but all progressives wrote that way, none more so than President Wilson himself, who spoke the language of moralism constantly. When Wilson said in 1913, referrring to foreign policy, "Morality and not expediency is the thing that must guide us," Morgan and his generation understood precisely. If not quite as morally outraged as their abolitionist antecedents, they were still committed, and the moral foundation for their view of the world was essentially Utopian, perfectionist, and religious. Moralism, then, permeated every individual

---

"A Philosophy of Race Relations," is printed in the *Congressional Record* 59 (Dec. 20, 1919), 963–69. In his obituary Smith is called "in politics as well as economics an ardent liberal, believing in the League of Nations and in the application of the Christian gospel to the problems of the social order." "Bolton Smith Dies, Friend of Scouts," *Christian Century* 52 (April 24, 1935), 555.

reform activity, and it appears to have been a distinctly Yankee Protestant moralism. The image of New England as a sort of cultural base for the progressives sometimes looms inescapably. Morgan and his fellow progressives constantly exhibited their Puritan strain, and for his part Morgan loved New England, the land of his mother.

Because, no doubt, of their political and economic reforms, it is easy to overlook the harsher side of progressive moralism. Prohibition, for example, was not simply a sad mistake best forgotten. It was a grand achievement of progressivism. The constitutional amendment did not come until 1919, it is true, and World War I was instrumental, but by then huge sections of the country were already dry. Prohibition was, in fact, a progressive attempt to legislate morality, a quite appropriate one from Morgan's point of view. A sort of paternalism, even authoritarianism, based on that bedrock of moral certainty, encompassed all of progressivism.

A rational, moral order seemed quite possible to the progressives, far more possible to them than to Americans today. Government could be put on an efficient, honest basis, just as corrupt businessmen could be converted back to the genius of free enterprise. They hated bribe-taking politicians and price-fixing "trusts" for the same reasons, and because both business and the public sphere were in desperate need of reform, the progressives set about to do it fairly, openly, respectably, and entirely within the legitimate process. If they never really came to grips with the reality of large-scale economic concentrations or the fuller implications of democracy, they achieved substantial, specific political reforms, most of them on the local level. Whether they were a generation of climbers or one reacting against perceived threats (and maybe they were both), they worked away at remaking their world. Morgan was ambitious and aggressive in his career in a world that he considered fundamentally endangered by copulating immigrants and other inferiors who, in their ignorance, were about to overrun his culture with their backward progeny.

With their faith in process, *the* process, progressives seem almost ritualistic in the manner of their reforms. Time after time, evil, inefficiency, and failures of civic duty were exposed and driven from the temple through the combined efforts of a free press and a public-minded citizenry. This process occurred at every level. Progressive officials armed themselves not only with the sword of righteousness, but with a staff of young, committed research assistants. Muckraking journalists and even editors thirsting for sensationalism were tolerated precisely because of the dirt they delivered. The duality of legislative investigations and news scoops became a trademark of the Progressive Era, one in which Morgan had the greatest confidence. The open, legitimate process would carry the day.

The progressives also look solidly middle-class and WASPish, though one can say the same thing of many of their enemies. But this was an aggressive middle class, and if they were fighting for survival they hoped to win by imposing their values on, and thus elevating, the filthy masses. From the time the non-Teutonic hordes of southern and eastern Europe had begun their descent on America in the 1880s, the masses had grown so indecent as to constitute a clear and present danger to the progresssive vision. These people had to be uplifted, educated, oriented, melted, and reformed from a threat into an asset.

There was an elitism in the progressives' uplift, their outreach, and their concept of social justice. There was also, and not just among the progressives but throughout society, racism, religious bigotry, xenophobia, and paranoia, the flames of which were fanned by pseudo-scientific concoctions and spurious speculations about the lesser races, the feebleminded, the poor, the criminal, the different. If many of the progressives' political reforms, such as the direct election of senators, the initiative and the recall, and the ballot itself were democratic, they were also designed to put the right kind of men into office. Literacy as a requirement for voting made absolutely good sense to progressives.

The influence of Social Darwinism, which pushed the Protestant ethic to new extremes, made it a matter of being socially fit—a matter of the fit managing—for their own good, to be sure—the unfit. Their elitism, moreover, had the force of law behind it. We see their nativism legalized with the final restrictions on immigration in the early 1920s, another legacy of the progressives.

They also regarded themselves as professionals in a new kind of way, in the modern sense. This can be seen beginning back in the late 1880s with the formation of a large crop of professional associations, and by 1912 the professionals had come of age. They organized, communicated, studied, planned, lobbied, set standards, devised tests and codes of ethical practice and technical uniformity. They regulated both admission into and the standards of countless professions. They loved efficiency passionately and gave us the efficiency expert, time and motion studies, and the assembly line. Bad government was inefficient, and so were profiteers, as was waste—waste of land, resources, public trust, the squandering of humanity. Inefficiency became so intolerable for the progressive mind that it seemed immoral.

In the same way, progressives hated intoxication, the absence of sexual restraint, poverty, ignorance, selfishness, impure food and drugs, all an immoral and disgustingly inefficient waste. It was the heyday of the home economics expert. With the development of their vast network of organizations, soon to bring them the franchise (a third progressive legacy), women were a powerful force in the Progressive Era. If Morgan's mother was characteristic of the Gilded Age middle-class lady, both his wives represented important aspects of the progressive woman.

Progressive is such a vague term that it came to be applied to any forward-looking agent of reform. Engineering, like so many other professions, had its progressive element. Morgan became just such a progressive engineer, part of a group of young men who wanted not only to unify their profession but to have it take an active role in social reform. Indeed, progressive engineers saw their profession and themselves as the logical leaders in the fight for a new civilization.

Edwin T. Layton, Jr., in his fascinating *The Revolt of the Engineers*, cites Morgan as one of the progressives urging his profession to take up the burden of social responsibility. Many engineers felt as Morgan did, and there was widespread discussion of ideals that at times sounded fully Utopian. It seemed obvious to them that as society headed for Armageddon, their technical elite would assume a larger responsibility and save civilization through their enlightened, scientific, and moral leadership.

Like many other progressives, these engineers harked back to the older, simpler life, and they envisioned a society destroyed by class warfare and moral irresponsibility. Despite the fact that they shared common traditions and values with other progressives, the engineers differed from them in one important aspect. Engineers, by their very profession, were linked to the big businesses that employed them. Tied to the corporate world, they expected to reform it from within and, eventually, to inherit control.

Progressive engineers such as Frederick Haynes Newell, founder and initial director of the Reclamation Service, could be blunt about the degree of social control required to forestall disaster. Here technical elitism was linked to conservation, a term that the progressives used in an extremely broad sense. Newell believed people could be organized mechanically, and it was the engineers who would undertake "the beneficial control of human forces and sentiments." For Newell, conservation was a moral effort, and the engineers' altruism would lead civilization to new heights.

The great-godfather in the drive for efficiency and the elimination of waste was Frederick W. Taylor, the founder of scientific management. Taylorism was applied to areas more indefinite than the assembly line, and the concept was so profoundly embraced by progressive engineers that they postulated the possibility of establishing a scientific basis for ethics. Scudder Klyce, like Morgan an engineer and moral philosopher, was so enthused by Taylor that he predicted a "complete and comprehensive standard of ethics." Taylorism became a new gospel preached with religious intensity, clothed in the language of morality.

This curious stage in the development of engineering did not long survive the Progressive Era. Soon formal collegiate training became the standard requirement for entry into the profession, and the emphasis on scientific ethics ended with the dominance of value-free science. Morgan himself left the engineering profession for all practical purposes after 1920, when he began new crusades, but he and some others retained the progressive aspects of engineering, including the propensity to assume a moral and scientific advantage over other people.[8]

Morgan was, then, a progressive—a moral, middle-class professional committed to universal reform. This attitude was exemplified in Memphis when Morgan learned of an injustice that seemed to him to threaten his professional credibility. He heard a call to action that quickened his progressive sense of moral indignation and public duty. He personally engaged evil, and his triumph once and for all cemented in him the assumptions and strategies of progressivism.

In early 1912 Morgan received word that his former superior in Drainge Investigations, Charles Elliott, had been summarily fired from his position. The official reason for the dismissal was related to some minor irregularity in the transfer of funds at the end of the budget year. As Elliott reminded Morgan, however, the real cause of his ouster was nothing less than a plot on the part of vicious land speculators out to swindle a gullible public. Some years earlier, during his days in the office of Drainage Investigations, Morgan had uncovered a scheme to produce a phony report on the easy possibilities of draining the Florida Everglades, a fraud engineered by land companies with the aid of one of Morgan's fellow officials. With Elliott away at the time, Morgan had on his own held up the publication of that report, and upon his return Elliott had concurred with Morgan's action. When he left government service, Morgan assumed that the Everglades affair had ended.

Now the barbarians were at the gate again, and Elliott's head was

8. This discussion of progressive engineers, including the quotations from Newell and Klyce, comes from an excellent study by Edwin T. Layton, Jr., *The Revolt of the Engineers: Social Responsibility and the American Engineering Profession* (Cleveland: The Press of Case Western Reserve University, 1971). Layton places Morgan firmly in the tradition of morality.

forfeit. The case was an irresistible one for Morgan, involving real estate swindlers, dishonest public employees, and corrupt politicians. With Morgan in private life, the conspirators had managed to secure Elliott's dismissal and had proceeded to resurrect the felonious report, which purported to prove the suitability of the Everglades for drainage. They were busily selling "land by the quart." Because Elliott had upheld his original recommendation to suppress the patently false report, Morgan easily saw his moral duty to set the record straight.

First, he wrote the U.S. secretary of agriculture, but the speculators had so entrenched themselves politically that no satisfactory action resulted. The typically progressive route, which Morgan then took, was to go public through the twin avenues of the press and the Congress. He exposed the entire sham before a Memphis press conference, possibly his first, and he zipped off a letter to his professional journal, *Engineering News*. He also wrote U.S. Rep. Frank Clark, a Florida Democrat.

This was the process of progressivism, and it produced instant action. The *New York Times* became exercised, and the House Committee on Expenditures in the Department of Agriculture decided to investigate the dismissal of Elliott and, upon Clark's urging, the whole question of the drainage of the Everglades. In the meantime formal charges against Elliott for "transference of public funds on false vouchers" were taken to a grand jury in the District of Columbia. Having already lost his job, Elliott was now subject to a fine of five thousand dollars and imprisonment for five years.

Morgan testified before the congressional committee for three days in February 1912. He seems to have made a good impression despite the opposition's attempts to find irregularities in his own reports and vouchers. The hearings were like most of that breed, long and tedious, and they continued until August, when Congress adjourned. The final verdict had been obvious for some time; Elliott was cleared, his dismissal criticized as "over-discipline," and the indictment quashed.

So the outcome was dramatic. Elliott was exonerated, and the evil government engineers were punished for conniving with speculators. Truth and justice prevailed, and the progressive belief in the efficacy of committees, investigations, and data gathering was justified, while the evils of land speculation were exposed and honest public servants were restored to office. Morgan believed in all of this, and it put his moral commitment into overdrive, for now he had hard evidence that a man of character could take a risk for the right, speak out publicly against injustice, and win.

To be sure, this was only a minor scandal, and there were others far more important that made it into the history texts as crises of the Progressive Era, yet the Everglades fight must stand as a model victory for the progressives. The sides were clear-cut, wrongs were made right, and the proper instruments (an enlightened private citizen, a free press, and a governmental investigating panel) were used. Morgan would never forget this time, nor this process, when progressivism was on the march.[9]

In Memphis, Morgan could very well have remained a successful businessman, and his marriage to Lucy must rank as one of the reasons he did not continue solely as an engineer. She came with a reforming heritage of her own, and she seems to have rekindled the vision of Morgan's youth. Together they dreamed of nothing less than establishing their own ideal community, which would serve as a model for the rest of society. They got their chance when they moved to Dayton, Ohio, where he would build the country's largest flood control project of the time, and where they would find an environment more suitable for a new moral order.

In the nineteenth century, ten major floods occurred in the Miami Valley, a fertile section of southern Ohio, with Dayton as the center. While an average of one flood per decade apparently was not sufficient to warrant the creation of a flood prevention system, the great flood of 1913 sufficed. On the morning of March 23, the waters of the Miami, Stillwater, and Mad rivers poured over their banks and flooded through Dayton. With ten feet of water in the main section of the city and additional problems of heavy snow and major fires, the final cost totaled

9. "Does the Punishment Fit the Crime?" *Engineering News* 67 (Feb. 22, 1912), 359–60. See Marjory Stoneman Douglas, *The Everglades. River of Grass* (New York: Rinehart and Co., Inc., 1947), p. 324; "Draining the Everglades," *Literary Digest* 64 (Feb. 17, 1912), 327; and *New York Times*, Feb. 12, 1912. An example of the advertising of the land companies is in the *Nashville American*, Nov. 28, 1909. See also Morgan to James Wilson, Jan. 29, 1912, and Morgan to Frank Clark, Feb. 7, 1912, Morgan Papers. The record of the hearings is in U.S. House of Representatives, Committee on Expenditures in the Department of Agriculture, *Everglades of Florida, Hearings before the Committee on Expenditures in the Department of Agriculture* (Washington: GPO, 1912). The report that Morgan and Elliott suppressed is J. O. Wright, "Report on the Drainage of the Everglades of Florida," in *Everglades of Florida: Acts, Reports, and other Papers, State and National, Relating to the Everglades of the State of Florida and Their Reclamation*, Senate document no. 82, 62nd Cong. 1st sess., 1911. The hearings were followed in the *New York Times* and the *Memphis Commercial Appeal* throughout February 1912, after which they were overshadowed by Theodore Roosevelt's entry into the presidential race. There is an exchange of letters between Mr. and Mrs. Charles G. Elliott and Morgan in the Morgan Papers and in the P. K. Yonge Library of Florida History, University of Florida Libraries, Gainesville, Florida.

more than three hundred lives and more than $100 million in property damage.

The reaction in Dayton was similar to that in Galveston, Texas, when in 1900 that city, having barely survived a hurricane, demonstrated a rare public spirit that resulted in an innovation in city government. In Dayton the response was immediate and equally innovative. The National Cash Register Company, on high ground and possessing its own power plant and water supply, became the center of rescue and relief operations. Shortly thereafter Edward A. Deeds, vice-president of NCR, became chairman of the flood prevention committee, which, on the rising crest of unity from a common disaster, raised two million dollars for a flood control program.

War chest in hand, the committee in May 1913 began a search for a chief engineer. Very quickly its members decided on Arthur Morgan in Memphis. Morgan dropped all his other projects, moved immediately to Dayton, and in fact may have treated his partner rather cavalierly, cutting him out of the picture altogether. With an excellent staff, he began a systematic collection of data on the flood in Dayton, floods in general, and flood control methods in this country and in Europe.

In a matter of months he submitted his preliminary plan calling for the creation of "conservancy districts," special-purpose agencies autonomous from city and county laws governing the construction of levees, canals, sewers, bridges, and other works neccessary for a complete, large-scale flood control effort. The Ohio legislature passed the enabling bill with dispatch, and Governor James M. Cox, a native of Dayton, signed it into law on February 7, 1914. The actual implementation went slowly at first because of opposition from towns north of Dayton that were fearful of excessive costs, did not want to lose their land to reservoirs, and were in general suspicious of dams—people still remembered the disastrous dam failure at Johnstown, Pennsylvania, in 1889. The flood prevention committee mounted a propaganda effort of its own, and in 1915 the Miami Conservancy District became a reality.

Morgan's first ideas on flood control for the Miami Valley went along the conventional lines of river channel improvement, but upon investigation he determined that a series of five dry, earthen dams and retarding basins would provide the greatest protection. The system he built still functions today, and these dams look like gigantic Indian mounds located in steep valleys, waiting to be used for storing floodwaters. At each of the five dams there is a granite block bearing this inscription: "The dams of the Miami Conservancy District are for flood prevention purposes. Their use for power development or for storage would be a menace to the cities below." Here is yet another indication of Morgan's attitude toward electricity. What presuppositions, if any, lay behind that cryptic comment linking electric power and menace? For all the technical truth the statement may have contained, it sounds judgmental, even defiant, in rejecting electrical power.

The use of dams to store water only during periods of actual flood, Morgan's engineers claimed, added to their safety and stability. "The thought of dams without water behind them," he wrote, "offended some people's intuitions of propriety. . . ." One of his first requests as chief engineer was that the board of directors secure a panel of consulting engineers to check his work: a typically responsible, professional gesture. Dry dams, as they were called, represented a new concept in this country, and Morgan was the first to put the principle into operation. After a flood in Pittsburgh in 1907, a study had recommended seventeen such reservoirs, but nothing had come of it. It was Morgan who ran with the idea, and subsequent evaluations of his design and construction of the widely hailed Miami system have been uniformly positive.

Morgan saw the Miami project as a social endeavor as well as an engineering enterprise, and he wanted to improve the men who would build the dams. In addition to specially designed bunkhouses that went far beyond the usual makeshift arrangements, his progressive engineer's characteristic sense of social responsibility led him to build small houses for workers with families. There is little doubt that he wanted to create a community, not just a shantytown. He even added an educational component, with day schools for children as well as night classes where immigrants could learn English, technical skills, and, not least, values. The workers also enjoyed a program of health and accident insurance and were encouraged to develop their own quasi government through community associations. Model communities appeared at each of the work sites, along with newspapers, recreational programs, and town meetings. Reform, both technical and social, was the order of the day, and no other major construction project could boast such enlightened leadership. Morgan was making his mark.

One of the most interesting features of the Miami Conservancy resulted from the large work force, which included numerous craft labor unions. While there was a tradition of unionism in urban construction, there were no precedents for such a huge program as the Miami Conservancy. Morgan, progressive engineer that he was, wanted to avoid the wasteful jurisdictional difficulties that could result from negotiations with so many separate unions. He developed a single labor code for the entire conservancy: a simple statement that guaranteed an open shop and union recognition by craft with collective bargaining. After an early and brief strike by two unions, the code remained in full force and encountered no other major labor problems. Morgan would later use the same approach to labor at the TVA.[10]

In Dayton, Morgan and Lucy began to find other ways to implement their reform ideas and to further their desire for an ideal community. Like other progressives, they loved the simplicity, the naturalness, and the interrelatedness of small-town life, a life they perceived as endangered. Influenced by Herbert Spencer's theory of the social organism, many progressives stressed the intellectual and moral validity of the organic community, which functioned harmoniously as a whole unit. Morgan shared this ideal with other progressives who wanted to restore the face-to-face communication of the small towns from which they had sprung.

In this sense, and for all his admiration for Edward Bellamy, Morgan seems less a Utopian and more a progressive communitarian who desired a simple, honest, self-supportive small community. These ideas were in vogue during the progressive period, after which they fell rapidly from favor as being nothing more than nostalgia for a lost age. But Morgan never changed, and after his experience with the Tennessee Valley Authority he gave most of the rest of his life to the cause of the small community.[11]

10. Arthur E. Morgan, *The Miami Conservancy District* (New York: McGraw Hill, 1951), is the best history of this significant engineering project. Other important sources are Arthur E. Morgan, *The Miami Valley and the 1913 Flood*, pt. 1 of the Miami Conservancy District's *Technical Reports* (Dayton: no pub., 1917), and Carl Bock, *History of the Miami Flood Control Project*, pt. 2 of *Technical Reports*. See also Morgan and Bock, "A History of Flood Control in Ohio," Ohio Archeological and Historical Society *Publications* 34 (1925), 474–503, and Morgan, "Building Up an Engineering Organization—with Special Reference to the Selection of Men," *Engineering News Record* 79 (Sept. 20, 1917), 552–53. Evaluations of the Miami project have been extremely favorable: "Present Status of Flood-Prevention Studies in Dayton," *Engineering Record* 69 (March 28, 1914), 356; Harold K. Barrows, *Floods: Their Hydrology and Control* (New York: McGraw Hill, 1948); Luna B. Leopold and Thomas Maddox, *The Flood Control Controversy: Big Dams, Little Dams, and Land Management* (New York: Ronald Press, 1954); and William G. Hoyt and Walter B. Langbein, *Floods* (Princeton, N.J.: Princeton University Press, 1955).

11. Jean B. Quandt, *From the Small Town to the Great Community: The Social Thought of Progressive Intellectuals* (New Brunswick, N.J.: Rutgers University Press, 1970). While Morgan is not included in this work, the nine progressives it studies are remarkably like him in terms of moralism, "the whole," and community mindedness. Quandt also notes that "their personal history suggests that the Protestant code of duty left a permanent imprint on their thinking, but that the conversion experience either eluded them or was rejected in favor of a purely ethical Christianity" (p. 11), much the same process Morgan endured. David E. Shi, in *The Simple Life: Plain Living and High Thinking in American Culture* (New York: Oxford University Press, 1985), places Morgan in the context of that tradition.

Soon after moving north from Memphis, the Morgans decided to put into effect a plan they had considered for some time. With a family of five (Ernest, from his first marriage, had rejoined him, and Lucy had borne a son and a daughter), they wanted a place that could serve as a permanent base throughout the frequent moves required by Morgan's profession. "We had also decided," wrote Lucy, "to start a school somewhere. . . ."[12] Their home and their school were to be the basis for their ideal community.

Morgan found a location for Utopia just as he developed plans for flood control. The site should, he and Lucy felt, be near a lake in the mountains, with farmland surrounded by wild country, all in a brisk climate. Instinctively looking to the Northeast, Morgan obtained maps of New England and made a list of areas that appeared to have the desired qualities. For more concrete data he sent, on bicycle, one of his young engineers, who reported on the sites selected so scientifically by Morgan.

At last they located and bought four hundred acres on Shaw Pond near Lee, Massachusetts. The house and three barns lent themselves to the founding of a school-community where the students would do a good deal of work. The rocks in the road leading to the proposed community reminded them of an Old Testament story and provided the name "Jacob's Pillow." For a variety of reasons, primarily a lack of time, their plans for this community never materialized. Otis Caldwell, director of the Lincoln School at Teachers College in New York, rented the place for a while, and eventually Morgan sold it to Edwin M. "Ted" Shawn, who developed it into the Jacob's Pillow Dance Festival. This became a leading center for instruction in and performance of the dance.[13]

Unsuccessful with Jacob's Pillow, Morgan moved to another reform idea that also was receiving serious consideration in the late progressive period—the attempt to establish a League of Nations. While Morgan's role in the development of the idea of a league and the fight to get it was a fairly minor one, it represents an interesting study of the movement on the state level. In the United States, the chief source of support for a league was an organization called the League to Enforce Peace, founded in 1915 by Hamilton Holt, editor of the *Independent* and a leader of the New York Peace Society, along with Theodore Marburg, minister to Belgium during the Taft administration. Taft himself served as honorary president of the League to Enforce Peace, and that league's campaign touched every state and collected nearly a million dollars.

12. Lucy Morgan, *Finding His World*, p. 97.
13. Morgan to Lloyd Marcus, Sept. 19, 1947, and Otis Caldwell to Morgan, Sept. 17, 1919, Morgan Papers. The story of Jacob's Pillow is in *Finding His World*, pp. 96–98.

When the Ohio branch was organized in 1916, Morgan became its secretary and gave the address at the initial meeting. Eventually he served on the National Executive Committee, along with his friend from Memphis, Bolton Smith. Traveling to Washington in May for his national installation, Morgan and Lucy joined two thousand others for a banquet at the Willard Hotel, later the temporary headquarters of the Tennessee Valley Authority, to hear President Wilson make his first public commitment to the idea of a League of Nations.

Back in Ohio, the league encountered a good deal of suspicion, especially after the United States entered the war in 1917. Some people had difficulty believing that the league stood for peace, not pacifism or a sellout to the Germans. Morgan eventually was forced to curtail his local activities for the league when the directors of the Miami Conservancy felt his connection "with some peace or pacifist movement" was endangering the progress of the conservancy. There was even talk of expelling him from the Dayton Engineers Club for his "German tendencies."[14]

Despite his setback with the league, there appears to have been a group of forward-looking citizens, primarily businessmen, in Dayton, and Morgan drew considerable aid from them when he ventured into educational reform, an effort that established him as a national leader in yet another field. As in engineering, there was also a progressive element in education. While Professor John Dewey was the philosopher-king of the movement, it was people such as Arthur Morgan and his comrades who created specific demonstrations of progressive education in action.

From his youth, Morgan had carried a vague notion about educational reform, but the greatest impact on him appears to have come from Johann Heinrich Pestalozzi, Charles Hanford Henderson, and Frederic L. Burk.[15] Pestalozzi wrote his famous *Leonard and Gertrude* in 1781, and in 1900 Morgan had read the story of Gertrude, a simple, honest, moral, hardworking woman who brought spiritual, economic, and political reform to an entire village. The revolution came primarily through an extension of the educational method she used in her home with her

14. The Morgan Papers contain a great deal of correspondence about the league, as well as minutes of the Ohio branch and the national Executive Committee. The fullest accounts are in Theodore Marburg, *Development of the League of Nations Idea: Documents and Correspondence of Theodore Marburg*, ed. John H. Latane (2 vols.; New York: Macmillan Co., 1932), and Ruhl J. Bartlett, *The League to Enforce Peace* (Chapel Hill: University of North Carolina Press, 1944).

15. Johann Heinrich Pestalozzi, *Leonard and Gertrude*, trans. and abridged by Eva Channing (Boston: Ginn, Heath, and Co., 1885); Charles Hanford Henderson, *Education and the Larger Life* (Boston: Houghton, Mifflin and Co., 1902) and *What Is It To Be Educated?* (Boston: Houghton Mifflin Co., 1914).

children, which was basically a combination of manual labor and education: the children learned while they worked at their spinning wheels. Morgan no doubt appreciated the triumph of morality and education, and building or remodeling an entire town was always his dream, whether in Minnesota, Tennessee, or Ohio.

While Morgan understood from Pestalozzi that education must have to do with real life and could not stand outside the daily experience of the student, he missed entirely the point that none of Gertrude's reforms would have come about but for the paternalism of the local prince. That failure to see paternalism for what it was ranks as one of the really serious flaws in Morgan's makeup and maybe in progressivism itself. The certainty with which he knew what was best for people sprang from a streak in him that was probably puritan and that at times seemed genuinely authoritarian.

Charles Henderson, a contemporary of Morgan's, had his own reformist school in Marienfield, North Carolina, which Morgan's older son, Ernest, attended. Henderson's educational philosophy involved freedom for students to choose and experiment, something he called "organic education," which somehow involved a fuller utilization of the senses and an emphasis on early reading and mathematics. Henderson saw each child as an individual who deserved to become master over his own life rather than as some dead soul caught in a corrupt, competitive society. Though definitely an antimaterialist, he preached that education must involve a study of industrial systems to teach survival and reform. "Personally most of my ideas," Morgan wrote Henderson in 1921, "as to education methods are closely related to the reading of your books . . . ."[16] The child as an individual was the same message Morgan received from Frederic Burk, president of the San Francisco State Normal School and a leading opponent of what he called "Lock Step Schooling." In his model elementary program at Normal, Burk developed the "Individual System," which was to have a great impact on progressive education.

Like the larger terms *progressive era* and *progressive movement*, *progressive education* is vague, and it has been applauded and condemned by a variety of people for many reasons. Generally, however, progressive education can be assigned three broad characteristics: recognition of the value of experimentation; belief in a basic and necessary relationship between school and society (involving no less than a commitment to social reform); and the principle that education should be child- rather than

16. Morgan to Henderson, April 5, 1921, Morgan Papers.

subject-oriented—although in varying degrees and practically never to the extent charged by its opponents.[17]

With these ideas as a basis for his educational theory, Morgan convinced several of his associates in Dayton to enter into plans for Moraine Park School. Such men as Edward A. Deeds, chairman of the board of directors of the Miami Conservancy; Charles F. Kettering, inventor of the electric starter for automobiles; and Orville Wright, coinventor of the airplane, joined with Morgan out of a desire for an alternative to the Dayton public school system, which they thought inferior. Deeds, of course, had worked with Morgan in the conservancy and had great respect for him, while Kettering began a relationship with Morgan that was to last the rest of his life. Wright's willingness to participate in this venture and serve as a trustee may have been unusual, in that he had virtually retired into seclusion after his brother's death in 1912.

Morgan gloried in knowing men like Kettering and Wright, seeing them as great Americans because they were creative inventors. In a few years he would meet and come to know America's best-known inventor, Thomas Alva Edison, who lived until 1931. Speaking of the rest of the group supporting the school, Morgan called them "manufacturers and merchants who realize somewhat indefinitely the imperfections of our school system. They will give our efforts very substantial financial support."[18]

Moraine Park School began its first regular term in June 1917 as a coeducational program with classes from kindergarten through college preparatory. Frank D. Slutz, former superintendent of schools in Pueblo, Colorado, served as headmaster at Moraine, which opened with sixty students. With a guiding principle that learning values was more important than learning facts, there was a clear moral tone about the school. "The object of education," Morgan wrote, "is not primarily to impart information, but to insure to the child the qualities, character and accomplishments he will need when he is a man."

One of the most unusual features of the school was the emphasis placed on self-reliance—most evident in the system of school governance and the business projects students were required to undertake to learn the

17. See Lawrence A. Cremin, *The Transformation of the School: Progressivism in American Education, 1876–1957* (New York: Knopf, 1961).

18. Morgan to Charles W. Eliot, Sept. 27, 1916, typed copy, Morgan Papers. This is the Eliot of Harvard, not the Elliott of Drainage Investigations. With Morgan's admiration for inventors and entrepreneurs such as Kettering and Edison, it is odd that he apparently never sought out or even discussed Henry Ford. The father of the Model T was a close friend of Edison's and one of the most fascinating individuals of this period. See Ford's role in the controversy over Muscle Shoals in chap. 4.

"arts of life." Kettering donated a large greenhouse as a classroom building, and each student had a private carrel for study. Instruction appears to have been fairly informal, with emphasis on student participation and extracurricular projects. In 1920 a handbook on private schools described Moraine Park as "one of the most promising educational experiments in recent years."[19]

Though Morgan had little to do with the school after he got it started, his association with it brought him a good deal of national attention, including a request from *Atlantic Monthly* to write an article on his educational philosophy. The resulting "Education: the Mastery of the Arts of Life" was Morgan's first nontechnical publication.[20] Here he condemned the separation of cultural and practical education. "The school-house," he insisted, "has received too much credit, and the barn not enough." He never quite suggested that the barn replace the school, but he did assert that "the two phases of education ought never to have been separated. . . ."

Morgan felt it stupid, if not psychologically damaging, to teach mathematics without having the student maintain a personal account of expenses, or, better still, to manage one's own small business. That was his original thought behind Moraine Park, and it would be the very same concept he used at Antioch College: get the student to develop a business that would support the community. Again in the Tennessee Valley it was his hope that, with training, TVA workers could develop their own businesses and create new small industries that would aid their small towns. That was what he, at least, meant by regional development.

Because of the national publicity associated with Moraine Park, Morgan came into contact with an organization called the Association for the Advancement of Progressive Education, which elected him its first president in 1920. One of his earliest acts was to suggest that the name be shortened to Progressive Education Association. Actually, Morgan had little time to devote to the PEA, as exciting a challenge as that might have been. He did arrange for the 1921 national convention to be held in

19. Arthur E. Morgan, "An Outline for a Proposed Boys' School for Which a Headmaster or Teacher is Being Sought," and "An Experiment in Educational Engineering," Morgan Papers. A description of Moraine Park School, and a comparison of it with other progressive schools, is in Lloyd Marcus, "The Founding of American Private Progressive Schools, 1912–1921," honor's thesis, Harvard University, 1948. The positive assessment of Moraine Park is in Porter E. Sargent (ed.), *Handbook of American Private Schools, 1919–1920* (Boston: P. Sargent, 1920), p. 266. While Morgan initially conceived of a boys' school, when established Moraine Park was coeducational.

20. Arthur E. Morgan, "Education: The Mastery of the Arts of Life," *Atlantic Monthly* 121 (March 1918), 337–46.

Dayton, where Moraine Park was the center of attention and where Kettering spoke on the nature of scientific invention.

With Morgan as president, the PEA in 1921 counted among its vice-presidents John Dewey, Hanford Henderson, and H. G. Wells. Its aims focused on natural student development, the teacher as guide, home and school cooperation, and experimentation. These principles and the Progressive Education Association were popular in the 1920s and 1930s, but in the next two decades a reaction set in which made *progressive education* a pejorative term. The association suffered accordingly, finally collapsing in 1955. Morgan served three terms as president of PEA, but later said, "I never got close to it."[21]

Morgan left Dayton and the Miami Conservancy in 1921 to become president of Antioch College, where he hoped at last to create his model community around a school. Even with all his civic service, his work for peace, and his educational reforms, his most important contribution from this period was clearly the Miami Conservancy. Completed in the summer of 1922, the Conservancy was unique in a number of ways. Morgan's successful utilization of the concept of a regional authority, the idea of the conservancy district, was certainly important. The use of dry dams as retarding basins was new in this country as a method of flood control, as was the labor policy in which management reached one agreement with a number of separate unions. Certainly the extent of the social services provided the workers was innovative.

Equally important as a development during this period was Morgan's emergence on the national scene. It was his work in education, not engineering, that led the *Atlantic Monthly* to seek him out, and for nearly twenty years that magazine's pages would be open to him. He had held national office in peace and education organizations, and his network of associates and supporters had widened accordingly. And why not? His progressive credentials were impeccable.

21. Patricia Albjerg Graham, *Progressive Education: From Arcady to Academe, a History of the Progressive Education Association, 1919–1955* (New York: Teachers College Press, 1967). See the correspondence between Morgan, Stanwood Cobb, and Gertrude Stevens Ayres in the Morgan Papers; also, *Definition of Progressive Education* (Washington: Association for the Advancement of Progressive Education, ca. 1919). Morgan's comment about the PEA comes from the author's interview with him, July 28, 1969, Yellow Springs, Ohio.

CHAPTER 3

The Antioch Scheme

As difficult as it is to imagine putting stern Arthur Morgan into the Roaring Twenties, it is fascinating to see how he and the old progressives handled this challenge. One would think they would have been crushed by the failure of idealism after World War I, but many of them seem not to have noticed that their age was over. In some respects they now appeared particularly conservative, but not because they had changed; society had shifted on them. Besides, Morgan had worried about decadence ever since 1896, when he called Max Nordau's *Degeneration* "the best book I have read."[1] Perhaps the overt materialism and loosening mores of the twenties only intensified his commitment to moral reform.

Considering how distraught Morgan must have been when he viewed the era's excessive waste of everything he held dear, and as much as the 1920s could not have been a pleasant time for him, it is striking how earnestly he pushed toward his goals. Far from being a crisis for him, the early twenties found him reaching for new heights. He was in his forties and still on the move, as determined as ever to reform the world. In fact, it may be that it was in the 1920s when he felt everything coming together for him. At last it was time to build his community, a time to express his vision. He was literally given a college and a town, to reform according to his views, to make a place for the conservation of values. H. L. Mencken called it "the Antioch scheme."[2]

Morgan turned Antioch College into a veritable monument to the moralism of the earlier progressive period. There is little doubt that his engineer's affinity for wealthy inventors provided him with plenty of admiration for the practical world of business, and Morgan never had

---

1. Morgan diary, Dec. 31, 1896. Max Simon Nordau, *Degeneration*, trans. from the 2nd ed. of the German work (5th ed.; New York: Appleton and Co., 1895).

2. Mencken used the term *Antioch scheme*, which he found "very pursuasive," in a May 22, 1921, letter to Hendrick W. Van Loon, Morgan Papers. Mencken felt that Morgan's biggest problem would be in attracting good students instead of "boneheads unable to pass the entrance examinations at Yale, Amherst and the Ohio Baptist University." Morgan had hired Van Loon, Munich Ph.D. and well known for his illustrated children's histories, as professor of social science. Van Loon, however, found the Yellow Springs pace a bit slow, and soon he left.

any difficulty with the prospect of making money. Yet for all his talk of creating entrepreneurs, Antioch was for him an experimental community expressing his own moral, idealistic vision.

The purpose had been there all along. Years later he explained to an Antioch psychologist that his first vision had come at the age of seventeen:

> I had a picture of a little community. . . . We'd be making our living. . . . We'd be selling things so we'd be independent. . . . The teachers would have their families there and the pupils would be living in the teachers' houses with them. . . . There would be nothing that we wouldn't be talking about . . . trying to invent new industries, new ways of making money. It would be a community of explorers and inventors and teachers and students. . . . I remember just being so taken up with that picture that I stood there on the footpath in the hazelbrush for possibly an hour. [3]

The 1920s was the time for the vision in the hazelbrush to be made manifest. The disciples were gathering at Antioch. There the muse of history produced a coincidence: this was the second time Utopia had come to that place.

Antioch College is located in Yellow Springs, Ohio, a sleepy village that had its start as nothing less than an Owenite Utopian community back in the mid-1820s. Robert Owen, the great British Utopian, was on his way to the wilderness of Indiana to create New Harmony as a model of right living. Stopping over in Cincinnati, he so aroused nearly a hundred of its citizens that they vowed to begin their own community based on Owen's principles of cooperation, equality, and freethinking. The Cincinnati communards bought land about seventy-five miles to the north, at Yellow Springs, and another Utopia was born. The Owenites of Yellow Springs stayed together for less than a year before departing "back into the selfish world from which they came."[4]

Now Utopia returned to Yellow Springs, and there was never any doubt that Morgan meant to reform both town and gown. Antioch and Yellow Springs were to fulfill his vision.

Antioch College also had a great reform tradition of its own. Founded in 1853 by the Christian Connexion with help from the Unitarians, Antioch was one of the earliest colleges to admit women. Moreover, its first president had been Horace Mann, the great educational reformer,

---

3. Audio tape of a conversation beteen Clarence Leuba and Morgan, June 4, 1966, Morgan Papers.

4. John Humphrey Noyes, *History of American Socialisms* (New York: Dover Pub., Inc., 1966), pp. 59–65. Noyes was one of the most successful American Utopians with his Oneida community and this is a reprint of his 1870 treatise.

and for a time the college looked forward to a bright future under its distinguished leader. Antioch was not, however, an unqualified success for Mann. He worked with sectarian and financial problems until his death in 1859, after which the school went into a decline, actually closing its doors in 1881 and 1882.

After the turn of the century, Antioch enjoyed a brief renewal under the presidency of Simeon D. Fess, who took office in 1906. Enrollment hovered at about 250, good for the small college, but the nagging problem of inadequate endowment remained. In 1912 Fess won election to the U.S. House of Representatives, but did not resign his Antioch post until 1917, going on to serve five terms in the House and two in the Senate. After his resignation, Antioch's enrollment dropped to ninety-seven. By 1920 only four seniors were graduated, and another and final closing seemed imminent.[5]

Antioch's modest physical plant consisted of College Hall, with thirty rooms for all educational activities; two dormitories, with seventy-two rooms for women and ninety-six for men; and a three-story brick home for the president. With tuition at fifty dollars a year, the college budget for 1920 was an uncertain fifteen thousand dollars. William M. Dawson, acting president, illustrated the problem with faculty. At Antioch for twenty years, he had taught Greek, Latin, German, English, history (medieval and modern European, American, and general), civics, general psychology, child psychology, educational psychology, principles of education, history of education, and ethics. Since the college could not pay him an adequate salary, he preached in a local church each Sunday.[6]

At their meeting in June 1919, after the failure of an attempt to sell the college to the Young Men's Christian Association, the Antioch trustees elected Arthur Morgan to the board. The story told by Lucy Morgan is that her husband was surprised to learn that he had become a college trustee, and the next Sunday they drove over to Yellow Springs from nearby Dayton to have a look. Morgan is supposed to have said, "I believe it is near enough dead to start over in the form I dream of."[7]

With that the Morgans gave up their plans for a school-community at Jacob's Pillow and concentrated on Antioch. In six weeks he presented a plan for the college's economic salvation, as well as a radical restructuring of its academic program. His idea for the survival of the college involved,

5. The best history of early Antioch College is Harvard Forrest Vallance, "A History of Antioch College" (Ph.D. diss., Ohio State University, 1936). Also available in the Antiochiana Collection, Olive Kettering Library, Antioch College, Yellow Springs, Ohio.

6. William M. Dawson to Morgan, Feb. 21, 1921, Morgan Papers.

7. Lucy Morgan, *Finding His World*, p. 100.

at first, a vague kind of practical industrial education. Morgan's ideas underwent fairly rapid change, and it is difficult to see any particular program, other than the concept he had introduced at Moraine Park— that cultural and practical education should be combined. Whatever his early plans, his fellow trustees apparently gave him complete freedom. After years of failing to come up with a solution to save the school, they seemed glad for someone with Morgan's reputation and energy to take the lead.[8]

Morgan's initial plan for Antioch sounds like something right out of Pestalozzi—he wanted students to coordinate their study in college with work in industry. He planned for them to spend four hours a day in class and four hours on the job, and he hoped the college would develop its own businesses to employ students and turn a profit. Even with the elimination of a number of liberal arts courses and the combination of others, Morgan estimated that it would take six years for a student to complete the new program.

Another innovation he wanted to introduce, from his earliest thinking about Antioch, involved what he called "autonomous courses," which would allow the student to work on a topic of his own choosing with only general supervision from the faculty. Today this idea would be termed independent study or research; most universities have incorporated the idea, and most faculty have learned how difficult it is to do really well. Morgan was thoroughly committed to the concept from the outset, and probably he arrived at it out of his own experience.

The idea of students doing practical work, the new concept that came to be called the "co-op," for cooperation with industry, did not entirely originate with Morgan. Herman Schneider, dean of engineering at the University of Cincinnati, had for some years required his students to work on actual engineering projects as part of their course of study. Morgan had employed some of these students in the Miami Conservancy, and this relationship, which dovetailed nicely with Pestalozzi, formed another basis for his favorable opinion of combining work and study.

What Morgan did that was innovative was to extend the cooperative concept to the liberal arts program. All students at Antioch would work, whether they needed the money or not. In making practical experience a core requirement, Morgan introduced the pioneering aspect of his work at Antioch and made his greatest contribution to modern American higher education.[9]

8. The minutes of the Antioch Board of Trustees for the Morgan period are in the Antiochiana Collection.
9. See Morgan correspondence with Bolton Smith, Allan T. Burns, Charles Elliott [Eliot], and James R. Angell in 1919 and 1920, Morgan Papers.

In 1919 and early 1920 Morgan formulated his plans for student self-support and completed his program of study. It seems certain that at this time he did not envision himself as president, intending to do as he had at Moraine Park by turning it over to others to administer. Yet his search for a chief executive officer proved unsuccessful, and in 1920 he agreed to accept the presidency offered him by the trustees. Morgan asked Dawson to continue in his acting capacity until 1921, when he would inaugurate the new curriculum.

In accepting the office, Morgan stipulated that the incumbent trustees and faculty must resign so that he could begin anew. The old trustees slowly sent in their resignations, and Morgan's people began to appear, while the small faculty wondered what would happen to it. Not many would be deemed suitable for the new order. There is a sad letter from Dawson offering to return to teaching German and asking if he could continue to teach ethics, since he had found it so rewarding. In typical fashion Morgan responded that at the new Antioch ethics would be a way of life, not a course.

The first person Morgan turned to as trustee was Charles Kettering, whom he described as "another Edison, but much more balanced and with a thoroughly good education." Next came Gordon Rentschler, a director of the Miami Conservancy and a manufacturer, followed by John C. Haswell and William Mayo, both industrialists. By the spring of 1921, he had completed his new board of trustees, and of the twenty men, thirteen were new. These included Frank Slutz from Moraine Park School and Ellery Sedgwick of the *Atlantic Monthly*. Most of the other members of the all-male board were capitalists.

When he took the helm at Antioch, Morgan also continued to serve as president of his engineering firm, chief engineer for the Miami Conservancy, president of the Progressive Education Association, and trustee of Moraine Park. By 1921 he would free himself of his other obligations, except for his engineering company, to devote himself to the college. "I have decided," he wrote in late 1920, "that this project offers greater promise of returns for the investment I can make than does any other work of which I can take part." Shortly thereafter, he informed the Progressive Education Association that he was considering resigning because of lack of time: "I *must* make Antioch go."[10]

In December 1920 Morgan sketched another preliminary plan for Antioch. He wanted self-support for the college through earnings from college industries, using student labor, and he wanted the students to alternate their study and practical experience. He also desired "cultural

10. Morgan to Mrs. M. V. Ayres, ca. Nov. 18, 1920, Morgan Papers.

education for the purpose of developing the texture of mind and character . . . rather than for the purpose of turning out persons who are simply well informed and academically minded." Morgan further included vocational courses that would develop self-reliance, and he insisted that students and faculty maintain a high level of physical fitness. Lastly, he vowed to instill in his students "a spirit of moral enthusiasm and social service."[11] Progressivism was to be alive and well at Antioch.

When the Progressive Education Association met in Dayton, Morgan gave a speech outlining his plan for Antioch. He had already given up the idea of four hours a day for study and four for work; the industries simply did not exist in Yellow Springs. Instead, he had decided to place the students with firms in the surrounding area, up to fifty miles away. He still hoped to bring small industry to his small town, but until then the students would have to leave the community for their jobs. This system allowed five weeks of study at Antioch and a similar period away at work. He continued to maintain that such a course of study would take six years.[12]

In another statement about this time, Morgan said that there were three types of students who would find Antioch worthwhile: those who wanted a general education and training in order to go on to a professional school; those who desired basic cultural training and the development of general administrative and business ability, but had no plans for additional study; and those who wished to find their vocations. Morgan also noted that lazy and immoral students, along with those "who aim to confine their study to musical or other art courses," would not be welcome at Antioch.[13]

There is an apparent inconsistency in these early meditations about the college's identity and mission. Morgan spoke almost entirely of business and administration, and at times Antioch sounded like little more than a business school that gave credit for practical experience. This tone is clearest in the first published statement about the new Antioch, which appeared in Morgan's home territory of the *Engineering News-Record*. Entitled "The Antioch Plan," it is the subtitle, "Training for Administration and Proprietorship at a Small College," that is in-

11. Arthur Morgan, "The Plan for the New Antioch," December 1920, mimeographed, Morgan Papers.
12. "Digest of the Second Annual Convention of the Progressive Education Association," 1921, Morgan Papers.
13. Arthur Morgan, "The Antioch Plan," Feb. 14, 1921, mimeographed, Morgan Papers.

structive. To make this early attitude even plainer, he stated that "an educational institution has certain points in resemblance to a factory."[14]

A reader complained: "Antioch is to be primarily a 'vestibule school' to the manufacturing and commercial field," and asked why Morgan did not train his students for social service. Morgan replied that the article had been reduced from a longer manuscript and that much of the emphasis on moral purpose had been eliminated. He claimed that his interest in Antioch would be considerably diminished were it not for the opportunity of "helping young people to define their social, economic and moral purpose." Antioch was to enable its students to reach financial independence so the expression of their ideals would be "economically feasible."[15] Morgan's reply was doubtless true, but it is also a fact that he had become enamored of the Dayton businessmen who had assisted him in so many of his projects. He appreciated men like Kettering, who was first an inventor and second a multimillionaire as a result of his creativity. Morgan had always admired self-reliance, initiative, and inventiveness in a personal, literary, or scientific sense; now he admired them for their economic success.

The wealthy entrepreneur of today could be the public servant of tomorrow; indeed, it was only because Morgan was a successful engineer and businessman that he could afford to take the financial risk of investing in the future of a small college. Remember, too, that the business of making money was very much a part of the spirit of the 1920s. Bruce Barton published his best-selling *The Man Nobody Knows* in 1925, which brought commercialism to a new, sacred level when he "proved" that Jesus Christ had been the best salesman in the history of the world.

Despite Lucy Morgan's contention that her husband went to Antioch to rebuild it according to his ideals, and despite our awareness of his vision, it seems certain that for the first few years the practical problems of keeping the institution alive and his concentration on training entrepreneurs tended to restrict his Utopianism. Later he did express the same goals for Antioch that he had for Jacob's Pillow. He failed in his hopes for two reasons: in the beginning he overemphasized the vocational training aspect, and he maintained the traditional structure of the typical American college. Had he gone to Jacob's Pillow he might not have succeeded in his vision, but at least he could have devised his own forms.

---

14. Arthur Morgan, "The Antioch Plan: Training for Administration and Proprietorship at a Small College," *Engineering News-Record* 86 (Jan. 20, 1921), 108–11.
15. "Antioch Plan Omits Public Service Training," *ibid.* (March 17, 1921), 480.

As radical as the co-op and autonomous courses were, they could not alter the fact that Antioch remained a liberal arts college.[16]

In an article in *Atlantic Monthly* in 1922, Morgan did less writing about creative entrepreneurs and more about building better lives and working for economic and social readjustment. He continued to maintain that self-support from the cooperative plan was incidental to its main purpose of developing "young men and women for management and pro-prietorship—for economic self-support and independence." He qualified this remark, however, by noting that monetary success was not an end in itself, "but an enlargement of opportunity for giving and getting life's highest values."[17]

This article gives Morgan's fullest statement of what he wanted to do at Antioch, of the kind of graduate he wanted to produce. Usually he relied on terms such as *entrepreneur* or *proprietor*, but here he introduced a new one: *the coordinator*. Morgan's ideal student would have the ability "to gather together the various tangled threads of forces, conditions, and affairs, which make up the elements of any potential human accomplish-ment, and to weave them into a perfect fabric, showing the texture and design of a preconceived plan." This ability to break with tradition, to bring separate parts together into a new whole, to see unity and purpose, was what Morgan meant when he spoke of creativity, innovation, and the entrepreneur. He never got more specific in writing of what he wanted to happen. Specifics were impossible because Morgan had more faith than facts, faith in the possibility of perfecting society. It was sufficient for him that Antioch's purpose was to serve as a bridge to the future, "with its perfect men and women."

At Antioch he thought he could educate people who would become philosopher-engineers, who understood technical affairs, who had a vision of unity and creativity to express, and whose only preconceived values lay in a dedication to truth. This theoretical student, combining most of the elusive progressive virtues, was to have good health, a well-proportioned personality, a keen appetite for knowledge, sound charac-ter, and "enlightened moral enthusiasm." These qualities would make him "an effective agent in the economic and social readjustment that is

16. The whole question of the cooperative plan remained quite vague in Morgan's early years at Antioch. He did much thinking about its utility insofar as it would provide economic support for the student. At the same time, he saw the co-op as an innovation with high merit in terms of basic education. This emphasis would continue over the years until money-making would be entirely disclaimed as a reason for the co-op. Doubtless some students selected Antioch because of the jobs, and the income, that were provided for them.

17. Arthur Morgan, "What is College For?" *Atlantic Monthly* 86 (May 1922), 649.

upon us," as well as a remarkable person who has found "the meaning and the significance of life as a whole."

In planning Antioch, Morgan was eager to solicit the advice and support of as many prominent people as he could, and he collected an impressive group. It included Jerome D. Greene of the Rockefeller Foundation and an Antioch trustee; Edwin F. Gay, formerly of the Harvard Business School and also a trustee; Charles W. Eliot, former president of Harvard University; Ellery Sedgwick, Angelo Patri (the educator), and John Dewey; historians James Harvey Robinson, Samuel Flagg Bemis, and Frederick B. Artz (a former professor at Antioch); Walter Lippmann, Ray Stannard Baker, and Ida M. Tarbell; David Starr Jordan, former chancellor of Stanford University; James R. Angell, newly installed president of Yale University; Bruce R. Payne, president of George Peabody College for Teachers; Lawrence Abbott, editor of *Outlook*; and John Patterson, president of the National Cash Register Company in Dayton.

By July 1921, Morgan had collected more than $100,000 in cash. He used $25,000 of that amount to buy Glen Helen, 180 acres of unusually beautiful land adjacent to the Antioch campus. Acquiring the Glen had been in his progressive mind since he first saw the college; such a natural area was a prerequisite, and he might very well not have come to Antioch had the Glen been unavailable. Nature remained, until his death, very important to him.

Morgan personally invested a good deal of money to buy land in town for faculty housing, and the trustees agreed to finance, through gifts and loans, the rest of the program for the first year. In all Morgan had more than $400,000 for renovation, construction, salaries, expenses, and land acquisition. The lack of a permanent endowment hampered the new president from the beginning, and future fundraising campaigns would continue to meet only immediate needs. He was to learn the real job of a private college president—finding money for general operations.

The new Antioch began with twenty faculty members, five of whom had taught at the college prior to 1921. Acting president Dawson had retired. In securing faculty members Morgan was as ambitious and audacious as he was in collecting money and advice. His progressive education sentiments meant by definition that he was a disciple of John Dewey. When Morgan mentioned to Charles Eliot that he wanted Dewey to join the Antioch effort, the old champion of the elective system at Harvard urged him to be cautious until he learned more about the famous educator. Despite his misgivings, Eliot and other friends of Antioch contacted Dewey, who was in China, and attempted to recruit him. One source indicated that Dewey would not consider a salary of less than fifteen thousand dollars, far above any figure Morgan could meet. For his demonstration school, Morgan wanted Dewey's daughter, Evelyn, but both father and daughter went unsigned. Morgan was equally unsuccessful in convincing Hanford Henderson to come to Antioch.[18]

In reorganizing the college, Morgan was greatly assisted by the man he placed at the head of his staff, Philip E. Nash. Moving to Yellow Springs before Morgan, Nash handled the details of the transition and became Antioch's dean. Also assisting were personnel from Moraine Park School over in Dayton.

In building his Antioch staff Morgan employed his usual and unconventional methods. He preferred to hire his people on an indefinite status as to rank and salary. Just as he never committed himself to a definite engineering plan before excavation, so he wanted to keep his organization fluid, avoiding permanent arrangements until each person had found his or her proper place. Whatever chaos and hardship this system may have produced, especially for the staff, Morgan felt that it worked. Such institutionalized confusion may have been his way of weeding out the uncommitted. By 1921 it was clear that a person followed Arthur Morgan because he believed in him and his ideas. To work for Morgan meant either to become his devotee or to leave. Only those who shared the vision could stay. His relationships, like his morality, were absolute, and he had a way of forcing conversion or rejection.

Over this staff, whether engineering, administrative, or academic, Morgan ruled with a heavy, paternalistic hand. He was in the habit of questioning himself until he decided something was morally right, and then he could not be moved. As he grew older it became easier for him to see the right, and he believed he had developed guidelines and intuitive powers that enabled him to make decisions that might appear arbitrary to others. As patriarch, Morgan was prepared to allow a good deal of freedom, provided one did not run afoul of his numerous and firm principles. "A college," he wrote in 1925, "should not be committed to any *a priori* theory of academic freedom from responsibility."[19]

By the fall of 1922, Antioch's enrollment had risen to about four hundred, and the faculty had doubled to forty, an expensive ratio. Enrollment, however, continued to grow as Antioch attracted a great deal

18. See the 1921 correspondence between Morgan and Angelo Patri, C. E. Erffmeyer, John and Evelyn Dewey, and Charles Eliot, Morgan Papers.

19. For an example of Morgan's attitudes toward faculty freedom, see Morgan to Fressa Baker Inman (his assistant), Feb. 10, 1930, Morgan Papers, and "College Government," *Antioch Notes* 2 (April 15, 1925).

of attention in newspapers and popular magazines.[20] The Carnegie Foundation provided funds for a new library, and Antioch, while never rich, no longer faced the prospect of closing. In terms of the curriculum, the system of autonomous courses about which Morgan felt so strongly was not put fully into effect until 1927, after which time Antioch offered a genuine program of self-directed study.

The Antioch catalogs reveal a slow but steady development of standard courses and divisions. Within the field of history, for example, Morgan had never wanted traditional courses. Indeed, he had hoped to develop one big, two-year course, "covering the entire field beginning with anthropology, giving a bird's eye view of history and ending with a general treatment of economics, sociology and possibly psychology." He had even gotten James Harvey Robinson, author of *The New History*, to attempt such a design.[21] By 1929, however, conventional history courses, taught by conventional historians to conventional history majors, were clearly in the ascendancy. For all his sincerity in seeing the college as an open and unstructured community, Morgan may have been unaware that the existence of departments, required courses, and prerequisites (all present at Antioch by 1929) worked against his ideal.

In 1929 the cooperative program became part of the newly created Extramural School, which was responsible for all off-campus educational activities. The college also redefined its aims for the co-op to strengthen the notion that student self-support was a by-product rather than a goal. Work experience, for its own sake, became a vital part of the Antioch experience, especially in providing a unique perspective for that education.

In the 1920s, Morgan no longer had to confine his thoughts to a private diary or journal, since his post as president of Antioch gave him a wonderful platform. Any fleeting thought now went instantly into print.

20. See Vallance, "A History of Antioch College." See also these articles about Antioch: Dickerson S. Miller, "The Antioch Idea," *Nation* 113 (Sept. 7,1921), 263, and Ida M. Tarbell, "Morgan of Antioch," *Colliers* 69 (June 3, 1922), 7–8, 20–21, 23. In addition to the articles on education by Morgan cited elsewhere in this chapter, the following are significant: "The Human Goal of Education," *Century* 106 (October 1923), 904–15; "What is a Cultural Subject," *School and Society* 20 (Nov. 29, 1924), 696–97; "Almus Pater: Antioch Introduces a Masculine Element into Higher Education," *Atlantic Monthly* 143 (June 1929), 774–82; and "Transforming the American College System," *Current History* 32 (July 1930), 717–20.

21. On autonomous courses, see Morgan, "The Antioch Program," *Journal of Higher Education* 1 (December 1930), 497–502. For the one big history course, see Morgan's correspondence with Samuel Flagg Bemis and James Harvey Robinson, January and February 1921, Morgan Papers.

Eventually he produced a shelf of books, but in the twenties his principal vehicle was the semimonthly *Antioch Notes*, with short essays expressing the president's views on a wide variety of subjects. Morgan wrote nearly all of the *Notes* personally, and they are an invaluable source for grappling with his thinking. Moreover, Morgan's growing reputation increasingly afforded him media coverage and additional outlets for his universalism. Never had Morgan had such an obliging system for the dissemination of his ideas, and he often abused it, writing too quickly, too poorly, too often.

Such is the interest in Morgan, however, that one must wade through this morass of meanderings in order to master his language. One learns to follow his nuances, his peculiarly progressive usages, and the images that abound. His most popular terms, by far, were *moral, vision,* and *ideal.* These images were central to his thinking. He easily manipulated particular words, giving his own special meaning. When he said "practical," as he often did, he never meant anything that limited idealism. When he said "expedient," he never implied an ethical concession. *Practical* simply meant basic and natural, while only universal values, such as honesty, could be *expedient.* Inferior minds used *practical* or *expedient* to mean compromise. Other words that carried Morgan's unqualified approval were *work, experience, self-reliance, efficiency, balance, symmetry, the whole, judgment* (good or bad), *aspiration, integrity, goodwill,* and *intelligence.*

On the negative side fell such terms as *waste, short-sighted, cynical,* and *disillusionment.* Morgan also felt genuinely negative about *sophistication,* which he held to be arrogant and insincere; or *instinct,* which he knew to represent only a base, animalistic impulse and which must be the enemy of the enlightened; or *individualism,* which he rejected as the wasteful selfishness of unchecked capitalism. Morgan might preach self-reliance for the individual and the community, but he loved even more the ideas of cooperation and association, just as the original Yellow Springs Utopians had loved them.

Another way in which this prolific Morgan is confusing is in his concept of time. The now is negative; the future, positive. If someone suggested that he be practical or expedient regarding a present situation, he heard a demand that he sell out, and he dismissed that person as a degenerate. When Morgan said, as he did for the next half century, that it is always practical and expedient to be straightforward and open in all situations, he spoke in terms of long periods of time. That a half-truth might serve a present purpose had no meaning for him. He was caught in the stream of life, the whole of it, which demanded that he think in the long-range terms of posterity. He was obsessed with the whole, and his overriding concern was for the long run.

A moral act was by definition, then, one that was good for all of society and the future as well as for the actor and the present. Morgan, however, never explained how we are to know the effects of an act before we commit it. Apparently if we are to be moral we must first be clairvoyant. Similar confusion exists with *fine purpose*, another of his favorite terms. That he desired this to be the basis of life is clear, but one never quite grasps just what he meant beyond a nice sounding generality.

One last ill-defined but basic concept in Morgan's thought involved *goodwill*. All men and women, one believes, despite so much evidence to the contrary, love goodwill, whatever it is. Morgan seems to have meant goodwill to be what Jesus spoke of in the Sermon on the Mount. "Good will toward men," he insisted, "is not a quixotic dream. It is the rule of economy, effectiveness, and power, and fate fights for it."[22] His view of the "universal competition for survival and increase" led him to predict the eventual triumph of the good because "the men of ill will ultimately will fail, along with the society they have weakened."

In saying that an ethical act is one whose long-run results are good for all concerned and that man could know these results, Morgan had to rely on intuition, which is what he probably meant when he talked about native intelligence. It seems clear that he believed people could develop and train intuition so as to know which act will have "good" consequences. This belief puts Morgan in the historic category of radicals who profess that the idea of good is basic to humanity. Men and women, by definition, have the capacity to know good. Inasmuch as most people do not use this capability, Morgan stressed "character building," by which he meant developing this ability to know good.

In a complex, mass society, Morgan insisted, most people would not be able to discipline themselves into enlightened character. The solution appeared clearly enough: those with character could construct a code of ethics that those without could follow. As a proper convert to Taylorism, Morgan saw such an enterprise as largely a technical matter, and as an engineer he felt eminently qualified for the task. Just as he had written numerous drainage codes, or a labor code for the Miami Conservancy, so he could write a code of ethics. In fact, as a progressive engineer he had the social responsibility to do so.

In 1926 he published in *Antioch Notes* a manifesto that he thought might find "universal acceptance in principle, and will cover almost every

---

22. Morgan, "The Future of Good Will," *Antioch Notes* 10 (Dec. 1, 1932). The entire issue of *Notes* 3 (Dec. 15, 1925) is devoted to goodwill. See also "Good Will is Good Sense," *ibid*. 3 (March 15, 1926).

circumstance of life." The statement, entitled "A Moral Code," seems sufficiently revealing to present in full:

1. *Good Will.* The good of the whole must prevail over that of the individual. The best motive of conduct is a controlling desire for the good of all life for all time.

2. *Health.* The human enterprise must be carried on in human bodies. Body and mind must be kept fit by omission of all harmful conduct, however socially entrenched, and by development of habits that add to their soundness and vigor.

3. *Eugenics.* The best lives should be perpetuated.

4. *Integrity.* Only as men can trust each other are they free to achieve life purpose. Integrity in all relations is essential.

5. *Inquiry.* Only as we learn the nature of the world, through unswerving search for truth, can we learn to live.

6. *Symmetry.* All values are relative. It is essential to strive always to see them in true relations.

7. *Aspiration.* Life purpose is potent only when pursued with desire. The nurture of aspiration is essential.[23]

"In ethics, as in every field," Morgan wrote in 1930, "genius sets standards which become authority to those who recognize excellence, even where they cannot create it," and that statement shows his paternalism about as clearly as any he ever made.[24] It is not surprising, therefore, that he included eugenics in his moral code, and in that area he was to observe almost literally that if the best lives should be perpetuated, the worst should be terminated. While modern genetics has proven a viable scientific field, the early eugenicists, of whom Morgan was one, were characterized more by enthusiasm than by science, and most of the studies that influenced Morgan in the early decades of this century have been discredited.

The first organization actively supporting eugenics was, appropriately enough, the American Breeders' Association, founded in 1903, with Secretary of Agriculture James Wilson as honorary president. Its committee on eugenics included David Starr Jordan, Alexander Graham Bell, Luther Burbank, and Charles Benedict Davenport, the principal leader of the eugenics movement in this country. After World War I other attempts were made to organize, eventually leading to the establishment of the American Eugenics Society, of which Morgan was a charter member.[25]

23. Morgan, "A Moral Code," *Antioch Notes* 4 (Dec. 1, 1926).
24. Morgan, "Ethics," *ibid.* 7 (Feb. 1, 1930).
25. There was a flurry of books and articles about eugenics in the 1920s and 1930s; a few were opposed. An excellent introduction to primary sources, including selections from Galton and Noyes (who with his stirpiculture anticipated eugenics) is contained in Carl Jay

In 1922 Morgan wrote, in the alarmist language of the eugenicist, "There are hundreds of thousands of feeble-minded now at large and breeding in the United States. . . ."[26] Ideas on the implementation of eugenic concern differed widely, and while several states actually passed sterilization laws, segregation of the "unfit" remained a frequent suggestion. In a famous Supreme Court decision in 1927 allowing the sterilization of a "feeble-minded" woman, Justice Oliver Wendell Holmes said, "The principle that sustains compulsory vaccination is broad enough to cover cutting the Fallopian tubes. . . . Three generations of imbeciles are enough."[27] Morgan, while urging a deliberate policy that would remove immediately the most unfit, used the aggressive term *elimination*, which suggests at the very least segregation or sterilization.

In 1935, after Morgan had served two years as head of the Tennessee Valley Authority, the American Eugenics Society asked him to become honorary president. He declined, but he did speak before the society's annual meeting. By that time his views had mellowed to the extent that he stressed learning to transmit the cultural heritage of the fit before concentrating on eliminating the unfit. Nazism soon gave eugenics a connotation that it never survived, and the society fell into decay.[28] Until his death, however, Morgan remained tempted by the promise of human perfection.

Morgan's ideas on eugenics are suggestive of his views on immigration restriction and on members of other races. His belief in national characteristics rendered him capable of condemning entire populations. In 1926 he told the freshmen of Antioch that because of past relationships with individuals of a particular nationality, not further identified, he had "come by experience to expect that in any business a native of this country will be dishonest." Obviously, Morgan had supported the closing of the floodgates of immigration. "In the exclusion of Asiatic immigration," he claimed, "we shall in the long run serve Asia as well as ourselves."[29]

Bajema (ed.), *Eugenics Then and Now* (Stroudsburg, Penn.: Dowden, Hutchinson, and Ross, Inc., 1976). More recent surveys of the movement include Mark H. Haller, *Eugenics: Hereditarian Attitudes in American Thought* (New Brunswick, N.J.: Rutgers University Press, 1963); Donald K. Pickens, *Eugenics and the Progressives* (Nashville: Vanderbilt University Press, 1968); and Daniel J. Kevles, *In the Name of Eugenics: Genetics and the Uses of Human Heredity* (New York: Alfred A. Knopf, 1985).

26. Morgan, "A Prospect," *Atlantic Monthly* 129 (March 1922), 382.

27. Quoted in Haller, *Eugenics*, p. 139.

28. See the Morgan–Ellsworth Huntington correspondence, Morgan Papers. In 1957 Morgan became a member of the board of directors of the nearly defunct American Eugenics Society.

29. Morgan, "To the Freshman of Antioch," *Antioch Notes* 4 (Sept. 1, 1926); "The Greatest Good," *ibid.* 4 (Sept. 15, 1926); "Population and Policy," *ibid.*

American blacks fared about the same in Morgan's regime. As early as 1910, he wrote that "the extreme and universal immorality of the negro is a bigger blight upon the country than people realize. . . ."[30] Blacks fell under the same eugenic shadow as Latin Americans (he called for ending immigration from south of the border, including Puerto Rico), Asians, and unfit Anglo-Saxons—all not intelligent or moral enough to meet Morgan's demands. Today we know this attitude to be plainly racist, but the Antioch president would have said that he was not opposed to them because of their color but because of their unfortunate cultural characteristics, which he had observed as universal to their race. Given the extensive racism throughout American society, especially in the 1920s, it is important to remember that Morgan's views probably seemed at least moderate and were not far out of line with the thinking of his contemporaries.

Morgan never achieved complete success in his dream of locating in Yellow Springs the industries he needed to support the college and educate his students. For several years he thought he had found the right project in the Antioch Shoe Company. He hired a man who could design shoes with both hygienic and artistic appeal, and the Antioch Shoe was to be both a reform and a moneymaker. Unfortunately, his craftsman proved to be mentally unstable, and Morgan had to let him and the project go. He did have some success, especially with businesses begun by students. The Morris Bean Company, the Antioch Bookplate Company, and the Antioch Press were all successful concerns located in Yellow Springs and founded by Antioch students. Morgan was also able to attract two large scientific centers to Yellow Springs. In 1925 Charles Kettering initiated the Kettering Research Institute for the purpose of studying photosynthesis, and Samuel Fels, a soap manufacturer, founded the Fels Research Institute in 1929 to study changes in the human body from birth to death. There was never enough work at home for all the students, and to this day Antiochians travel around the world on their co-ops.

If Antioch was becoming more and more a traditional college in terms of its curriculum (except for the co-op system), it appears also to have been attracting students given to the time-honored practices of collegians everywhere. Morgan's puritanical attitude made it impossible for him to comprehend why a student would smoke, much less drink alcohol. "College students seem inclined to gossip," he noted in 1926, and he

30. Morgan diary, March 1, 1910.

admonished the freshmen: "Do not indulge in the small evils that steal away the margin of quality." While recognizing the inadvisability of restricting students and not allowing them to learn by experience, Morgan felt some regulations necessary because students arrived at college with standards and interests, acquired by inheritance and imitation, which were not necessarily good. To him this was no great problem: "With integrity and mutual good will, respect for authority will grow along with self-direction and independence." For undergraduates, the matter was never so simple.[31]

Sometime in the 1920s, the Antioch president shifted his emphasis on what he desired for the college. The old idea of creating coordinators and entrepreneurs found less expression in his writing, while he spoke more often of the necessity of developing an enlightened lifestyle. "Current and transient social manners and standards in general," he said at the Antioch commencement in 1928, "tend more to receive naïve uncritical acceptance as being unquestionably desirable and authentic." He went on to chastise the Antioch community for not having aroused "aspiration and will, and the resulting failure to mobilize all the spiritual resources of life and to completely commit them to great purpose."[32]

At least as early as 1926, Morgan was serious in promoting Antioch as an attempt to revolutionize American culture. The college, he thought, should be a place where standards were set and an ideal created that society could emulate. "Nothing less than that," he said, "is an adequate aim for higher education." To the freshman class of that year he put the point directly: "My hope for Antioch is that through great desire disciplined by knowledge, and through great commitment to fine purpose, its students may be a powerful force for remaking human life."[33]

What appears to have happened is that in moving from building enlightened proprietors to reforming humanity, Morgan lost many of the faculty and students. He came to believe that they did not appreciate his deep seriousness of purpose. Doubtless the students and faculty members felt pride in Antioch's achievements, having demonstrated the efficacy of the co-op, created a real community government going far beyond the standard college "student government," and pioneered in

31. Morgan, "To the Freshman of Antioch," and "Freedom at College," *Antioch Notes* 1 (June 1, 1924).

32. Morgan, "Intensity and Rightness," address at Antioch commencement, June 23, 1928, typed manuscript, Morgan Papers. Also available in Morgan, *Purpose and Circumstance* (Yellow Springs: Kahoe and Co., 1928).

33. Morgan, "Standards," *Antioch Notes* 4 (Sept. 1, 1926); "To the Freshman of Antioch."

core courses and independent study. Antioch in those terms was a success. It had become a college with a unique identity and a mission, and it must have been hard for others to follow the president when he spoke of Antioch's failure to achieve great purpose.

Morgan simply did not understand the college mind, and that incomprehension isolated him. The impression one gets of him at Antioch after the first few exciting years is again that of a sad, depressed, lonely man. Unfortunately, this depression lent itself to a feeling of suspicion—primarily suspicion that the smoking student and the bridge-playing instructor (clear evidence of their lack of fine purpose) were not willing to give what was necessary. Morgan became paranoid in his belief that the failure to end these habits and to become more like him actually represented personal opposition to him. Anything short of total acceptance of his rules meant complete rejection and outright antagonism.

In Arthur Morgan's papers there is a series of letters from Edward Mathews, creator of the Antioch Shoe, whom Morgan had fired. Mathews was an amazing character, clearly unbalanced, certainly a brilliant designer and craftsman. He eventually established his own Utopia, the Homestead Guild Communities in Antrim, New Hampshire. One of the most interesting arrangements of this unsuccessful venture was what Mathews called the "Contract of Life Tenure," a marriage system which afforded him several wives. Experimenting with marital and sexual arrangements, one notes hastily, is not without precedent and does not by itself indicate an unbalanced mind. Men of the caliber of Joseph Smith and John Humphrey Noyes were among the best-known experimenters of the nineteenth century. On the other hand, Mathews's letters to Morgan are at times little more than the ravings of a maniac. He had a recurring image of Morgan as King Saul and himself as the young David. Other fantasies had Morgan as The Judge pronouncing sentence. Perhaps Mathews's lunacy gave him license to say what other faculty members could not, and his missives provide a fascinating picture of the small college and village ruled over by Arthur and Lucy Morgan. "When you become suspicious," Mathews warned Morgan, "you actually create delusion and trouble for yourself. The evil you fear comes upon you."[34]

In 1926 and 1927 Morgan began to express more forcefully his great concern for morality, and the faculty started to squirm, as faculty will. Early in 1926 the college president devoted an entire issue of *Antioch Notes* to a defense of moral restraint, or in Morgan's terms, a conservation of vital energies. Those who could not control the desire for gambling, sex,

34. Mathews to Morgan, May 6, 1926, Morgan Papers.

idle recreation, or pleasures with any complexity whatever, were guilty of wasting the force of their lives. Since vitality can be so easily depleted, moral responsibility demanded that it be conserved and used only to the best advantage of the whole social organism.

Morgan's position in the tradition of restraint is unmistakable: desires should be curbed and the search for pleasure should be in genuine accomplishment, not in dissipation. Gambling gave a sense of daring and thrill that should come from more creative endeavors with authentic adventure. The use of tobacco, alcohol, and drugs was wrong because it wasted human resources. Sex was only for home-building; it was meant to be restrained, and should never be gratified for its own sake. "It is a sound social demand," he explained, "that the resources of the sex impulse throughout life be conserved for the creation, preservation, and enrichment of the home, and for other creative accomplishment."[35]

His hypermoralism isolated him from a substantial part of the college and the town. Once again he felt unheeded, misunderstood, unloved. He began to contemplate drastic measures. "Seven years is long enough," he told Lucy, "to try out the method we have been working on."[36] He tinkered with a plan to revitalize Antioch by dismissing about half the students and keeping only those he felt were making a definite contribution. Presumably he would have done much the same with the faculty. In 1928 a leave of absence and a trip to Europe, ancient techniques for a president in trouble, calmed the situation for a while.

A note is in order here on the customs and manners of college presidents. It is, in fact, a lonely job. College administrators, especially those at the top, are uniformly and profoundly unappreciated by faculty and students, who tend to regard them as superfluous to their several purposes. Morgan's difficulties at Antioch were not substantially different from those of hundreds of other college heads, then and now. Most of them spend a large part of their time raising money. They are expected to provide the wherewithal for the college's support, but they are seldom loved when they attempt to stay at home and run the place. There has probably never been a collegiate chief executive officer who did not know the value of an extended vacation or the virtue in occasionally firing a dean. The most important—sometimes the only—loyalty a president must absolutely maintain is that of his board of trustees. Morgan continued to have the full confidence of the Antioch board, but he was beginning to get the feeling that the Antioch experiment was over.

35. Morgan, "Conserve the Creative Impulse," *Antioch Notes* 3 (Jan. 15, 1926).
36. Morgan to Lucy Morgan, March 7, 1928, Morgan Papers.

The Great Depression after 1929 brought matters to a breaking point, and when the president returned from Europe he found the college in another budget crisis. The time he had to spend as a financial agent furthered his isolation, for Morgan could not exist as a fund-raiser for a project he increasingly regarded as a failure. Another point of contention involved the system of autonomous courses. Morgan felt that the faculty had not given the plan the spirit and dedication it deserved. He expressed his deep discontent once again and in June 1931 departed for another trip to Europe. He left behind a faculty angry over salary reductions, and rumor had it that Morgan would not return to Antioch.[37]

He and Lucy traveled by automobile through Europe, collecting observations on politics, agriculture, and lifestyles. On October 18, 1931, Lucy sailed for home, while Morgan located in the small town of Cintra, Portugal. He planned to stay in this beautiful spot, widely known for its picturesque buildings, abundant vegetation, and climate. Deeply troubled and in poor health, he wrote his wife, "I feel somewhat at a loss to know how to proceed."[38]

The product of Morgan's meditation reached Antioch in early December. Known as "The Letter from Portugal," this remarkable document directed to the faculty was Morgan's appraisal of Antioch after ten years. Declaring himself unwilling to work to sustain Antioch unless that college contributed significantly to civilization, he felt there were already too many average colleges, and if that were all Antioch aspired to be he could no longer remain there. His hope, he told the faculty, had been to create at Antioch a community that exhibited a large degree of spiritual quality and "a marked and sustained difference of purpose and of commitment from those of society at large." He had found only disappointment: "It is the aim of achieving a great pattern of life that we have to a large degree failed at Antioch." In a reflective moment of self-analysis he admitted that he bore part of the responsibility for that failure: "I know I am and have been inadequate for such leadership. Lacking educational and cultural background, with unstable temperament and bad judgment, I did not expect that I should for long be leader of the enterprise."

After this self-flagellation, reminiscent of his morbid thoughts as a youth, Morgan began a catalog of Antioch's faults. He covered the territory from faculty parties to student "petting" and immoral theatrical productions, concluding that "I believe it is a fact that in the Antioch student body there is a fear to express generous purpose." His main

37. Vallance, "A History of Antioch College," pp. 260–63.
38. Morgan to Lucy Morgan, Nov. 1, 1931, Morgan Papers.

concern was that he saw no effort on the part of the faculty to develop a life purpose and to impart that purpose to the students. He saw no moral code. A more specific criticism in the letter had to do with education at Antioch. Morgan exhibited three papers (one of which, curiously, was the work of his younger son, Griscom) which had received very low marks, but which he felt represented unconventional thinking. Why should creativity, he asked, be punished? Such an Antioch, he told the faculty, was not the fulfillment of his hopes.[39]

The faculty held a series of meetings to discuss the letter and appointed a committee, as faculties will do, to bring together the ideas coming out of their sessions and to write Morgan, urging his return. While admitting that Antioch was in the midst of a crisis, that Morgan was indispensable to the college, and that they evidently had not fully understood his aims and aspirations, the faculty response insisted that Morgan might "not be fully aware of our real attitude toward and concern for the Antioch program." "We admit failures," they said, "we do not admit failure." The faculty members agreed that Morgan should not have to carry the burden of raising money and begged him to return immediately to direct the educational effort.[40]

This first letter represented a fairly weak and vacillating attitude, but in a second missive they grasped the nettle (although this letter appears to have been mailed without approval by the entire faculty). They opened the question of Morgan's complaint that Antioch had failed to produce graduates of moral discrimination and unselfish purpose, raising the whole subject of the aims and goals of the education offered at Antioch. The faculty members asked the president whether having a definite moral code to impose on students was not inconsistent with other values, such as open inquiry, advocated by Morgan. The faculty went further and inquired whether the problem of understanding what Morgan wanted at Antioch was due to a failure to perceive on its part or to a change of emphasis on his. They raised a valid point. Morgan's criticism of Antioch in 1931 was a long way from his plan for producing enlightened proprietors ten years earlier. "Is it possible," these professors asked, "to conduct a college with definite moral aims on democratic principles?"[41] There lay the real problem: Morgan's tendency to dictate a moral standard instead of allowing each to find his own. He could kick against the

39. "The Letter from Portugal," Morgan to the Antioch faculty, Dec. 3, 1931, Morgan Papers.
40. The Faculty of Antioch College to Morgan, Dec. 15, 1931, Morgan Papers.
41. The Faculty of Antioch College to Morgan, Dec. 22, 1931, Morgan Papers.

pricks of relativism for all he was worth, but the moral certainty of his progressive world no longer functioned adequately.

In early 1932 Morgan returned to Antioch, ostensibly under new arrangements that would allow him to work on his ideas for education, but it must have seemed clear to most observers that his work there was over. He wrote Lucy that he was again considering taking a remnant of faculty and students "to do more nearly the job we dreamed about." His one concern was his obligation to Kettering, who had donated so much money to the college.[42]

Morgan brought back with him from Portugal what would be his last attempt to communicate with the Antioch faculty. It was a play, of all things, and he had the college press rush it into print. It was his answer to the charge that he lacked specificity in his plea for noble purpose, and he called it *The Seed Man; or, Things in General*.[43] In all that Morgan was and could do well, he was no playwright, and his decision to publish *Seed Man* was unfortunate, since his story of John and Mary Smith and their triumph over evil opened him to ridicule. On the other hand, the play is remarkably revealing about Morgan's view of proper living, and in a more subtle sense about himself. John's strict mother teaches him fairness and honesty, even when the other boys tease him. John resists the temptations of a corrupt society, and resolving to follow the higher road, he quits a job because his employer is dishonest.

Even the title can be construed as an unconscious sexual image, and *Seed Man* is Morgan's frankest attempt to deal with the sexual revolution. Before John marries Mary, he faces the challenge of saving himself for her. John stalks the hills at midnight "because my passions drive me." He encounters a doctor who advises him to "go find a woman." John, however, cannot accept the "loss of uniqueness." He refuses the doctor:

> Can a man spend his life as he will, and then find it whole and unspoiled to offer as his great gift? Can full tenderness and affection and trust grow on the ashes of spent desire? When the fires of passion are spent that might have purified his life and driven it to higher levels, shall he offer the residue as all he has?

No maiden ever showed more concern for virginity. Convinced that John will not ruin himself for marriage, the doctor recommends long, hot baths. But Morgan does not let the sexual theme go. John is next accosted

42. Morgan to Lucy Morgan, March 22, 1932, Morgan Papers. An excellent example of Morgan's continuing disappointment with Antioch is his "A Talk to the Antioch Alumni," June 24, 1932, typed manuscript, Morgan Papers.

43. Morgan, *The Seed Man; or, Things in General* (Yellow Springs: Antioch Press, 1932).

by Letitia, "a girl of the town," who proposes a rendezvous, and our hero almost succumbs only to be saved by the fortunate appearance of Mary, who makes him a better offer—an evening of music on the lawn. John and Mary have found each other, and not a moment too soon.

John comes up with a new idea to clean garden seeds, a wholesome small business. With the slogan, "A few more seeds in the grower's package. A few cents less from the grower's pocket," he becomes a success. When he decides to turn his entire business over to the more fit of his employees, he refuses to worry about the charge of paternalism when fewer than 10 percent are deemed sufficiently proper to hold the company's stock. "Let's find out what is good," insists John, "and call that democratic."

John, retired, enters his last great fight. He discovers that an old friend is under attack as a state factory inspector. His comrade had developed an inspection code (Morgan did not hold back in *Seed Man*; he used every one of his heavy symbols), the standards of which had so alienated corrupt manufacturers that they were determined to have him fired. The case is obviously based on Morgan's own experience with the Everglades scandal back in 1912, when he had aided his former superior in a fight against evil land speculators. The battle in *Seed Man* is won by taking the issue to the public and educating it on the need for factory inspection, but John and Mary use all their savings on the campaign. Wealth, however, means nothing to them, and they happily return to their original and simple cottage where John, as an old man, develops new varieties of plants.

We have no record of the *Seed Man*'s impact on Antioch and Yellow Springs. The play may have been so poor and didactic that sensitive people overlooked it. We do know that years later copies of it were extremely difficult to find. Some kindly staff or family member may have suppressed it, but for those of us eager to peer into what is clearly now a deeply complex and troubled mind the little play is a wonderful discovery. How tortured Morgan must have been, so committed to fine purpose and so easily misunderstood.

When *Seed Man* appeared, Morgan was only a year away from appointment to the Tennessee Valley Authority. The siren call of Franklin D. Roosevelt spared him what would otherwise have been a painful separation from Antioch. Yet there is little doubt of Morgan's profound disappointment with the Antioch scheme. In some ways it seems a shame that Morgan did not set a more modest goal for himself. He literally saved Antioch from extinction, saved it rather dramatically and boldly with a brave new idea of work-study that caught the imagination of the American public for a time before the depression. He gave to Antioch a tradition of experimentation, social consciousness, unconventionality, and community. He brought to the institution what every small, private college must have: a clear sense of mission and an easily understood identity. He never understood an Antioch that could refuse his moral code, but his achievements there were truly remarkable and they provided a definite legacy that has stood the college in good stead.

One cannot easily dismiss the Utopian nature of Morgan's hopes for Antioch. How could he have insisted that one small college save humanity? How could he have blundered into the contradictions the faculty spotted so easily? Perhaps he was himself a contradiction, driven by a complex dualism spanning this century and the last: a money-making Utopian, an intuitive scientist, a freethinking moral dogmatist.

Could Morgan have characterized in a personal sense the contradictions of the 1920s? Of modern America? The iron law of historiography kindly prevents making such claims for the man, but it does seem that Morgan had a way of internalizing, more perhaps than any other recent figure, the Utopianism of the nineteenth century. He fell into the pit of contradiction because he represented so well the technicalism and scientism of our time. The demands he placed on Antioch doomed his scheme, and there is a sort of fatalism about Morgan that suggests that his failure was self-fulfilling. He must have expected a wicked world to reject his nobility.

Despite the seeming obviousness of the fact, Morgan never guessed that moral codes could not be written as easily as engineering plans. The beauty of the code concept overwhelmed him and permeated in a powerfully fundamental way his view of the world. Within three months after becoming the first chairman of the board of the Tennessee Valley Authority, as well as its chief engineer, Morgan would produce "An Ethical Code for the Staff of the TVA." Repeated rejections of his code would not stop him. When, at the age of ninety-six, alone and largely forgotten, he would come to the last chapter of his last book, he would include "Elements of an Ethical Code."

CHAPTER 4

Morgan Meets the Electric President

Leaving Arthur Morgan tense and unhappy in Yellow Springs, the story turns to focus on the development of that power which offered him another chance at Utopia. If Morgan had given up on Antioch as the fulfillment of his dream, he had not forsaken the larger vision. He needed a new site for the next experiment. It was electricity that gave it to him—another town and another institution, and this time he was able to start from scratch.

To understand how electricity had grown so, scan the statistical tables that Americans compile with such intensity. Our records do not begin until 1902, and one can see the remarkable development of the electric power industry over the next three decades. Electricity, produced by hydroelectric dams, coal, or internal combustion, became very big business. By 1929 the net production of electric energy had increased twentyfold, after which the Great Depression forced a slight decline until 1935. In terms of the average American, this process meant that more and more of them had electrified homes. By 1925 more than half of the country's residential units had electric service. This progress was, however, essentially an urban phenomenon, and in that same year over 96 percent of America's farms still had no electric lights. Indeed, most farms remained powerless throughout the New Deal years. Even as the price of power steadily decreased, and usage just as steadily increased, rural America was deemed unsuitable for electricity, largely because conventional wisdom held it uneconomical to run transmission lines into the countryside.

By 1925 nearly 70 percent of nonfarm residences had electric lights, but most of those families could hardly afford the great amounts of energy post–World War II Americans used. For a small family in the 1920s, being very careful with electricity and burning only a few lights, and maybe a radio, but certainly going without an electric range or washing machine, the monthly usage averaged about fifty kilowatt-hours. Although prices varied, in 1920 that use level meant an average cost of about $4.20. By 1940 that figure had dropped to $2.72 and usage had increased dramatically. In the 1920s and 1930s, however, most Americans used the comparatively expensive electricity sparingly.

It is also interesting to see who owned the capability to produce electricity. Back in 1902 privately held electric utilities outnumbered publicly controlled ones by well over ten to one. The progressive era soon produced a spate of public utilities, as many municipalities began to operate their own water and power systems. This movement of municipal socialism, as it was called, stalled during the 1920s, and by the end of that decade the ratio between private and public ownership had increased to nearly twenty to one. Comparing the generating capacity between the two forms of control produces similar ratios, as the private sector clearly outstripped the public sector.[1] The thought that the people should own the utilities on which they so increasingly depended was a notion that actually declined in the 1920s. Still, the idea did not disappear altogether, and it is to a small group of old progressives, most of them in the Republican party, that credit goes for keeping the concept of public power available as a legitimate option. The private power companies naturally held that such public ownership was outright Bolshevism, and the country's leadership generally agreed with them. For all its indignation, however, the already massive private electrical industry soon had its hands full defending itself against revelations of substantial abuses of its power.

It frequently happens in history that such large debates over matters of philosophy and policy are fought out in terms of specific, and sometimes minor, test cases that serve to symbolize the issues. In the 1920s the debate over public versus private ownership of the capacity to produce and transmit electricity came to be discussed almost entirely in terms of one small town in northern Alabama.

Muscle Shoals became the center of this significant controversy because of its location on the Tennessee River. As beautiful as the Tennessee was, and still is, for that matter, it was not a "good" river. Years ago the glaciers had deformed it and made it downright evil at points. Meandering out of the Appalachian Mountains, the river begins its 650-mile course above Knoxville, then heads down into Alabama, where it takes a sudden turn to the northwest and runs through Muscle Shoals. The river then continues north, through West Tennessee and into Kentucky, where it hits the Ohio River near Paducah, just before the Ohio joins the Mississippi at Cairo. The Tennessee Valley itself consists of some forty thousand square miles, and in 1920 it was home for a population of about

---

1. This brief statistical overview is based on *The Statistical History of the United States from Colonial Times to the Present* (Stamford, Conn.: Fairfield Pubs., Inc., 1965), pp. 501–12B.

two million people. The Tennessee was what the engineers called a "flashy river." It could rise from a creek of fewer than eight thousand cubic feet per second to a monster of nearly half a million. Muscle Shoals was the most terrifying stretch of all: thirty-seven miles of treacherous rocks and crazy water with a total fall of 130 feet, almost as much as Niagara Falls.

Situated about midway in Alabama's Colbert County, equidistant from Nashville and Birmingham, Muscle Shoals was nothing until the Great War. As the United States faced entry into World War I, national officials became concerned that the country's ability to produce munitions involved an unhealthy reliance on nitrates imported from Chile. To end such dependence, which might become disastrous in wartime, a section of the National Defense Act of 1916 enabled the president to build plants that could produce synthetic nitrogen, to power those plants by hydroelectric means, and in peacetime to use the nitrogen to produce fertilizer. The act also allowed the government to make such improvements in navigation as would support the nitrate production.

In the early fall of 1917, with the United States in the war, the Wilson administration used the National Defense Act to begin building near Muscle Shoals two nitrate plants, at a cost of at least eighty-two million dollars, and an adjacent hydroelectric dam as a source of power. The first nitrate plant never worked at all, and the second was not finished until the end of the war. The dam, later known as Wilson Dam, was still under construction when peace came. After the war, and especially when the Republicans took over the White House in 1921, the Muscle Shoals property became a genuine white elephant for Washington. Most of the surplus war materiel was sold at bargain prices, and it seemed reasonable to expect that Muscle Shoals would be disposed of similarly.

In the early 1920s there were a number of proposals to sell or lease Muscle Shoals, and it is interesting that in those years the value of the installations was seen almost entirely in terms of their ability to produce fertilizer. Southern farmers may be forgiven if most of them thought only of getting a bigger cotton yield for less money. They accepted the untested belief that the government could deliver cheaper fertilizer from Muscle Shoals and did not grasp quickly the fact that the real miracle was in the electricity that Wilson Dam could produce. Electricity was, after all, "citified."

The great hubbub about Muscle Shoals came in the summer of 1921 when no less a figure than Henry Ford, the genius of Detroit, offered to take over the whole enterprise from the federal government. Ford thought that slightly less than six cents on the dollar would be an attractive figure to bail out Washington. Given the ridiculously low prices the government had been getting for surplus ships and planes, Ford's offer was seen by many as fairly reasonable. Just what he had in mind for Muscle Shoals is difficult to say, for he remained vague about his plans. He brought in his close friend Thomas Alva Edison to sanctify the project with science, referring to some secret plan to produce fertilizer cheaply, something the federal government had never decisively demonstrated. But the whole episode was clouded with Ford's extravagance. Somehow he related the success of his scheme to an end of domination by Wall Street financiers, and he tied his hatred for bankers to his rather strong anti-Semitism. It was the Jews, Ford insisted, who controlled the gold supply and who dominated the hated gold standard, and it was in fact the Jews who were responsible for the Great War.

By early 1922 Ford had gone so far as to announce plans for a wonderful new city, some seventy-five miles long, in the Muscle Shoals area. He even intimated that eventually he intended to turn over the whole project to the local inhabitants, who would at last be free from want. The result was one of the country's greatest real estate booms, as speculators poured into northern Alabama. The frenzy of speculation, the obviously low price that Ford offered, and the opposition of lingering progressives in the Senate, led by Nebraska Republican George W. Norris, delayed any decision on the Ford bid. In the meantime, as further offers to lease the property came forth, Senator Norris developed his own proposal for Muscle Shoals.[2]

In the spring of 1922 Norris introduced his first Muscle Shoals bill, calling for the creation of a government corporation that would sell fertilizer and power at cost. Norris also paid lip service to the prospect of a unified development system for the Tennessee River that would include improvements for navigation and flood control, but these aspects remained vague in the early 1920s, as did the question of whether the government could build transmission lines to carry the surplus power. Attention continued to focus primarily on the fertilizer dimension.

It was Norris, more than anyone else, who stopped the Ford plan, which he called "the most wonderful real-estate speculation since Adam

2. The complete story of the Muscle Shoals debate is told in Preston J. Hubbard, *Origins of the TVA: The Muscle Shoals Controversy, 1920–1932* (Nashville: Vanderbilt University Press, 1961; reprinted by Norton in 1968). For more on Ford, see Allen Nevins and Frank Ernest Hill, *Ford: Expansion and Challenge, 1915–1933* (New York: Charles Scribner's Sons, 1957). Norris's role in this and other progressive causes has been exhaustively examined in Richard Lowitt, *George W. Norris: The Persistence of a Progressive, 1913–1933* (Urbana: University of Illinois Press, 1971).

and Eve lost title to the Garden of Eden."[3] Ford was fantastically popular during this period, having put the country on wheels, and as early as 1922 a serious Ford-for-President movement had emerged. Norris, however, had sufficient power on the Senate Agriculture Committee, which had jurisdiction over Muscle Shoals issues, to beat Ford through contrived delays until the latter eventually withdrew his offer. Moreover, by 1924 Norris had introduced another bill, which clearly saw that Muscle Shoals was just one spot in an entire river system that could be developed. By then Norris wanted not only fertilizer and power production, but government-built transmission lines and a series of dams along the whole river for more power, as well as flood control and navigation enhancement.

By 1925 the Muscle Shoals matter had been debated and studied thoroughly. In that year a special commission appointed by President Coolidge recommended that the project be leased to a private concern. Coolidge himself remarked that he failed to see what all the fuss was about since the government's holdings at Muscle Shoals were not worth "much more than a first-class battleship."[4] Norris was as stymied in his plan as was Ford, and if the Nebraska senator succeeded in fending off attempts to unload the property, he could do very little about the White House.

Whatever Coolidge might have thought, the fact of the matter was that the idle complex the government had down at Muscle Shoals was truly impressive. The nitrate plants were gigantic by any standard, and the nearly completed Wilson Dam was simply fantastic, the largest concrete dam in the world at the time. The U.S. Army Corps of Engineers had five thousand laborers working three shifts a day to complete the project, and they were using enough concrete to build a highway from New York to Chicago. Holding back a magnificent fifteen-mile lake was a structure twice as tall as the Woolworth Building and longer than twenty football fields. Wilson Dam was projected to generate power equivalent to one-eighth of the nation's existing capacity.

No wonder the real estate market went berserk. The promise of power was evident in the structure itself. In regard to real estate speculation, consider one sensational example of boosterism. This is no mere pamphlet here, but 254 pages in Martin Clary's 1924 *The Facts About Muscle Shoals*. This period piece was so obviously commercial that it refused to take sides on the public-versus-private angle. Insisting that Ford might

3. Quoted in Hubbard, *Origins of the TVA*, p. 77.
4. Quoted in *ibid.*, p. 177.

still lease Muscle Shoals, Clary noted other bids from Union Carbide and the Alabama Power Company, concluding: "It will be a splendid thing if the Shoals are leased to any one of the three. It will be a splendid thing if the Shoals are never leased and if the Government undertakes to operate them instead." One sees clearly from *Facts About Muscle Shoals* that by 1924 power was the real story, for there is only one perfunctory chapter on the miracles of cheap fertilizer for farmers too long oppressed by Wall Street. Clary provided these wild estimations of the value of Muscle Shoals:

> The golden touch of Midas and the mines of Solomon represent but a widow's mite when compared with the penned-up productiveness of Muscle Shoals . . . greatest single factor in the future development of the United States . . . future site of the greatest commercial and manufacturing community in the world. . . . Power will be cheap at Muscle Shoals. . . . So soon as the power is developed manufacturers will flock to the Shoals like flies to a sugar barrel . . . all contained in the magic word "power."[5]

In 1928 Norris managed to move his bill through Congress, only to have Coolidge kill it with a pocket veto. The president simply could not envision the federal government involved in the production, distribution, and sale of power. If Norris had come to see the Muscle Shoals issue as a multipurpose program centered upon making a case for the efficiency and economy of public power, he continued to face disappointment in this era of Republican domination. The one success he did have was in shifting the debate away from fertilizer to electricity and in introducing the concept of the comprehensive development of the Tennessee River basin. Engineering and conservation circles had for some time, as we have seen, endorsed the concept of unified river development. In 1930 the Army Corps of Engineers completed a survey of the Tennessee system and reported that it was ideal for a series of dams that could generate power, facilitate navigation, and control floods. The corps was even aware that with so many dams it could achieve other benefits, such as the elimination of malaria through lowering the water table during the mosquito breeding season.

In 1931 Norris successfully guided his bill once again through Congress, only to have it face President Hoover's veto. "The power problem," Hoover said, "is not to be solved by the Federal Government going into the power business."[6] By then, however, the depression had ended the

5. Martin Clary, *The Facts About Muscle Shoals* (New York: Ocean Publishing Co., 1924), not to be confused with a similarly entitled document put out by the National League of Women Voters in 1927 and cited in Lowitt, *Norris*, p. 201.
6. Quoted in Hubbard, *Origins of the TVA*, p. 293.

ascendancy of the Republicans, and Norris looked forward to November 1932, when he was confident of the election of a friend of public power.

Before the election of Franklin D. Roosevelt in 1932, the private power industry had already done much to ruin its own image with the American people. The moral and political rout started in 1928 with lengthy and terribly damaging investigations by the Federal Trade Commission. Along with the hearings themselves, a number of books extremely critical of the private utilities appeared. Most Americans were deeply shocked to hear that the industry had a systematic propaganda campaign, which had even invaded the public school system. What looked like good public relations to the utilities seemed so much indoctrination to consumers already convinced that their electric bills were inflated.[7]

By 1930 more people were ready to believe the charges that the power companies had watered their stock and passed on false charges to their customers. It was easy to see the magnates in cahoots with the corrupt bankers, buying and selling legislators. The private utilities seemed nothing more than greedy hypocrites who had gained control of the very process that was supposed to regulate them, and who in fact represented a power trust conspiring to smash the public ownership movement. The electric industry had, in its dynamic growth, emerged as the new symbol of a Trust, replacing the older combinations in railroads and steel as a threat to the American way. Vast empires had been created, using the holding company as a technique of control. Holding companies were stacked on holding companies to create a "pyramid," where a small group controlled vast power and properties totaling in the billions of dollars.

The greatest of these monsters was the Insull pyramid. By 1929 Samuel Insull was seventy years old and head of the world's biggest power conglomerate, an array of electric and gas holding companies that gave him effective control of nearly 15 percent of the power produced in the United States—almost as much as any other nation consumed altogether. Some four million customers in twenty-two states depended on him for power, and his investors totaled more than a million. In 1929 Insull's personal fortune was $150 million. In three years it would be zero.[8] A combination of public ill will and corporate infighting led to

7. Examples of contemporary attacks on the power companies, all of them based on the Federal Trade Commission's investigation, include Jack Levin, *Power Ethics* (New York: Alfred A. Knopf, 1931); Carl D. Thompson, *Confessions of the Power Trust* (New York: E. P. Dutton and Co., 1932); and M. L. Ramsay, *Pyramids of Power: The Story of Roosevelt, Insull, and the Utility Wars* (New York: Bobbs-Merrill, 1937). Wendell L. Willkie, who ought to have known, placed the beginning of the attack on electrical pyramids and holding companies with William Z. Ripley's "More Light!—and Power Too," *Atlantic Monthly* 137 (November, 1926), 667–87.

8. Forrest McDonald, *Insull* (Chicago: University of Chicago Press, 1962).

Insull's downfall in the spring of 1932. The crash of his empire was sudden and drastic, leaving his investors with worthless paper. In October 1932 he was indicted for embezzlement and larceny, and he fled to Greece with only a few thousand dollars in pocket change. In 1934 the United States pressured Greece into ordering him out of the country. Sailing in the Mediterranean, Insull was kidnapped by the Turks and eventually returned to America to stand trial. Found not guilty, he exiled himself to Paris, where he died of a heart attack in 1938.

By 1932 the battle lines between the interests of private power and those favoring public control were drawn. For Franklin Roosevelt, the fight was an old one. He had earned his progressive spurs back in 1912 when as a young New York state senator he had helped regain for the people the hydroelectric rights to the St. Lawrence River. Roosevelt was a public power man all the way. When he was elected for the first of two terms as governor in 1928, he had great hopes for the St. Lawrence as a source of cheap electricity. "It is our power," he said in his January 1929 inaugural address, "and no inordinate profit must be allowed to those who act as the people's agents in bringing this power to their homes and workshops."[9] Two months later he went before the legislature to make a direct appeal for the hydroelectric development of the St. Lawrence. He clearly stated that New York could, if the private utilities failed to compromise, build its own transmission lines. From then on he was a committed public power man, in its most advanced form.[10]

In 1930 Governor Roosevelt got the Water Power Law passed in New York, and in 1931 he appointed Frank P. Walsh as head of the State Power Authority. Already relying on skilled advisers, as he would in the White House, Roosevelt also appointed Morris L. Cooke to the authority. If Norris was the political leader of the fight for public power, Cooke was its technical proponent. He had been Gifford Pinchot's consulting engineer when that old forester was governor of Pennsylvania in the 1920s, and there Cooke had proposed his concept of giant power. Although his electric pooling proposal was not necessarily limited to state power, Cooke eventually became a strong advocate of public utilities and was highly regarded in progressive circles. In 1935 President Roosevelt put Cooke in charge of the Rural Electrification Administration.[11]

9. Quoted in Bernard Bellush, *Franklin D. Roosevelt as Governor of New York* (New York: Columbia University Press, 1955), p. 209.

10. *Ibid.*, pp. 208–42.

11. Morris L. Cooke's papers are housed in the Franklin D. Roosevelt Library at Hyde Park. They reveal contact with Arthur Morgan beginning in the 1920s. Additional correspondence is in the Morgan Papers. Two biographies of Cooke exist: Kenneth E. Morris,

Because the St. Lawrence project involved cooperating with Canada, Governor Roosevelt found himself forced to deal with President Hoover's State Department in attempting to work out the treaty required to allow development of the river that formed part of the border between the two countries. He found it a frustrating experience. From Hyde Park he watched very carefully Hoover's handling of the Muscle Shoals case, and with the president's veto of that project, Roosevelt knew that the New York program was endangered. He was all too correct: the St. Lawrence project did not become a reality until the 1950s.[12]

For all the work done on behalf of public power by Norris and Cooke, and for all the credit that Norris deserves as the father of the TVA, it takes nothing away from them to suggest that Roosevelt also contributed significantly in the conversion of the Muscle Shoals issue into the TVA concept. It was no doubt Roosevelt who really grasped just how multi-purpose the development of the Tennessee River could be. To Norris's ideas of power, fertilizer, flood control, and navigation, Roosevelt added even more functions: soil erosion control, reforestation, land management, and something vaguely wonderful called social and economic development. Such expansive ideas went back to his days as governor. By the spring of 1933, Roosevelt's vision of what the TVA could do would be broad enough to enthrall Arthur Morgan.

As 1933 began, and despite the revelations of the Federal Trade Commission and the emergency of a depression that brought new energy to antitrust agitation, the utility companies were hardly defeated. One of the most energetic spokesmen for private power had emerged on the national scene. Only thirty-six years old that year, Wendell L. Willkie was well into a remarkable career that made him the Republican presidential nominee in 1940. In 1933, after service as a corporation lawyer, Willkie became president and chief executive officer of the Commonwealth and Southern, a billion-dollar holding company with large ter-

---

The Life and Times of a Happy Liberal: A Biography of Morris Llewellyn Cooke (New York: Harper and Brothers, 1954), and Jean Christie, *Morris Llewellyn Cooke: Progressive Engineer* (New York: Garland Pub., Inc., 1983). For a sound study of the Rural Electrification Administration, see D. Clayton Brown, *Electricity for Rural America: The Fight for the REA* (Westport, Conn.: Greenwood Press, 1980). Another fighter for public power in the 1920s was Judson King, director of the National Popular Government League, established by La Follette and other progressives in 1913. King's interesting views of the entire period under study are in his *The Conservation Fight: From Theodore Roosevelt to the Tennessee Valley Authority* (Washington: Public Affairs Press, 1959).

12. Roosevelt's gubernatorial papers are available on microfilm at the Roosevelt Library in Hyde Park. From them Roosevelt's great concern for the case of Muscle Shoals, particularly as it might affect his plans for the St. Lawrence, is obvious.

ritories in the South. Brilliant and amiable, Willkie was the best of the spokesmen for the private interests, and he could be eloquent in his description of the ruin public power would bring to the widows and orphans who had invested in private utility stocks. One anti-Power Trust writer called him "the power industry's outstanding front man."[13] The Tennessee Valley Authority was a definite threat to Willkie's pyramid, and he would fight it tooth and nail.

Another young professional demands our attention before we turn to Roosevelt's New Deal. David E. Lilienthal, one of Harvard Law School's finest and a protégé of the great Felix Frankfurter, had earned his stripes as an attorney with the liberal Donald Richberg in Chicago, where they battled the Insull interests. Richberg, later himself a controversial New Dealer in the National Recovery Administration, recommended Lilienthal for a job in Wisconsin, and in 1931 Governor Philip La Follette appointed him to what became the Wisconsin Public Service Commission. In Wisconsin, Lilienthal made a name for himself as an aggressive supporter of the public's right to regulate utilities, and he achieved substantial recognition as an enemy of the power companies. After La Follette's defeat in 1932, however, it became apparent that Lilienthal's appointment would not be renewed. In 1933, then, Lilienthal was looking for another challenge, another place to fight for the public interest. He, like Morgan, would find that place in the Tennessee Valley Authority, where he would meet Willkie head-on in a series of legal battles and political wars that decided the fate of public power. The arena for that contest was set with the inauguration of Franklin D. Roosevelt.

After his election in November 1932, Roosevelt planned furiously for the beginning of his administration the following March. One of the things he wanted to do was visit Muscle Shoals and see firsthand what all the controversy had been about. As a progressive Republican, Norris had crossed over in 1932 and supported Roosevelt. There was not so much a debt to be paid as a tribute to be made, and on January 1, 1933, the president-elect announced that he had invited Norris to accompany him on a trip to Alabama later in the month. There, with tears in his eyes, Norris heard Roosevelt make his commitment: "With the help of Congress we are going to put Muscle Shoals and the Tennessee River back on the map."[14] Roosevelt soon labeled his scheme the Tennessee Valley Authority.

13. Ramsay, *Pyramids*, p. 36.
14. Quoted in Lowitt, *Norris*, p. 568.

Roosevelt's great plans for the New Deal had not been obvious in the campaign of 1932. As far as the major political parties were concerned in preparing for the election, there might as well have been no depression. The disaster was so total that the parties as institutions hardly knew what to say. So they argued about booze, with the GOP willing to give prohibition another chance and the Democrats calling for outright repeal. After a hard fight for the Democratic nomination, Roosevelt made his acceptance speech and included the term *new deal*. Even though he had not intended anything special by the phrase, it stuck. In the presidential campaign, Roosevelt was vague and contradictory, and many observers found him unimpressive. He produced no particular plan for recovery, but he did promise to balance the budget, something dear to his heart no matter what has been said about him. At the same time he pledged some sort of help for the farmers, a conservation program employing young men, and controls and safeguards in banking and financing. Along with general references to the need for planning and government cooperation with business, Roosevelt specifically vowed to develop public power projects and to regulate the unruly private utilities.

What he did not do in the campaign of 1932 was to make any mention of the Tennessee Valley Authority, the National Recovery Administration, or any of the other major programs that came to make up the New Deal. In a way, it did not matter that he seemed to lack specifics, because the most important thing he promised the people of the United States was action. Unlike Hoover, whose very philosophy of limited government tied his hands, Roosevelt was going to do something. With this sense of action he restored a modicum of confidence to a nation in the throes of the worst depression in modern history.

It helps to focus a moment on the severity of the country's situation in the winter of 1932–1933 while Roosevelt waited for his inauguration on March 4. Americans are accustomed to economic fluctuations, and they have learned to fear double digits whether in inflation or unemployment. In a depression, as the name suggests, inflation is not a problem; indeed, we have come to appreciate that reflation is part of the solution. But when a recession bottoms out into a first-class depression, it is terribly difficult to restart the economy. Priming the pump in hard times means you have to haul a lot of water. In 1933 fully 25 percent of American workers were unemployed. At that level, one can imagine what the rate was for the underemployed. There were also those with jobs who were being paid irregularly, if at all. Barter was common in small towns and rural areas, and in the cities the garbage bins became supermarkets for hundreds of thousands. For all too many the situation was simply hopeless, as evidenced in the vacant faces in countless photographs. The condition became so common that it gained a name: depression psychosis, a generalized despair crippling the mind of the country.

If Roosevelt promised to do something, the country was willing, in its lethargic fashion, to let him try. Confidence-building was his top priority, and he did it in extraordinary fashion. It was in his March 4, 1933, inaugural address that he used his famous line about fear being the only thing we had to fear. He called Congress into special session on March 9, and he gave his first fireside chat three days later on a Sunday night. The original media president, he had at his disposal an electrical gadget his cousin Theodore Roosevelt had lacked, and he came across on the radio in a deeply reassuring, caring, and humane manner. He got the banks open again in short order, and within slightly more than a month he had the country drinking legal beer.

It was obvious to liberals and at least to some old progressives that the Hundred Days, as this special session of Congress and its honeymoon with Roosevelt is called, was another opportunity to enact many of their ideas so long stymied by the conservatives. Ancient programs were to be dusted off for another attempt at a rational ordering of the social and economic fabric of American society. Now was the time for George Norris to win with his Muscle Shoals bill. On April 10, 1933, five weeks after taking office, Roosevelt asked Congress to create the Tennessee Valley Authority. Passed by a wide margin, the president signed the measure into law on May 18 and announced that Arthur E. Morgan would head the project.

Now comes the delicate matter of the relationship between Morgan and Franklin Roosevelt. Less than a third of the way through the Hundred Days, before the TVA bill was passed, the president offered the chairmanship of the new agency to Morgan. There must have been some very special feeling on the part of the president that led him to such an early decision. He must have had Morgan in mind, must have had some fascinating tie with him that explains precisely why he turned to the moralizing engineer-educator.

Archivists assert that the worse the crisis, the worse the record-keeping. The country was in its greatest crisis since the Civil War, and the surviving records of the Hundred Days show it. That wonderful collection of papers in the Franklin D. Roosevelt Library at Hyde Park, New York, helps only marginally. One cannot, for example, establish with any certainty just when Roosevelt offered the leadership of TVA to Morgan. With only a handful of secretaries, Roosevelt's office was unable even to maintain an accurate list of who came to see the president. Unforgivable? Not when one considers the nature of the Hundred Days. Everything in Washington was topsy-turvy in the early moments of the New Deal.

In this narrative, the contact man in the White House is Marvin H. McIntyre, known to the president and friends as Mac. Along with Louis M. Howe and Marguerite ("Missy") LeHand, Mac had been with Roosevelt since his vice-presidential campaign in 1920. One recent examination of his role says that McIntyre was "in charge of political appointments, insofar as anybody was."[15] He was Morgan's liaison with the White House, and it was through him that the Utopian got to see the president. It did not take him long to realize that a letter, telegram, or phone call to Mac was as good as talking to FDR himself. McIntyre had the most direct access to President Roosevelt, and it was his neatly typed list of items that Roosevelt dealt with each day. His agendas for the president's attention were invariably cryptic, but they represent for us the best view we have of Roosevelt's daily management style. McIntyre had no time for detailed records. He called deserving matters to the president's notice, got his instructions verbally, and in many cases appears to have carried them out over the telephone.

How did Morgan come to Roosevelt's attention? The two men had never met personally, but Morgan had seen Roosevelt once, back in the gubernatorial days when the New Yorker addressed a group of college and university presidents. The jovial governor's unflattering comments about the New York legislature had put off the stern Morgan, who found him too political and insensitive. We know that Morgan did not vote for Roosevelt in 1932, for that he freely admitted. He voted for the engineer, Hoover. Roosevelt had not shown his charisma in the campaign, and it was natural that Morgan would not yet have warmed up to a politician from New York. Hoover had been a wonder back before the depression, and he obviously still had appeal to old progressives such as Morgan. Yet many of them had at least a brief honeymoon with the new president once he swung into action.[16]

15. "McIntyre, Marvin Hunter ('Mac')," in Otis L. Graham, Jr., and Meghan Robinson Wander (eds.), *Franklin D. Roosevelt, His Life and Times: An Encyclopedic View* (Boston: G. K. Hall & Co., 1985), pp. 254–55.

16. Otis L. Graham, Jr., *An Encore for Reform: The Old Progressives and the New Deal* (New York: Oxford University Press, 1967). Graham samples a large number of progressives and finds that most of them had given up on reform after World War I. Of those remaining, the majority had severe difficulties in accepting the new role of the state inherent in the New Deal. It is not surprising that Arthur Morgan voted against Roosevelt in 1932. It is,

In many ways Morgan was an obvious choice for Roosevelt, best seen in the complete ease and dispatch with which the Senate confirmed his nomination. Morgan was, after all, a national figure of nearly two decades' standing. It seems likely that Roosevelt had run across some of Morgan's writings, perhaps even *Antioch Notes*. Morgan always maintained that it was through Eleanor Roosevelt that he came to Roosevelt's attention. There is some brief correspondence between Eleanor and Morgan at Hyde Park, but it shows only the fairly mundane work of a college president seeking to enlist the aid of the rich and famous for his campus. Morgan asked Eleanor Roosevelt to serve on a New York committee to support Antioch, but this effort appears never to have gotten off the ground. He also urged the Roosevelts to visit Yellow Springs, but when they did in the spring of 1931 Morgan was out of town. Morgan had faith in Mrs. Roosevelt, respecting her for much the same reasons that many other Americans came to love her. For Morgan, it was always through Eleanor that Roosevelt knew about him.[17]

Roosevelt also may have heard of Morgan from Morris Cooke, his chief adviser on matters electric. Cooke and Morgan were part of the elitist engineering community from the late progressive period into the twenties, and they had corresponded professionally since 1922. Roosevelt trusted Cooke, giving him major positions in New York and in Washington, and even if Cooke never mentioned Morgan to Roosevelt, the president probably asked Cooke's advice about the appointment. He also may have consulted with Senator Norris on who was to become TVA's first chairman of the board of directors; there is, however, no evidence that Roosevelt discussed Morgan's appointment with either Norris or Cooke.[18]

There is one man who claims to have been responsible for Morgan's selection—James M. Cox, Roosevelt's old friend and 1920 running mate. Before their disastrous campaign for the White House, Cox had been governor of Ohio, back in the days when Morgan was developing the

---

however, somewhat shocking that five months later he embraced him with such intensity. Whether or not this move makes Morgan any less a progressive than we have considered him is difficult to say. Perhaps it emphasizes the sense of energy and high aspiration that the New Yorker offered and that Morgan required.

17. Arthur Morgan to Eleanor Roosevelt, April 11, 1931, and Eleanor Roosevelt to Morgan, April 15, 1933, Eleanor Roosevelt Papers, Roosevelt Library, Hyde Park. Morgan's great affection for Eleanor and the fact that he attributed his appointment to her is obvious in his *The Making of the TVA* (Buffalo, N.Y.: Prometheus Books, 1974), pp. 4, 7–8, 175.

18. Lowitt, in his thoroughly researched *Norris*, finds no reason to believe that Norris knew about Morgan's appointment before the fact.

innovative Miami Conservancy. Perhaps Cox discussed the conservancy and Morgan with his vice-presidential candidate. As a state governor, Roosevelt must have known about the great Ohio idea. At any rate, after 1920 Cox and Roosevelt remained very close, despite their defeat, and the New Yorker wrote Cox the warmest of letters from the White House. In his memoirs Cox specifically recollected Roosevelt inquiring in early 1933 about a good hydraulic engineer. Cox gave him Morgan's name, and the president had Louis Howe call Morgan to set up an interview for the very next day. "I remember well," Cox said, "remarking to the President that Morgan would be honest and efficient but had no patience with politics in matters such as this."[19]

Is one to believe that the president of the United States, searching for an appointee to a major position, based his decision on a single recommendation from an old comrade in a lost election? It seems amazing, but perhaps it does only because history knows far more about Morgan than the new president did. Today we understand the hint that Cox gave Roosevelt, and we might not have taken the risk with Morgan. But those were not ordinary times. They did not allow ordinary searches, and Roosevelt was no ordinary president. Even with considerably more information on Morgan, Roosevelt still might have appointed him. That is part of the enigma that is Roosevelt. Part of him liked the Utopian. Within twenty-four hours after discussing Morgan with Cox, Roosevelt offered the Antioch College president another chance at building a new moral order.

Back at Antioch, with all the problems that it held for him, Morgan naturally had turned to renewing his engineering practice. He still remained president of the college, but essentially this was in name only. Sometime in late March or early April 1933, Morgan visited Washington to lobby for a replication of his Miami project, called the Muskingum Conservancy. It seemed certain to Morgan, from his reading of Roosevelt, that large relief measures were in the offing, and he, along with the Ohio congressional delegation, wanted their share for Ohio. According to Morgan's story, a few days after returning to Yellow Springs from Washington, where he had met with various congressmen, he received an invitation to the White House. Assuming that the president wanted to talk about Muskingum, Morgan returned to Washington on or about April 13, 1933.

19. James M. Cox, *Journey Through My Years* (New York: Simon and Schuster, 1946), p. 176.

Lacking any hints from Roosevelt's files regarding the nature of his meeting with Morgan, one must refer to the latter's accounts of his interview with the president. Morgan always insisted that in his conversation with Roosevelt, the Muskingum concern was never mentioned. Instead, the president launched immediately into a monologue about his plans for the Tennessee Valley Authority. After a lengthy discussion of the multiplicity of programs the new agency would offer, the president asked Morgan to become chairman of the board of the TVA.

At this point Morgan made a salient observation: "But, Mr. President, you do not know me." The answer Morgan always heard, as he went over and over that fateful encounter for the next four decades, was, "Haven't I been reading *Antioch Notes* all these years? I like your vision." Morgan always made a note of that: the president shared the vision. Morgan was equally convinced that at that initial meeting he secured from Roosevelt a promise that the Tennessee Valley Authority would be entirely free from politics. The president is supposed to have pounded the table, "There is to be no politics in this!" Morgan recalled near the end of his life: "I felt then that I wanted the job."[20] Even while picturing the president easily nodding his agreement to Morgan's moralisms, one knows, as Roosevelt did, that nothing was ever completely free from his need for reelection. Everything was political.

It is difficult to leave this dimly lit scene where Roosevelt and Morgan came to terms with each other. There is no reason to think that Morgan's version is false. Honesty was for him a universal expedient. He was incapable of lying. He could misinterpret, though, and Roosevelt could be so disarmingly agreeable. Note, too, with some suspicion, that Morgan's accounts of the meeting get more detailed as he gets older, as they do for most people. Possibly his first meeting with Roosevelt was so central to the whole history of their relationship that, for Morgan, it entered the realm of fantasy. That was the meeting where he would have used his sound judgment to make a quick but accurate appraisal of Roosevelt. He had bragged on his ability to evaluate anyone after only a few minutes, as he had told the Antioch student body often enough. Morgan would have intuited Roosevelt's character right then and there. Knowing that Morgan embraced Roosevelt and became a New Dealer, the inescapable conclusion is that something happened in that meeting to give Morgan a wonderful glimpse of the president's vision. By 1933 Morgan was desper-

20. Morgan grappled with the meaning of his first meeting with Roosevelt for the rest of his life. His initial account was written five years after the occasion: "A Statement of My Relations with the President," July 1, 1938, Morgan Papers. His last recollections were recorded in his final book, *The Making of the TVA*, pp. 6–7.

ate to regain intensity and rightness, to be about some noble purpose, and he heard Roosevelt offer it to him.

One cannot help wondering how the two men looked together. They must have seemed an odd pair: Roosevelt with that flashy smile, and Morgan with his aggressively simple demeanor. Morgan turned fifty-five shortly after the end of the Hundred Days. His hair was almost completely gray, and it had thinned, exposing a forehead that seemed all wrinkled brow. His nose had become a prominent figure, and its hawklike aspect added to his forbidding quality. All in all, given the times, it was a quite respectable look. If the conservatively dressed, well-to-do man of 1933 seems a bit overstarched, it was then regarded as nothing more than dignified. Morgan was immensely dignified.

"I tell you, Henry," Morgan had John say in *Seed Man*, "Humor's dangerous. A man of dignity and responsibility must beware of it." Morgan was completely serious, and he never joked. He had a kind of total commitment to the great task at hand that reminds one somewhat of Lenin, who in his dedication excluded any private life at all. Lenin, however, was a very good politician; events will show how good Morgan was. For the moment, one wonders if Morgan had on his customary look, that visage that could make one feel so uneasy, the face that the Antioch Shoe designer saw when he imagined Morgan as The Judge.

It is easy to picture Roosevelt with that ready hand and that patented buoyancy, but was he smoking a cigarette in his jaunty holder? Did he call for a cocktail in what seems to have been a lengthy meeting? Morgan's last estimate had it up to ninety minutes. Smoking and drinking were clear signals to Morgan not to trust the offending individual. In his reminiscing years later, he told of a trip he once took to meet a man who came highly recommended for a position. Morgan found the fellow at home, out in the backyard using his twelve gauge to fire birdshot into a piece of furniture to make it look like antique wormwood. Morgan instantly saw deceit: an outright, deliberate lie, along with a violation of the code of the simple life that allowed no such pretense. Somehow what this man had done was wrong, destroying in some way Morgan's equilbrium. From that single episode Morgan believed for the rest of his life that the man was dishonest. Case closed. When Morgan found dishonesty, he had found the worst. Far from being a matter of knowing that he could not believe anything the man might tell him, being dishonest was to Morgan an absolute crime. Morgan saw no such deceit in Roosevelt. He saw a comrade in Utopia.

Before allowing Morgan to be too firmly in control during this first meeting, however, consider that he would have been very much impressed with being in the presence of the president, as would we all. Apparently the offer of a major appointment took him completely by surprise. No doubt Morgan heard duty call, saw fate reaching out to him. Such a feeling would be normal when the president asks for one's help, and Morgan had been in agony for the past few years, waiting for his aspiration to return. Was his need for a new mission so important, his response so immediate and emotional, that he neglected to listen closely? Morgan needed Roosevelt. As for the president's feeling for Morgan, and how they changed, there shall be ample opportunity for consideration.

CHAPTER 5

Launching The TVA

A rthur Morgan walked out of the White House and began work on the Tennessee Valley Authority. There was nothing he loved so much as a sense of urgency involving a great project. From the spring of 1933 Morgan forgot Antioch, and he was delighted to focus all his immense energy on the Tennessee experiment.

One of the interesting aspects of the Muscle Shoals drama was that while the rural Alabama town was the essential antecedent in the creation of the TVA, the new agency would be primarily a Knoxville phenomenon. The TVA act called for headquarters to be located at Muscle Shoals, but the center of attention shifted to Tennessee, where the U.S. Army Corps of Engineers had been planning for some time to build the next dam in its effort to control the river, a dam on a tributary in the hills of East Tennessee at Cove Creek. Alabamians occasionally expressed their resentment, and the TVA established an office at Muscle Shoals, but the New Deal action was always in Knoxville because of its proximity to Cove Creek. Tennessee Valley Authority headquarters have, of course, remained in Knoxville.

Shortly after his conversation with Franklin Roosevelt, it occurred to Morgan that he still had the opportunity to participate in the writing of the Tennessee Valley Authority statute, then in the conference stage in Congress. Morgan wired the president, asking for permission to introduce himself to the members of the committee working on the final draft. FDR's aide, McIntyre, responded: "Suggest you discuss matter you mention with Senator Norris and Chairman McSwain."[1] Norris, for so long the Tennessee Valley's champion, was working on the bill with Rep. John J. McSwain of South Carolina, who had guided it through the House. Although the TVA bill, what with Norris's experience, was well along when he arrived on the scene, Morgan's engineering success and his work with state legislatures enabled him to make numerous technical suggestions, which were incorporated into the measure. At least one of Morgan's recommendations was of greater importance than the technicalities he corrected.

1. Telegram from McIntyre to Morgan, April 13, 1933, Roosevelt Papers.

Morgan wished to make certain that the TVA would not have to depend on the Army Corps of Engineers for the construction of its dams. The corps had built the facilities down at Muscle Shoals, and it was well along on planning for the Cove Creek dam. There is every reason to believe that, since the army had been so heavily involved in what was to be the TVA, Morgan's intervention on this point was decisive. Because having his own dedicated work force was an essential part of the plan he was forming, he certainly did not want to rely on the military. Moreover, he had a long-standing antipathy toward the corps, having fought with it over flood control methods. He battled it for the rest of his life.[2] Morgan's suggestion that the TVA do its own engineering and hire its own employees without reference to civil service was included in the act.

Morgan also supported the adding of the section that gave the TVA authority to extend its transmission lines in order to create its own system for delivering power, thus avoiding any reliance on Wendell Willkie's private utilities. Morgan always took a good deal of credit for this feature of the bill, and it was the subject of debate, but the idea had been around since Norris's early proposals. Morgan's support of this approach may have carried weight, but it was unlikely to have been critical. By 1933 virtually all public power enthusiasts understood the necessity of transmitting as well as of producing power.

When Morgan approached the conference committee, he found that its members intended to pay the chairman of the board a thousand dollars per year more than the other two directors. In a typical gesture, Morgan urged that the three directors receive the same remuneration, and so the bill was changed to provide an annual salary of ten thousand dollars to each board member.[3] The several collections of materials that yield information on the very early life of the TVA—the Morgan papers in Yellow Springs, the Roosevelt papers in Hyde Park, and the central files of the Authority itself—combine to show Morgan's intense work on behalf of the measure before it was finally passed by Congress, and certainly before his appointment had been confirmed by the Senate. No

2. Morgan's long fight with the Corps of Engineers began in the 1920s and is best summarized in his *Dams and Other Disasters: A Century of the Army Corps of Engineers in Civil Works* (Boston: Porter Sargent, 1971).

3. Morgan, "Suggestions Concerning H.R. 4859," Morgan Papers; author's interview with Morgan, April 26, 1966. See also U.S. Congress, Joint Committee on the Investigation of the Tennessee Valley Authority, *Hearings, May 25-December 21, 1938*, pursuant to Public Resolution no. 83 (75th Cong., 3rd sess.) (14 parts; Washington: U.S. Government Printing Office, 1939) p. 337. Hereinafter cited as *TVA Hearings*.

New Dealer worked harder in the Hundred Days than did Morgan, and by the end of May he was well into establishing the Authority.[4]

After Roosevelt signed the TVA bill into law and announced Morgan's appointment on May 18, 1933, the latter's effort for the TVA was full-time. The army engineers working on plans for Cove Creek Dam wished to know how and when the TVA would assume work on that project. The Geological Survey and the Weather Bureau wanted to know who would handle the stations located in the Tennessee Valley. The U.S. Treasury inquired as to how the TVA desired its accounts maintained. It seemed obvious to Morgan that these matters could not wait. It did not occur to him that he had been given no solitary control over the Authority. The act called for a three-person board of directors. At this point only Morgan had been named. He could quite reasonably have waited for the board to constitute itself, but he was in the white heat of high aspiration. This was the next experiment. Utopia waited for no man.

To deal with these several problems, Morgan, at his own expense, got together a group of trusted associates. He sent Samuel M. Woodward, an old friend and engineering colleague, to St. Louis to go over plans for dams in the Tennessee Valley with the Corps of Engineers, which had telegraphed urgently requesting a statement of policy. Morgan dispatched Carl Bock, his chief assistant from the Miami Conservancy and vice-president of his engineering company, to Chattanooga to discuss with the corps the Cove Creek Dam, planning for which was so far along that it was obvious that this would be the TVA's first construction project. Another engineer who had worked with Morgan previously, Barton M. Jones, went to Muscle Shoals to prepare for the Authority's takeover from the army.

Upon signing the TVA act, the president had announced his selection of Morgan to head the new government corporation. On the following day, FDR held a press conference, and the reporters asked about Morgan and "the Muscle Shoals Commission." The president responded by noting that Morgan was president of Antioch College, by citing his great work with the Miami Conservancy, and by calling him one of the nation's foremost hydraulic engineers. It is interesting to note that Roosevelt himself did not use the term TVA, but referred instead to "the Muscle

4. For Morgan's account of his early activities on behalf of the TVA, see Morgan to Nathan Bachman, Oct. 9, 1933, TVA Files, Knoxville, Tennessee.

Shoals Authority."[5] Public interest was once again stirred over the fate of Muscle Shoals, as was curiosity about this first chairman. A flood of congratulations poured in on Morgan. Through his work at Antioch he had made acquaintances all over the country, and many of them wrote to express their faith in him. Clyde R. Miller, director of the Bureau of Educational Services at Columbia University, wrote: "For many years I have been hopeful that we could have a larger degree of socialization of natural resources. The Muscle Shoals development appears to be a realization of that hope, and with yourself in charge chances for that realization seem particularly good."[6]

Hundreds of such letters appeared, and together they show that Morgan was held in high regard by many Americans. One admirer wrote: "Perhaps some future wise student of the philosophy of history . . . will pronounce a verdict, receiving general approval, that 'American Civilization really began in 1933 when Arthur E. Morgan began his work in Tennessee Valley.' "[7] Ellery Sedgwick, longtime friend and editor of *Atlantic Monthly*, claimed that "the perfect indifference to politics shown by the appointment is a lesson to the country, but the appraisal of your individual capacity is, on the part of the administration, little short of a work of genius."[8] Norman Thomas, not the famous socialist but a twenty-eight-year-old black schoolteacher in Tuscumbia, Alabama, wrote: "This development, we realize, should affect our people as much as any people; and with a man of your type who advocates fairness and justice to all, I am confident that we shall get our share of consideration."[9]

Weeks before Morgan's skeleton engineering staff began work on the technical aspects of the transition from Corps of Engineers to TVA, the new chairman undertook the task of selecting the other two board members. Morgan fancied himself a past master in the location and selection of top personnel. He claimed that when he founded Moraine Park School in Dayton, back in 1916, he had considered some fifteen hundred men before hiring the headmaster. His years on the Miami Conservancy had given him files on hundreds of engineers, along with a work force that was unsurpassed. It seemed to Morgan that the same

5. *Complete Presidential Press Conferences of Franklin D. Roosevelt*, 25 vols. (New York: Da Capo Press, 1972), vol. 1, 288.
6. Clyde R. Miller to Morgan, July 13, 1933, Morgan Papers.
7. James A. Haight to Morgan, May 29, 1933, *ibid.*
8. Ellery Sedgwick to Morgan, June 6, 1933, *ibid.*
9. Norman T. Thomas to Morgan, May 23, 1933, *ibid.*

Arthur E. Morgan, president of Antioch College, 1921–1933

The first TVA board members: Harcourt A. Morgan, Arthur E. Morgan, David E. Lilienthal

(Above) Chattanooga, Tennessee, during the great flood of 1867
(Below) The same view of Chattanooga in 1967, after TVA dams up-
stream had eliminated the danger of such devastating floods.

Cutting crew members examine the saw-filer's library.

Washday at a nonelectric home near Norris, 1935

The small homes of Norris ten years later

These cartoons are representative of the many that appeared during hearings on the TVA.

methods would be applicable in searching for TVA directors and other staff members.

On April 18, a matter of days after he first saw the president, Morgan sent him a memorandum indicating that the success of the TVA would depend largely on its key people. "I presume that prompt and vigorous action will be desirable," he noted before he proposed beginning a "very confidential inquiry" regarding men qualified to serve as directors. He further indicated that he would not bother the president until he had "definite opinions to present as to the other proposed members of the Board." Roosevelt gave Morgan his head.[10]

In searching for people to work for him, whether engineers, faculty, trustees, or board members, Morgan had a standard method of operation. From nominations received from people in whose judgment he had faith, he compiled a list of names. Next he sent assistants to do the legwork, while he started culling based on the reports from his agents in the field. Those candidates who survived the cut were interviewed personally by Morgan, and he was as likely to travel to visit them as he was to call them in. It was as if he wanted to see them in their natural habitat. This interview was critical, for there Morgan would determine the candidate's vision and the direction of his life. A man's character was more important to Morgan than were technical qualifications. As he once explained, in the short time available for an interview he could seldom change a person's life purpose. That focus had usually been set by years of habit, so what Morgan did was to present his own philosophy and then monitor the candidate's reaction. Morgan felt that this simple process gave him a pretty clear picture of a person's vision, direction, and character.[11] Knowing his manner of operation, one wonders again if he used it in his meeting with the president; or did FDR use an entirely different method, the Roosevelt style, on him?

Apparently Roosevelt had already made several suggestions to Morgan about possible board members for TVA. Morgan began checking out the list. Some of the president's recommendations, however, were unacceptable to Morgan. A former grand wizard of the American Legion might have been a wise political choice, but Morgan rejected him immediately. Toward the end of April, Morgan traveled across the country following

10. Morgan to Roosevelt, and FDR's reply, both dated April 18, 1933, Morgan Papers and Roosevelt Papers.

11. Morgan, "To the Antioch Faculty: On Being Practical," Aug. 8, 1932, Morgan Papers.

up on leads suggested by Roosevelt. The most promising appeared to be Ezra F. Scattergood, head of the Los Angeles Power Bureau and a man who had been near the forefront of public power utilities for some time. His name, for example, had been brought up by reporters at the May 19 press conference when FDR fielded questions about Morgan's appointment. Morgan subjected Scattergood to a thorough background investigation, using friends in California as operatives. Initially he found Scattergood a promising prospect, "a man of unusual character and ability." But there was something about Scattergood that bothered Morgan, a nagging feeling that he was too given to expediency, that his means for good ends were often questionable. Morgan was especially suspicious of Scattergood's militant attitude toward private utilities. He was convinced that negotiations with the likes of Wendell Willkie were going to require a thoroughly honest, open, straightforward attitude. For Morgan, how a person did something was as important as what he did. "Questionable means" could ruin the Tennessee Valley Authority. Morgan eliminated Scattergood from consideration, and the president acquiesced.[12]

Llewellyn Evans, another power man Morgan looked up while on the West Coast, was not at all like Scattergood, and Morgan disqualified him for precisely opposite reasons. It seemed to him that Evans, while a technical expert on utilities, and just the man the TVA needed in that respect, did not have the personal stamina to stand up against the onslaught that Morgan expected from the private utilities. Later Evans joined the Authority in a technical capacity, as did Scattergood, but for the moment he was out. Scattergood was too extreme; Evans, too soft. Morgan wanted a man with proper balance, and he had every reason to believe that Roosevelt desired the same.[13]

The new chairman consulted with Supreme Court Justice Louis D. Brandeis, a reader of *Antioch Notes,* and from him got the name of David E. Lilienthal, a member of the Wisconsin Public Service Commission. Morgan initiated an investigation of Lilienthal, sending his Antioch dean to Chicago, where Lilienthal had formerly been a partner in the law firm of Donald Richberg, an early New Dealer who later reacted against Roosevelt. Morgan's man then went to Wisconsin to interview Lilienthal and late in May submitted a lengthy report on the young public power

12. Morgan to Roosevelt, April 30, 1933, Morgan Papers.
13. See Morgan, "Relations with the President," and Morgan to Albert Lepawsky, November 1965 (exact date not given), Morgan Papers. This last is an eighty-five-page transcription of a tape made by Morgan for Lepawsky, hereinafter referred to as Lepawsky transcription.

advocate. Most of the extensive comments garnered about Lilienthal were quite favorable. Lilienthal was said to be a hardworking, brilliant, liberal lawyer. The most negative impression came from one of Morgan's old friends, Antioch trustee and Chicago lawyer Edwin H. Cassells. "Would he be a person to throw monkey wrenches? Type of man who gets lots of publicity—makes rash statements? Starts things? . . . Always shooting off mouth in a way that is embarrassing."[14]

With Marvin McIntyre making the arrangements out of the White House, Morgan met Lilienthal in Chicago on May 30. Morgan summed up his expectations before the interview in a wire to McIntyre, a telegram to which has been added sufficient punctuation to make it readable:

> If personal interview supports favorable report already received from careful investigation, I shall recommend him as a member of Tennessee board. Reports indicate he is brilliant, thorough, accurate, aggressive, fair, loyal, and committed to public interests. Has raised Wisconsin utility commission to new high level. Where former commissions disciplined little companies and let large ones go, he is requiring all companies to consider public interests. His shortcomings are reported to be personal ambition and publicity. General tone of reports excellent.[15]

Lilienthal seems to have been prepared for contact with the White House. Despite getting Morgan and McIntyre confused, as his journal shows, he carried the interview off perfectly. Whatever test it was Morgan administered to Lilienthal, he came away impressed. He telegraphed the White House: "Lilienthal is fine. I heartily recommend his appointment on Tennessee Board."[16]

There is some evidence that Morgan did not have complete control over the appointment of Lilienthal to the TVA board. It appears that Roosevelt, independently of Morgan's investigation, decided that Lilienthal was a logical person for the effort. In talking with Senator Norris before Morgan's enthusiastic report, Roosevelt is reported to have said, "If we could get Lilienthal, it would be a ten-strike."[17] Roosevelt may have heard of Lilienthal through Robert M. La Follette, Jr., then

14. Algo Henderson to Morgan, May 25 and 29, 1933, Morgan Papers.

15. Morgan to McIntyre, Morgan Papers. This telegram is dated "June 3 or 4, 1933," but both dates are obviously incorrect because the conference with Lilienthal took place on May 30.

16. Morgan to McIntyre, May 30, 1933, Morgan Papers. See also David E. Lilienthal, *The Journals of David E. Lilienthal*, 3 vols. (New York: Harper and Row, 1964–1966), vol. 1, 33.

17. Morgan, "Relations with the President"; Lilienthal, *Journals*, vol. 1, 38, 102; Willson Whitman, *David Lilienthal: Public Servant in a Power Age* (New York: Henry Holt and Co., 1948), p. 18.

carrying on his father's work in the Senate and a strong supporter of Lilienthal's in Wisconsin. Well before the White House called, Lilienthal had already put his feelers out regarding the new TVA, and he had contacted La Follette.[18] It is not improbable that Roosevelt saw an opportunity to increase his support from two strong, liberal Republicans (Norris and La Follette) by appointing their choice. Be that as it may, Lilienthal was in.

Roosevelt specifically instructed Morgan, through his usual conduit McIntyre, that the third spot on the board of directors should go to a man from the South who was interested in agriculture.[19] The leading contender, as Morgan viewed the situation, was George G. Crawford, former president of the Tennessee Coal, Iron and Railroad Company and since '1930 president of the Jones and Laughlin Steel Corporation in Pittsburgh. While living in Birmingham, Crawford had done much for agriculture in Alabama, and he was a leader in encouraging and practicing progressive labor policies. Crawford no doubt reminded Morgan of the amiable, mildly progressive businessmen with whom he had associated in Dayton, but Roosevelt refused to make the appointment because of that business link. Crawford passed out of the picture.[20]

Morgan's next recommendation for the remaining director's post was the president of the University of Tennessee, Harcourt A. Morgan (no relation to Arthur E. Morgan). Born in Canada, H. A. Morgan had a long history of tireless work in southern agriculture. He had been dean of the University of Tennessee School of Agriculture before becoming president, and he had a sound scholarly reputation for his work on the life cycle of the boll weevil.[21] In investigating Harcourt Morgan, Arthur Morgan talked with several experts in the U.S. Department of Agri-

18. Thomas K. McCraw, *Morgan vs. Lilienthal: The Feud within the TVA* (Chicago: Loyola University Press, 1970), p. 22. Roosevelt was aware of Lilienthal's difficulties in Wisconsin (Milo R. Maltbie to Roosevelt, Dec. 29, 1932, Roosevelt Papers), and Lilienthal was lobbying for a federal appointment from him (Lilienthal to Adolf A. Berle, Jr., Nov. 4, 1932, Berle Papers, FDR Library).

19. McIntyre to Morgan, June 2, 1933, Morgan Papers.

20. Morgan to McIntyre, May 30, 1933, the file marked "Correspondence Previous to the Appointment of the Other Two Directors," and Morgan, "Relations with the President," all in the Morgan Papers.

21. For information on Harcourt A. Morgan, see Mouzon Peters, "The Story of Dr. Harcourt A. Morgan," book 5 of Louis D. Wallace (ed.), *Makers of Millions: Not for Themselves—But for You* (Nashville: Tennessee Department of Agriculture, 1951). These "books" on famous Tennesseans are paged separately, with the one on H. A. Morgan running eighty-nine pages. His fairly metaphysical views on agriculture and nature are presented in Ellis F. Hartford, *Our Common Mooring* (Athens: University of Georgia Press, 1941). Apparently his central ideas involved "the need for southern agriculture to observe the fundamental natural relationship among minerals, plants, and animals through a

culture, from whom he had first heard of Harcourt, and with presidents of other land grant universities. He found glowing recommendations concerning the ability and personality of the university president, except for one extremely negative report from Antioch trustee Bruce R. Payne, president of Peabody College in Nashville. Payne called Harcourt Morgan "a typical political college president who manipulated Land Grant College politics without scruple."[22]

After a personal interview, Arthur Morgan disagreed, wiring Washington:

> He sees the President's purpose as few other men in the South and has worked consistently for it. . . . He is absolutely sincere and modest and would work just as hard and loyally off the board as he would on it. His appointment would carry high approval in Tennessee and everywhere in the South among agriculturalists. He has common sense, talks the people's language, and makes money go a long way. . . .[23]

Roosevelt found Harcourt Morgan acceptable, and the board was filled.

The TVA act required that the terms of the directors be staggered, and as chairman, Arthur Morgan received the nine-year term. Harcourt Morgan drew the six-year spot, and Lilienthal as the junior member received the three-year appointment. From the start the board was confusing to the public, what with two Morgans, both of whom were college presidents. The emerging TVA staff solved this problem in a typically informal way. To separate the Ohio Morgan from the Tennessee Morgan, staff members invariably referred to Arthur E. Morgan as "A.E." and to Harcourt A. Morgan as "H.A." David E. Lilienthal was known simply as "Dave." Outside the authority, this nickname for the chairman never stuck, and to the friends of Antioch he was always known as Arthur Morgan. Assuming that a college president automatically possessed a doctorate, the press always referred to him as Dr. Morgan. He had received an honorary degree from the University of Colorado back in the twenties, but Arthur Morgan quite appropriately never used the title.

---

program of balanced farming" and "the desirability of a decentralized industrial development dispersed throughout an agriculture economy as a balancing factor." *Our Common Mooring*, viii.

22. Lepawsky transcription. A similar evaluation of Harcourt Morgan was provided by a later TVA director, Frank E. Smith, in an interview with this writer on March 18, 1966. See also "Opinions about Pres. H. A. Morgan (Compiled by Arthur E. Morgan from personal interviews or phone calls)," Norris Papers. For an early biographical sketch of H. A. Morgan, see the Nashville *Tennessean*, May 27, 1919.

23. Morgan to McIntyre, May 30, 1933, Morgan Papers.

The members of the TVA board were diverse in background and interests. At sixty-five, Harcourt Morgan was nearly twice the age of Lilienthal. He had a grand reputation with southern farmers, and he could be expected to concentrate on agriculture. Presidents of state universities are never less than a peripheral figure in political circles, and Harcourt Morgan was often more. There was even talk of his running for governor, and though the boll weevil specialist turned down this offer, he remained important in the inner workings of the Democratric party of Tennessee. As one Authority employee said, "Anyone who thought H. A. Morgan was simply an old farm lobbyist past his prime just couldn't have been more mistaken."[24]

David Lilienthal, at thirty-three, was relatively unknown nationally. He had an excellent background, which included the firm support of Felix Frankfurter, the La Follettes, and Senator Norris. He was sharp, aggressive, and likable. He found a home in the New Deal, where he made friends in high places with astonishing ease, along with a certain amount of cultivation. Lilienthal's letters to his mentors and confidants verge on sycophancy. As a young man he once thanked a prominent lawyer for sending him a personal photograph by saying, "It takes an honored place on the walls of my room with the other dwellers on my private Mount Olympus: my Father, Abraham Lincoln, Justice Holmes, and my fiancee."[25] Nevertheless, he had a genuine respect for progressive ideals and a willingness to give his all for the triumph of the people. In the early 1930s Lilienthal referred to himself as a progressive, and he encouraged and donated to efforts to revitalize the progressive wing of the Republican party, to which he was tied because of the La Follettes' support. He emerged from the New Deal as one of the leaders in the liberal coalition that Roosevelt forged.

Morgan had a predictably complex task in getting the proper funding accounts set up for a new agency in the federal bureaucracy. We suppose it was of some importance to him in that he was paying salaries and expenses from his personal funds. On June 9, 1933, he wrote the White House enclosing a copy of an executive order for the president to sign. McIntyre mulled over the proper procedure and finally decided that a simple letter from the president to "My dear Mr. Chairman" would suffice. Roosevelt thus gave Morgan, on June 13, the authority to hire

24. James Rorty, "TVA's H. A. Morgan," *Commonweal* 47 (June 18, 1948), 226–30. The quotation about "couldn't have been more mistaken" is in McCraw, *Morgan vs. Lilienthal*, p. 16.

25. Quoted in McCraw, *Morgan vs. Lilienthal*, p. 19.

people and incur expenses to meet emergencies and to protect the public interest in relation to the Tennessee Valley Authority previous to the official organization of the Board." But Roosevelt kept the power of the pen, insisting that all appointments and proposed expenditures be submitted to him for prior approval. As much as FDR was willing to delegate, the TVA was a federal agency reporting directly to him, and he wanted to keep his finger in the pie for a while.[26]

In early June, Morgan had his first encounter with the federal political process, and it was an incident of major significance for him. The Democrats had been out of the White House for twelve years, while the Republicans had dominated politics, and the fruits of victory, throughout the 1920s. With the Democrats back in power there was for the first time since Wilson the opportunity for government jobs for Democrats. Patronage was one of Morgan's most dreaded fears about his new position; the chairman was afraid that he would be pressured to hire TVA employees on the basis of political affiliation.

The Tennessee Valley Authority Act specifically outlawed such politicizing of the new agency, and Senator Norris was a devout believer in hiring on merit, on a nonpartisan basis. Morgan shared the senator's emotional fervor on this matter of principle. He had been delighted when the act read "no political test or qualification shall be permitted or given consideration, but all such appointments and promotions shall be given and made on the basis of merit and efficiency."[27] Indeed, Morgan had taken the liberty of forcing a commitment from the president on this very point. It was no doubt with some apprehension, then, that Morgan, on June 7, in response to a telephone invitation, paid a call on the man most responsible for dispensing Democratic patronage.

Postmaster General James A. Farley represented the tough political side of Roosevelt's administration, and he had been put in the postal department because that was where the most jobs were. As chairman of the Democratic National Committee, Farley was FDR's chief political operative, and it was his job to help loyal Democrats and to oust Republicans. Morgan did not like at all the exchange he had with Farley, and he prepared a memorandum shortly afterward describing the meeting. Morgan was ushered into Farley's office to meet the postmaster general and his three top assistants. After a few casual remarks, Morgan record-

26. Morgan to McIntyre, June 9, 1933; McIntyre to Roosevelt, June 9, 1933; and Roosevelt to Morgan, June 13, 1933, all Roosevelt Papers, with copies in the Morgan Papers. This interchange offers a glimpse of how McIntyre handled matters, and his several notes to the president regarding the subject are in the Roosevelt Papers.

27. U.S., *Statutes at Large*, vol. 48, 63.

ed, Farley came right to the point: "Appointments should be made so as not to embarrass the administration." By this, Farley explained, he meant that the TVA "should get men recommended by Congressmen and senators, and should get democrats [*sic*] or Roosevelt Republicans."[28]

Morgan never stopped to see that Farley was merely doing his job, business as usual, spoils for the winners. Farley was sinning. Farley was being shortsighted, expedient, and totally without sound character. Morgan abruptly declared that he would get "the best men available regardless of party affiliation." He mentioned that the law itself required the TVA to be beyond politics. Farley and his assistants "brushed that aside as though it was unimportant." Morgan quite clearly saw that the four men were "very vigorous, very forceful and very insistent that I appoint Democrats." For his part, Farley observed that if Morgan pursued this policy he would get into "a great deal of trouble." Morgan felt extremely disturbed by their "brutally frank and cynically direct" remarks. To him "they talked much sophistry about saving civilization through supporting the party that elected President Roosevelt, and about overcoming the evil deeds of Republicans, but for the most part it was a straightforward demand that appointments be given to Democrats." The meeting concluded with Morgan feeling that he had been "very definitely and explicitly told what to do, and that there would be trouble" if he did not heed instructions.

Here is one of the early New Deal events for which there is more than one account, for Farley wrote up his version of the incident some six years later. Farley's view had him counseling Morgan that "it would be wise to avoid appointing people down there who would be unacceptable to the Senators and Representatives from that area. . . ." Such little alienations could haunt the Authority later, and "after all it was a smart practice in government to avoid antagonizing the men who vote the appropriations. I didn't suggest that he appoint anyone." From Farley's perspective Morgan got "exercised and promptly replied in what seemed to me discourteous fashion that he would appoint whom he liked and that he had no interest whatever in politics." What made Morgan "a bit more wrathy" was Farley's note that the TVA chairman was himself a political appointee. Farley admitted that he got a trifle upset himself, finally telling Morgan "that for all of me he could go out and do what he pleased."[29]

28. Morgan's memorandum of June 7, 1933, which covers his meeting with Farley in great detail, is in his papers.

29. James A. Farley, *Behind the Ballots: The Personal History of a Politician* (New York: Harcourt, Brace and Co., 1938), p. 232.

Morgan went straight to the White House and got an appointment to see the president the next day. He informed on Farley, and FDR calmly observed that Farley had meant no such implications. Morgan reiterated his commitment to nonpartisanship, and Roosevelt "showed no signs of disapproval and definite evidence of approval."[30] The upshot of the whole affair was that Roosevelt sent Morgan back to see Farley, and the matter was smoothed over.[31] Some months later, in December, the syndicated column "National Whirligig," by Paul Mallon, carried an account of the Morgan-Farley discussion. Farley's later story employed much the same language as the column, which probably means no more than that Farley clipped the article and used it when writing his own book. What is important here is that the nation learned of Arthur Morgan's stand against patronage, and newspapers all over the country supported his position.[32]

The press also responded favorably on June 15 when Morgan presented to the secretary of state a financial statement of all real and personal property and other assets owned by the chairman and his family. No other prominent government official had done this, and editors were pleased with Morgan's insistence on absolute openness. The *St. Louis Post Dispatch* declared: "What a refreshing and wholesome contrast. . . . Dr. Morgan sets a precedent that the American people as a whole will be happy to applaud."[33]

The fight over political patronage was just beginning, however. This was the depression and jobs were scarcer than ever. Morgan continued to disregard political references as a criterion for employment. Soon his director of personnel, Floyd W. Reeves, and his assistant, Gordon R. Clapp, set up a standard system for hiring. All prospective employees were required to file "Form 10," an application to take the TVA merit examination and a household word in the valley. Since the Authority was not under civil service, they devised their own merit system. With only a few exceptions, important only because of Morgan's hatred of them, the TVA was remarkably free from the taint of politics.

30. Morgan, "Memorandum of a Conference witih President Roosevelt," June 8, 1933, Morgan Papers. It was also at this conference that Roosevelt asked Morgan to join a sort of second cabinet made up of heads of agencies, various advisers, and some regular cabinet members. It is not clear from the records just how large a role Morgan played here. Because the offices of the TVA were soon moved to Knoxville, his service was probably limited. FDR liked to see people who came to him with a concern go away happy. This suggestion that Morgan was to be included in Roosevelt's inner circle may be just another example of how he handled problems and people.

31. Morgan, "Memorandum of a Second Visit of Arthur E. Morgan with Postmaster General Farley," June 10, 1933, Morgan Papers.

32. "A. E. Morgan" newspaper file, TVA Technical Library, Knoxville, Tennessee.

33. *Ibid.*

The reaction of politicians was somewhat different from that of the press. Consider these statements culled from Morgan's congressional file:

. . . Congress is not going to stand for such a procedure. . . . They are the men the political leaders are most anxious to place. . . . In passing these laws we made it possible for you people to have jobs yourselves, and a lot of us congressmen are getting mighty, mighty sore. . . .[34]

Morgan had relatively little difficulty with these outcries. He had faced Farley, and with the president's support had won. These were people who simply had not yet gotten the message. He patiently responded to each letter, noting the requirements of the TVA, as well as the fact that many people with congressional endorsements had been hired but only because they were the best qualified. "I cannot see my way clear," he told Rep. Jed Johnson of Oklahoma, "to depart from this policy. I believe you will agree with me that we should not."[35]

It had been under the condition that there be no politics in TVA that Morgan had accepted its leadership. He hated political patronage, hated it as only a progressive could, calling it a "sinister . . . evil force."[36] If patronage were not ended, "it will destroy our government, locally and nationally." Otherwise, "democratic government will sag and sag until some form of dictatorship takes it over and wipes the slate clean of that mess."[37]

Morgan did make one appointment that he always listed as his single capitulation to political pressure. R. Harold Denton, a victim of paralysis, had spent two years at Warm Springs, Georgia, where he met the Roosevelts. The president's wife took an interest in this student at Yale Law School, and sent him to see Arthur Morgan. Denton, like the president able to stand only with the aid of two canes, wobbled into the chairman's office, and Morgan took him on as a research assistant.[38] Denton later collected Morgan's numerous TVA speeches and bound them for subsequent perusal by historians.

34. See Gordon R. Clapp, *The TVA: An Approach to the Development of a Region* (Chicago: University of Chicago Press, 1955), pp. 32–34, on the TVA's hiring practices. For congressional nominations for TVA employment, see a file in the Morgan Papers marked "Important Congressional Letters, Personal File of A. E. Morgan."

35. Morgan to Johnson, Jan. 12, 1934, *ibid.*

36. Morgan, address before the Public Ownership Institute, Chicago, Ill., Sept. 30, 1933, "Speeches and Remarks" (Knoxville, 1940), typewritten speeches collected and bound in two volumes, vol. 1, 3; available in the Morgan Papers and the TVA Technical Library.

37. Morgan, address before the Ohio Society, New York City, November 13, 1933, "Speeches and Remarks," vol. 1, 13.

38. Charles E. Clark to Eleanor Roosevelt, March 27, 1934, and Marguerite Owen (TVA Washington representative) to Malvinda T. Scheider (secretary to Mrs. Roosevelt), April 7, 1934, both in the Morgan Papers. See also interview with Morgan, July 27, 1966.

By the summer of 1933 Morgan seemed to have won his battle against the politicians. It remains to be seen how much he had lost. From a practical standpoint, in refusing to play the appointments game, Morgan not only failed to make important political friends, but he created more than a few enemies. As one student of this period observed, "Morgan was not just apolitical, but antipolitical."[39]

The Tennessee Valley Authority board of directors held its first meeting on June 16 that year. This meeting, at which David Lilienthal and Harcourt Morgan met for the first time, took place in the Willard Hotel in Washington. Office space was at a definite premium, what with FDR's alphabet agencies appearing nearly every week. It took some time before anything resembling a routine operation was established for the TVA. After going through the formalities of declaring the board fully constituted, the chairman took it into a lengthy discussion of the practical matters at hand. Morgan had selected his fellow directors, and he felt confident that they shared his understanding of their mission. There was work already accomplished that required the board's retroactive approval if all was to be in order, and there was a sizable correspondence that had to be reviewed. Philosophical issues had been settled. Now was the time for action.

His codirectors demurred. Harcourt Morgan later complained that at that organizational meeting the chairman made no mention of the TVA act or of the major objectives of Congress. Instead, he led them into a mass of details about which they were hardly well-informed and that must have overwhelmed his colleagues, who were still winding up their personal and professional affairs. H. A. Morgan had not terminated his work at the University of Tennessee, and Lilienthal was leaving that very night for a ten-day trip to Wisconsin, where his son was to have an operation. From Morgan's point of view, he had to act while he had the board together for this one meeting. Time was wasting. A few months later he described to a senator that day when the TVA officially began:

> We hadn't any space yet. There was mail piled around in stacks, and in burrowing through that, we would find an important letter from the President, piled up under a 3-foot stack of mail; we would find letters from Congressmen, department heads, wanting to know what to do about this appropriation or that.[40]

39. McCraw, *Morgan vs. Lilienthal*, p. 107.
40. *TVA Hearings*, pp. 98–99, 301. See also Morgan to Nathan Bachman, Oct. 9, 1933, TVA Files.

Regardless of Morgan's approach, the board decided several things of importance at the first meeting. It elected Harcourt Morgan vice-chairman, authorized a seal for the TVA, resolved to request twenty-five thousand dollars from the U.S. Treasury, authorized surveys of the land around the Cove Creek Dam site, and appointed Carl Bock as an aide to the chairman. Observing that with the other directors away someone needed to be in a capacity to accomplish the work, Morgan proposed that the board make him temporary general manager.[41]

Along with the title thus given him, and in addition to being chairman of the board, Morgan was also chief engineer, for Roosevelt had so designated him. It was natural that much of the work should fall upon his shoulders. During the next six weeks, Lilienthal and H. A. Morgan would be available for only part-time service. The launching of the TVA was up to Morgan, and he accomplished a great deal. By August he had the transition from the Corps of Engineers nearly completed, and despite his animosity for the corps, the transfer continued smoothly and efficiently through the efforts of the team of engineers he had dispatched to corps headquarters in St. Louis. In Washington, Morgan acquired a few rooms in the Interior Building, and there a staff was organized to consider some forty thousand applications for jobs, which were arriving at a rate of nearly two thousand per day.

Out of the controversies in the 1920s, the Tennessee Valley Authority had inherited a large research program in fertilizer, and this too was assimilated into the TVA program. In these early days Morgan showed a great interest in fertilizer research. He also began to work on the possibility of trading TVA electricity for land needed as future dam sites. In addition to an avalanche of congressional visits, letters, and requests, Morgan found that the several missions of the Authority required considerable coordination with other federal programs. Secretary of the Interior Harold L. Ickes wanted plans for the construction of a cement plant. The Civilian Conservation Corps planned to move South for the winter and expected the TVA to prepare the way for its New Deal cousin. There was also an emergency program of subsistence homesteads that desired TVA cooperation.[42]

When H. A. Morgan and Lilienthal reported for permanent duty in late July 1933, they found that the chairman had accumulated a great deal

41. TVA Minutes of the Board of Directors, June 16, 1933. The Morgan Papers contain photostatic copies of the board minutes during his tenure. Originals are at TVA headquarters in Knoxville.

42. Morgan, "Memorandum on Progress toward Organization to August 5, 1933," Morgan Papers and *TVA Hearings*, pp. 107–9.

of power directly in his hands. Both men had specific concerns about areas they regarded as professionally theirs. For the Tennessee Morgan it was agriculture, and for Lilienthal it was electric power. They were coming to understand that the chairman possessed a much broader, and to them vaguer, vision of the Tennessee Valley Authority. Having vision is one thing. Being a visionary is another. Arthur Morgan was, to his fellow directors, beginnning to look every bit the visionary.

In mid-July the chairman had proposed an ethical code for TVA employees, which shall be analyzed in detail later, and the board had found it puzzling, a bit bizarre, and unnecessary. Another memorandum on July 30 really got their attention. Here was Morgan's preliminary plan for the Authority. The Utopian aggressively assumed all the missions set forth in the act, and he interpreted them as broadly as possible. Then he went further. Lilienthal must have winced at Morgan's vague scheme for the total integration and planned development of all power sites in the Tennessee River system. The concept, as such, was not new, but here was Arthur Morgan looking years ahead when the TVA had not yet built its first dam. He went even further. He proposed that the Authority make and sell portland cement and dry ice at one of the plants in Muscle Shoals. He described a sweeping forestry program that transcended other federal and state agencies. He wanted to create a cooperative distribution system for the products of local industry. Most of all, he wanted something called social and economic planning.[43]

Genuinely shocked by Morgan's broad gauge, the two directors expressed their concern. Later they said that to them many of Morgan's proposals seemed "impracticable and highly visionary." They devised a plan that not only limited Morgan's authority, but awarded them specific areas of control. They gave him their suggestion, received his rebuttal, and the board met on August 5 to discuss their differences. They assembled in the Andrew Johnson Hotel in downtown Knoxville, and when they met H. A. Morgan and Lilienthal were in agreement. Two votes to one. It was not a happy session for the chairman. Later he described the meeting where his wings were clipped:

> . . . the atmosphere was a very hostile one. It was aggressively resentful and dictatorial. I was being told this is what is going to be done. I was not asked shall we do this, but I was explicitly told, as explicitly as I would tell a servant to do anything, except there was discussion, and I secured modifications, but some of these were nullified. It was a case of being told and not discussing, primarily.[44]

43. *TVA Hearings*, p. 102.   44. *Ibid.*, p. 337.

As much as he hated what they had done, as much as he felt they had betrayed him, the Utopian still voted for the measure as a demonstration of goodwill. Besides, the division of responsibilities agreed on at the August 5 meeting gave him plenty to do. Essentially what happened was that each member was made responsible for certain TVA missions. H. A. Morgan got, as he desired, control over "all matters relating to agriculture." Lilienthal became responsible for all aspects of power, all legal matters including land acquisition, and the economics of transportation. Here Lilienthal gained everything he wanted, for he knew that power was the secret of the Authority. As chairman, Morgan became responsible for overall coordination of these missions, for all engineering and construction work, for educational and training programs excluding agriculture, for land and regional planning, housing, forestry, and "matters relating to social and economic organization and planning."[45]

Was this tricephalous arrangement a meaningful expression of the board's natural tendencies? It did allow each member to concentrate on the area in which he was most interested, and it excluded from those areas any meddling by the visionary chairman; but it still gave the chairman ample room in which to operate. And when Morgan operated, he was something to behold. "Mr. Morgan has 'came and went,' " his Antioch secretary wrote during this period. "He was here yesterday just for the day. It's like a cyclone hitting us. Woof."[46] Back in Washington, one of the Antiochians Morgan had installed in the TVA provisional headquarters commented: "It's still pretty much of a madhouse here. No one knows anyone else's name, and it's a lucky person who gets the right party when he calls this place on the phone."[47]

The tempo of the Tennessee Valley Authority, and of all the early New Deal agencies, was amazing. In the summer of 1933 a paper organization became an actuality. Arthur Morgan guided the fledgling agency during this formative period, and he made critical decisions, particularly in selecting personnel, that affected it for years to come. Since his first conversation with the president, Morgan had been considering the manner in which the TVA should go about hiring the huge

45. TVA Minutes, Aug. 5, 1933. For a more complete discussion of this divided authority arrangement, see Charles Herman Pritchett, *The Tennessee Valley Authority: A Study in Public Administration* (Chapel Hill: University of North Carolina Press, 1943). While aware of its problems, Pritchett concludes that, under the circumstances, this arrangement may have been the best. J. Dudley Dawson, in an interview with this writer, Aug. 3, 1966, indicated that Morgan's supporters in the TVA were terribly disappointed with the Aug. 5 decision.
46. Jean C. Hanson to Herbert Gough, Oct. 3, 1933, Morgan Papers.
47. Herbert Gough to Eleanor Dyer, June 28, 1933, *ibid.*

number of men needed to construct the Cove Creek Dam. As early as May 16 he had written out by hand "A Suggested Method for Determining the Qualifications of Persons Being Considered for Employment by the Tennessee Valley Authority." Morgan observed that conventional civil service often failed because it was unable to judge the whole of a candidate. While measuring technical competence, no existing test gauged even more important factors. What were these mysterious traits that Morgan would judge? They are right out of his plan for Antioch: physical, mental, and ethical fitness, personal habits, cultural characteristics, and public-service-mindedness.[48]

By early June 1933, before the first meeting of the board, Morgan had developed a fairly definite idea of what he would do with his work crews once he assembled them. Again, he drew directly from his experience with the Miami Conservancy District. The men would use their time wisely if they were worth helping at all, and the one thing they needed the most was training. Why not establish near Cove Creek a training school? While the men were working or studying, the TVA could train their wives in housekeeping and the fundamentals of home economics. Lucy Morgan was more than glad to preach the benefits of whole-wheat flour to the mountain folk. To training in a craft for the men and in right cooking for the wives would be added, for both, instruction in "hygiene, community interests, and in liberal interests."[49]

Morgan had already picked the man he wanted to run his training program: J. Dudley Dawson, from Antioch, where he had taught mathematics and worked with the cooperative program. Morgan drew many of his initial staff from Antioch. Some were young, such as Slim Gough and Felix X. Reynolds. Others were former associates such as Barton Jones, an engineer from the Miami Conservancy days and a professor at Antioch. Morgan was always a bit sensitive about the number of Antiochians he hired, and well he might have been, for he brought in some thirty. For their part, the Antiochians seem to have done very well at TVA.[50]

Morgan himself developed the form letter to be sent to the references offered by job-seekers. "In the case of the present applicant," he frequently added in a postscript, "we are interested in knowing what evidence he has given of public spirit and social mindedness. In what

48. Morgan, "A Suggested Method for Determining the Qualifications of Persons Being Considered for Employment by the Tennessee Valley Authority," May 16, 1933, Morgan Papers.

49. Morgan, "TVA Memorandum," June 5, 1933, Morgan Papers.

50. J. Dudley Dawson interview with this writer, Aug. 3, 1966.

activities has he engaged which were primarily in the public interest and not for financial profit?"[51]

On July 30, at the suggestion of Arthur Morgan and apparently without the approval of the president, the TVA board voted to name the proposed dam at Cove Creek in honor of Senator Norris. Henceforth the dam the engineers were planning was known as Norris Dam, built by Chief Engineer Morgan and his two able assistants Carl Bock and Barton Jones, both of whom had worked with him for years. Jones became the construction engineer at Norris Dam. On October 1, fewer than four months after the board's first meeting, the building of Norris Dam commenced. In very few construction projects, either municipal, state, or national, was there as great progress as in the TVA, with an excellently organized construction program and men and equipment used to their full possibilities. Work went along so well that the four-year construction plan originally proposed by the army engineers dwindled to two and one-half years, and the Authority moved ahead of schedule on even that shortened program.[52]

Not only the engineering staff but also the labor policy of the TVA was almost a direct carry-over from the Miami Conservancy. The official policy was not announced until 1935, but in these early months the Authority followed an *ad hoc* approach based on the Miami Conservancy system developed by Morgan some twenty years earlier. Lilienthal himself gave Morgan credit for the eventual Authority labor policy: "Under the leadership of Chairman of the TVA Board, Arthur E. Morgan . . . an effort has been made to formulate TVA labor policies into a brief, clear statement of principles."[53]

The initial success of the TVA can be traced directly to the work of Arthur Morgan. As general manager and chief engineer, he handled most of the funds, and his engineering staff directed the work of the most evident symbol of progress, Norris Dam. Moreover, it was Arthur Morgan more than anyone else who set the tone for personnel, and his influence resulted in one of the most highly praised staffs in government history. Morgan had launched the TVA, but not without difficulty. He could take some pride in having fought off the politicians, and the hiring of employees seemed to be going his way. He had again a pool of men he

51. A sample of the TVA reference letter is Morgan to Helen Torte, July 13, 1933, Morgan Papers.

52. Morgan to Joseph C. O'Mahoney, Dec. 8, 1933, *ibid*.

53. Lilienthal, "Advance Text, Remarks of David E. Lilienthal, Labor Day Celebration of Detroit and Wayne County Federation of Labor, Detroit, Michigan," Sept. 2, 1935, Morgan Papers.

could train for skills and community building. Soon he would have another town. It is true that relations with his fellow board members had not gone well. By the end of the summer of 1933, he had seen his colleagues in action sufficiently to revise his initial estimates. Harcourt Morgan he could trust. The chairman felt that instinctively. Lilienthal was another matter. There was something about the man that bothered Arthur Morgan.

CHAPTER 6

TVA Utopia

Much is known today about how Franklin D. Roosevelt viewed the Tennessee Valley Authority. As part of that conglomeration termed the New Deal, his essential goal was to show action and build confidence in a depression-stricken America. Moreover, the work on the Muscle Shoals legislation was virtually done. Already there to be approved, the TVA was simply one more thing FDR could do very quickly. To be sure, Roosevelt added his own rather expansive definition of regional development, giving the TVA a myriad of tasks, and allowing it to replace many other federal agencies in the region. Roosevelt also saw the Authority as a fairly wide-open experiment in regional planning. If it worked, he would replicate it in other areas and maybe in the country as a whole. While he, like his contemporaries, never fully explained what he meant by social and economic development, he certainly wanted the TVA to demonstrate a more efficient, coordinated, and thus better way of doing things.

Something is known, too, about how the people of the valley felt about the Authority. The TVA was the presence of the federal government, essentially alien, but to be tolerated because the valley needed the work. If the strangers could tame that wild river and in doing so bring lights and cheaper fertilizer, then hillbillies and rowcroppers alike were willing to suspend the harsher aspects of their judgment.[1]

What is not known is how Arthur Morgan viewed the Tennessee Valley Authority, and this is a question of immense importance to this narrative. Should one simply dismiss Morgan as some kind of accident of history who passed through the New Deal, but whose impact was so insignificant that he can be safely ignored? Or does the Morgan story reveal something about the New Deal, FDR, and the early TVA? Morgan was pretty strange by 1933, yet Roosevelt gave him an extraordinarily free hand, at least until 1936, when the president faced reelection. The fact of the matter is that Morgan was there, and the Authority,

---

1. Michael J. McDonald and John Muldowny, *TVA and the Dispossessed: The Resettlement of Population in the Norris Dam Area* (Knoxville: University of Tennessee Press, 1982), provides an excellent view of the TVA from the bottom up.

at least for a while, was his. He cannot be ignored. One can only examine the evidence, attempt to sift out Morgan's vision, and in the end speculate about what that vision shows about America in the 1930s.

Morgan would, after all, lead the Tennessee Valley Authority for the next five years, virtually the entirety of the New Deal period. Surely, understanding his vision of the TVA can tell much about what that agency was like before World War II, back before it had to grow up, back when it was part and parcel of the meaning and activity of the young and idealistic New Deal. Maybe Morgan's story will even shed some light on that mysterious "Man in the White House" and the nature of the Roosevelt program.

It is time to begin this process by examining what Morgan said about the Tennessee Valley Authority and by analyzing what he did as its head. There is a great deal of information in this regard, inasmuch as Morgan continued to be a prolific writer and speaker, particularly in 1933 and 1934. The nation's press eagerly published his articles, and the young paralytic sent to him by Eleanor Roosevelt meticulously filed away his speeches. From these sources and from Morgan's numerous memoranda can be pieced together what he wanted to do with the Authority and how he went about it. Having examined Morgan's earlier life and thought, one can expect to find a TVA considerably different from the one of today. That expectation will not be disappointed.

Morgan's TVA was to be nothing less than the culmination of his life work, and for that reason it was a combination of what he had done before. It was all there: the young idealist hoping to have proletarians read good books; the hydraulic (and social) engineer designing better lives for his workers building better dams; the revolutionary educator; the plain-living enthusiast; the creator of small communities; the destroyer of waste; the moralizing, character-building writer of ethical codes. Especially the ethicist. The moral code came first.

In July 1933, Morgan had been anointed by FDR, and the time for his dream had come. The disappointment at Antioch was behind him, and he eagerly faced his new opportunity to remold an entire region. Confident that he possessed the mandate of the president, Morgan had no intention of being bound by the conventional definitions of government agencies, especially when he knew that those methods and activities were demonstrably wrong and in the long run morally degenerative. His agency, a new experiment, would blaze trails, set precedents, become an example. It would discover, or so he thought in a vague and extremely general sort of way, what new things required doing and how best to do them.

It shall be seen that Morgan had a particularly broad view of what the Tennessee Valley Authority might do. It could, and should, do anything that rational, moral people determined needed to be done.[2] There were no sacred cows for Morgan . . . windmills, maybe, but no forms or functions that he dared not criticize. Already shown is that Morgan talked too much and too vaguely, and that he wrote too quickly. He never faced the simple human reality that we all need a good editor. Hence, one anticipates that this rambling, confused, high-toned vision of the TVA will cause him some difficulty. But before focusing on this sort of mushy definition—indeed, what his detractors came to call his vagaries—it is important at this point to note the one fundamental requirement Morgan had for the new order he envisioned for the Authority. For all of his ideas that can, and shall, be listed as encompassing his TVA vision, nothing was more important to him than that these tasks be approached from a sound ethical basis. Take away all the Utopianism, all the eccentricities, and even all the things that Morgan's Authority actually did, and what is left is Morgan the moralist. The ethical foundation was his prerequisite for the Tennessee Valley Authority. Absolutely. In 1933 he was still the Morgan he had been at Antioch. For him nothing had changed except the location. The Morgan principle: Ethical development precedes socioeconomic development.

On July 15, 1933, Morgan traveled by train from Washington back to Yellow Springs. No doubt his hopes for the TVA and the goals he wanted to accomplish there were much on his mind. As the train rumbled along, he took out his pen and sketched another list of essential moral standards: "An Ethical Code for the Staff of the Tennessee Valley Authority." Once in Yellow Springs, he gave the code a last, quick revision before his secretary typed it, as she had so many others. It was just in time for the next meeting of the board of directors.

The code sprang directly from Morgan's conviction that only ethical means could produce desirable ends. Morgan was surpassed by no other New Dealer in insisting that radical change must be firmly rooted in morality and uncompromising ethics. He understood better than anyone

2. In addition to the articles and speeches cited elsewhere in this chapter that demonstrate Morgan's expansive view of the role of TVA, see the following unpublished documents: "A Study of the Succession of Authority and of the Genius of Organization," TVA memorandum, June 5, 1933; "To Heads of Departments Concerned with Planning Activities of the Tennessee Valley Authority: An Expression of Opinion by Arthur E. Morgan of the Proper Functions of Special Agencies, Such as the Tennessee Valley Authority," Nov. 3, 1933; and "A Statement of the Personal Attitude of Arthur E. Morgan Concerning a Sound Basis for Economic and Social Development in the Tennessee Valley Authority and Under Its Direction," Nov. 10, 1933. Morgan Papers.

else, including the president, that the TVA would undertake many new and grand things, but he believed fervently that if the people who comprised the Authority were lacking in personal conviction and sound character then its purposes would be defeated from the very beginning.

As one of Morgan's earliest statements of his view of the New Deal and the TVA, his ethical code deserves careful attention. Morgan opened the document with a listing of the TVA's values:

> . . . the control and orderly development of material resources . . . a full and wholesome development of the region and its people in accord with wise design . . . widespread understanding and appreciation of the possibilities of the region and of the possibilities of personal, social, economic, legal, and cultural development which would be made possible by intelligent design . . . the development of ethical attitude and conduct, so that our efforts shall be cumulative . . . and shall not be wasted and dissipated in the internal conflict, distrust and friction which result from inethical habits.[3]

Morgan defined the New Deal as simply "the new social and economic order we are striving for," which required nothing less than "actual changes in deep seated habits, social, economic, and personal" brought about "by conscious deliberate effort." To him it was fundamental that "unless we realize that ethical attitude and conduct are the very foundation of a new order, we will resent changes in habits and attitudes, and our talk of a new social and economic order will be nothing but talk." All of this was by way of a preamble, and Morgan's introduction to the ethical code is nearly as long as the document itself because he was trying almost desperately to prove his point that, if "we should leave an example of deceit, exploitation, favoritism, patronage, extravagance, bad personal habits, and selfish personal ambitions, our efforts might do more harm than good."

Morgan was a Utopian from the very start of the TVA; indeed, he had been one from his youth. His Utopianism was essentially of the early-nineteenth-century type that stressed that people must relate to each other in an open, honest, cooperative, harmonious fashion. "Poor ethical habits," he insisted, "are the chief preventive of a better civilization." Again he added his curious, long-term definition of the ethical act: "conduct which is best in the light of its total consequences." Truthfulness, he said, "is good because it is fundamentally efficient and economical when we take the whole result into account."

3. Morgan, "An Ethical Code for the Staff of the Tennessee Valley Authority," July 15, 1933, Morgan Papers; also available in Roy Talbert, Jr. (ed.), "Arthur E. Morgan's Ethical Code for the Tennessee Valley Authority," East Tennessee Valley Historical Society's *Publications*, No. 40 (1968), 119–27.

There is much of Robert Owen here, the Utopian who so ignited the citizens of Cincinnati that they headed off for Yellow Springs. There is also a good bit of Charles Fourier, the French Utopian who inspired, briefly, the famous American community of Brook Farm. With Morgan's emphasis on planning, organization, and efficiency, and with his admiration for the inventor and entrepreneur, there is more than a hint of Count de Saint Simon, the early nineteenth century Frenchman who, among other things, suggested that society might well be organized like a smoothly running factory. The Utopian Edward Bellamy, Morgan's hero of the 1890s, continues to lurk everywhere in his thinking.

As he had done so often in *Antioch Notes*, Morgan felt obliged to observe that some authority would be required in developing proper ethical behavior. "It is not true," his code claimed with typical ignorance of the authoritarianism others inevitably would read into it, "that each person should determine his own ethical standards." If not each individual, who? Morgan felt himself to be as sound an ethicist as he was an engineer, and he had no doubt that he could write "principles that most well informed, intelligent, reasonable and well intentioned men agree are desirable." So it was that he prepared the following code as a "guide to help persons of good intentions to clarify their minds as to what conduct is desirable."

Item one: "General and enduring interest should control over special or temporary interests." Here he opposed especially "ambition or selfish rivalry," either between the Tennessee Valley Authority and other agencies or between departments of the TVA itself. "If it starts to develop," he said, "it should be openly faced and eliminated, and not allowed to smoulder." He urged his employees not to resist the promotion of someone else when that person was obviously better qualified, and he specifically outlawed promotion by seniority, which "will have little place where high character and a good spirit are in control." He insisted that the TVA should see that "self seeking ambition does not succeed in advancing itself." The agency should guarantee that "the able person who habitually puts the general good ahead of his own shall be recognized and put in positions of responsibility."

Item two: "The affairs of the Tennessee Valley Authority shall be conducted in all respects with honesty and openness." Such a policy, he said, "may be revolutionary in business and government, but once established it will count strongly for good will and economy in living." There were to be no "secret investigations, spying, or espionage in any form. If we cannot get information by straight forward honesty, we shall go without it." Such a process might cause some problems, "but the increase in self respect, mutual confidence and dignity will far outweigh the loss." As Morgan put it: "a man who will lie for me will lie to me." Again: "Straight forward openness is not only more self respecting, but in the long run is more effective." Item two contained a number of specific examples of how the TVA would operate. No haggling over land purchases or other business arrangements. "Complete openness of dealing should prevail." Similarly, subtle strategies designed to confound the opposition were forbidden: "no false moves shall be made to mislead or confuse the firm, person, corporation, or public organization concerned." And again: "No evasive or misleading statements should be made." He included a special note on expense accounts that was truly revolutionary: "items should appear to be what they really are."

Morgan concluded this section on honesty by insisting that even to the press "only true and representative statements should be made"—with the caveat that "this does not mean that information should be published prematurely or that a person must tell everything he knows." Good advice, which Morgan usually failed to heed himself.

Item three: TVA employees "should not take gifts, favors, hospitality or any other benefits from any persons who might in any way profit by giving such benefits." After taking a swipe at Europe, "honeycombed with such practices," Morgan gave the following illustrations of his principle. Never take anything from investment bankers. Never let a contractor pay for lunch. Never "accept meals, gifts or any favors from persons who have goods or services to sell." When traveling to appraise land (the TVA would be buying or condemning millions of acres), use only official transportation and never ride with the person whose land is to be sold. "The same general principle should apply everywhere with all employees." Sometimes, he added, "acceptance of a favor or of hospitality from a person one is doing business with is suitable and proper and an evidence of mutual respect." But such hospitality had to be reported within a month. Under no circumstances should a TVA employee accept a tip. If a gratuity is left and cannot be returned, it "should be turned over to some such organization as an Employees Relief Association." Authority administrators should file, upon their appointment, "a complete list of the real and personal property of himself and of his dependents or immediate family," to be updated periodically.

Item four: A curious note on time and effort. "What an employee of the Tennessee Valley Authority has to offer is not primarily hours of time, but rather it is insight, judgment, interest and enthusiasm. A Thomas Edison might be worth as much in a day as a careless plodder would be in a year." People in poor physical and mental health cannot contribute fully; consequently: "Dissipation and other habits which destroy health and the full possession of one's powers are in direct conflict with any reasonable ethical code."

Item five: An employee who comes by monetarily valuable information during the course of his work should turn it over to the TVA and make no attempt "to personally profit by his discovery."

Item six: "Employees of the Tennessee Valley Authority should live moderately and economically, avoiding competitive expenditures." In so living they would "avoid many temptations to improper use of funds or influence. Integrity needs to be thus fortified by thrift and foresight. Free spending is infectious, and the standard here presented can be maintained best if it is generally and openly adopted." Furthermore, no employee should expect to get rich, because working for the agency represented "a conscious and deliberate surrender of the expectation of acquiring wealth." The staff's satisfaction should come "from doing good work in their chosen fields, from economical and thrifty living, from deserving the respect and good will of their associates and of the public and from reasonable security for old age or in sickness." If an employee accepted a position with the feeling that it was only temporary until he could "escape into another economic class," then that person "should leave the Tennessee Valley Authority service."

Item seven: "Tennessee Valley employees should maintain wholesome and self respecting standards of personal conduct. Intemperance, lax sex morality, gambling, and the use of habit forming drugs are not in keeping with the spirit of the Tennessee Valley Authority personnel." No ambivalence here. Morgan expected to rule the TVA as sternly as he had Antioch.

Item eight: "A spirit of friendliness and good will, with readiness to cooperate and to bear one's full share of the load, or more than one's share when occasion demands, is essential to the job we have on hand." Welcome to Utopia.

Item nine: "The Tennessee Valley Authority aims to develop a staff of men and women who are whole heartedly and enthusiastically committed to the project of helping build a new social and economic order. . . . Where such sincere effort exists, arbitrariness or harshness in dealing with mistakes or failures is out of place." Even if an employee has committed no precisely illegal act, should he demonstrate "calculating, selfish ambition, or habitual cheapness of conduct," he would be "eliminated."

That was the code, and that was a major part of Morgan's TVA. He wanted every member of the Authority to sign it. It is important to remember that this code represents much of Morgan's very early thinking about the TVA. In July of 1933 the agency was hardly organized. The board had only recently been selected, and in fact the operation had yet to move to Tennessee in any real sense. It is obvious from the outset that to Morgan the TVA was far more than flood control, agriculture, power generation and transmission, or any of the other specific actions allowed by the act. It was for Morgan nothing less than an opportunity to build, in his words, a new order, one that would not only involve radical changes in the social and economic structure but that would provide an improved moral foundation for society. In a moment the impact of such ideas shall be described, but first, consider other examples of the world that Morgan intended to fashion.

With the moral code firmly in place, the next step for the Utopian was to settle on a specific demonstration where these principles could be tested and, upon their justification, adopted by the rest of the country. Morgan needed a community, a town, a village for Utopia. He had moved quickly to make sure that the Authority would not only handle all the engineering work in building its dams but that it would hire directly its own work force rather than relying on contractors. The planning for the dam at Cove Creek above Knoxville had been virtually completed by the Corps of Engineers. Work on it could begin immediately, and thousands of employees would be assembled, to buy the property to be flooded, as well as a protective barrier around the reservoir, to clear the land, and to build the dam itself.

The workers would provide the inhabitants for his new town, and there Morgan's demonstration of right living could take place. Rather than inherit an existing village, as he had in Yellow Springs, this time he could start afresh. Morgan made his suggestion for a model village at Cove Creek at the very first board meeting on June 16, 1933, and it was for him an obvious idea, the extension of what he had attempted at Yellow Springs and nearly twenty years earlier with the construction camps of the Miami Conservancy District. His fellow board members hesitated, aware that temporary housing would be far cheaper than the permanent town the chairman proposed. Work began, and for the initial period the employees had to live in barracks or commute long distances over poor mountain roads to get to their new jobs.

Finally, on July 29 the board gave full approval for the construction of the town. One of Morgan's assistants recommended that it be called New Deal, Tennessee, but the chairman rejected that suggestion and, with the board's approval, called the village Norris, after the famous senator who had fought so hard for the Muscle Shoals project that became the TVA.

In addition, the Cove Creek dam was also named Norris, and so the first major project of the Authority was the building of Norris Dam with the town of Norris adjacent to it. Like the ethical code, the village of Norris represents a vital part of Morgan's TVA and deserves an equal level of scrutiny.

The Norris Dam is up on the Clinch River, a tributary of the Tennessee, slightly more than twenty miles from Knoxville. Norris was designed chiefly as a storage dam to hold back the waters during the flood season and to release them during the dry months. With its obvious navigational and flood control aspects, Norris Dam also could use the power of the released water to generate electricity. Its primary purpose was to regularize the river's flow and thus to increase the power efficiency of Wilson Dam, the soon-to-be-constructed Wheeler Dam, and the others planned downstream.[4] Located four miles from Norris Dam was the town of Norris.

In planning Norris, Morgan contemplated a population of about two thousand. Eventually the town had more than three hundred family dwelling units, a dormitory for single workers, and the usual requirements for a small town: administration building, firehouse, telephone exchange, post office, school, grocery store, drugstore, creamery, barber shop, beauty parlor, and gas station. Eschewing concrete sidewalks, Morgan ordered natural footpaths constructed and additional beauty maintained by a two thousand-acre greenbelt surrounding the village. Overall planning and architectural design was assigned to Earle S. Draper, a nationally known landscape architect and community planner primarily identified with regional and resort planning in the South. Draper, assisted to a degree by the chairman's wife, Lucy Morgan, began the planning of Norris.[5] Despite the less than enthusiastic support of his fellow board members, Morgan pushed ahead with making Norris a model town.[6]

Within a year the low-cost, but well-planned, modern, efficient, comfortable houses were completed. At least, that is the way the contemporary media always described the Norris homes. Actually, most of

4. A capable account of the construction and engineering techniques used at Norris Dam is in Barton M. Jones, "Norris Dam," *Scientific American* 152 (January 1935), 24–26.

5. For the early planning of the town of Norris, see Tennessee Valley Authority Press Release, June 22, 1933, TVA Files. The involvement of Lucy Morgan in the development of Norris is evident in her correspondence with Earle Draper, *ibid*.

6. For Lilienthal's concern over Norris, see his "Memorandum of Inquiry on Norris Dam Townsite Project," Oct. 13, 1933, Morgan Papers.

them—the ones the workers could afford—were rather drab cinder block. It is necessary to view the photographs of these houses along with those of the shacks from which the workers moved in order to appreciate the 1934 enthusiasm over them. Cinder block, electric lights, indoor plumbing, and an electric cookstove sure looked like Utopia to the folks of East Tennessee.

Most of the homes in Norris consisted of four or five rooms, and the monthly rents were low, ranging from fourteen to eighteen dollars, with an additional charge of five dollars for an electric range, refrigerator, water heater, and space heaters. Several larger homes rented for as much as forty dollars per month. These apparently low rents seem less desirable when we remember that TVA workers were on a thirty-three-hour week, for which the unskilled laborer received forty-five cents an hour. Roughly one-quarter of their income went for rent, more if they opted for the appliances. Still, those percentages can be regarded as reasonable. A worker and his family, moreover, could eat all they wanted in the Norris cafeteria for twenty-five cents a meal.[7]

In fact, TVA wages were substantially higher than those in the surrounding area, making it an attractive place to work, but with the disadvantage that the town's cooperative stores and service agencies (whose employees were paid TVA wages) never could turn a profit. Morgan had made money by being hardworking, honest, and fair, and being in the right place at the right time. He never did understand why his hopes for small businesses and cooperatives were realized so seldom. By 1937 red ink had overwhelmed the stores and shops, and they were all turned over to private operators who could pay lower wages.

Norris homes were completely electrified, and each family had available to them a four-acre plot for subsistence farming outside of town. One house was designated the home economics demonstration cottage, "where all types of electrical labor savers are put into practical use" and where Lucy Morgan crusaded on behalf of whole wheat and plain living.[8] Rental rates continued to increase, especially as Knoxville began to experience a housing shortage, and by 1937 rents ranged from $19.90 to $60.00 a month.[9]

Earle Draper, the TVA director of land planning and housing, was an

7. "Norris, Tennessee: A Symbol of Economic Change," *Literary Digest* 118 (Nov. 17, 1934), 9. See also Walter E. Myer, "The Tennessee Valley Looks to the Future," National Education Association *Journal* 23 (December 1934), 233–48.

8. Ruth Peck McLeod, "A Modern TVA Electrically Heated School Building at Norris, Tennessee," *American School Board Journal* 92 (January 1936), 64.

9. Charles Stevenson, "A Contrast in 'Perfect' Towns," *Nation's Business* 25 (December 1937), 115.

ardent New Dealer and planner, who wrote glowingly of his Norris project. In December 1933 he called it "a community based upon the orderly combination of industrial work and subsistence farming." He shared Morgan's vision of a "work-school system of guiding the native people," and his expansive plans included hotels and hospitals. Norris, he said, was "but one phase of that vast system of regional planning in the Tennessee Valley which is destined to bridge a social and economic gap of almost a hundred years."[10]

Two aspects of Morgan's dream for Norris and the Tennessee Valley Authority received special attention in the national press. Most exciting was the very handsome, progressive, and totally electric school, the first in the world to be heated electrically, with even the lights being operated automatically by an electric eye. Norris School must have been heavily influenced by Morgan, for it was thoroughly progressive and resembled nothing so much as Moraine Park back in Dayton. Consider the goals established by the faculty: "subject matter should be used as it applies to real life situations, not as having virtue in itself. . . . Functional values, such as appreciation, ideals, self-direction, etc. [are most important]. . . . Curriculum should be society-centered. . . . Marks, honor rolls, contests, and other forms of rivalry and competition should be eliminated as far as possible."[11] Vintage Morgan. Vintage progressive education.

The large, brick, Georgian-style school operated for eleven months a year, with all teachers on a twelve-month contract. With cheap TVA power, the "largest building in the world to be entirely heated by electricity" ran an electric bill of only two thousand dollars per year.[12] Of the numerous articles on the school, not one was in any way negative, and most reporters observed that the building served as a genuine community center, opening its doors in the evening for adult education and offering its 580-seat auditorium for community events, including church services and movies twice a week.

The clearest progressive and Morgan-related component of education in Norris was the fact that students were encouraged to develop their

10. Earle S. Draper, "The New TVA Town of Norris, Tennessee," *American City* 48 (December 1933), 67–68. Other interesting reports on Norris include Joseph K. Hart, "Building of a City," *Journal of Educational Sociology* 8 (January 1935), 298–308; M. H. Satterfield, "Government of Norris, Tennessee, Studied," *National Municipal Review* 28 (November 1939), 799–800; and Larston D. Farrar, "Norris, Tennessee: An Abandoned Experiment," *Public Utilities Fortnightly* 15 (Nov. 20, 1947), 686–92.

11. Quoted in "Education News and Editorial Comment," *Elementary School Journal* 39 (April 1939), 569.

12. Hugo Giduz, "The Norris School," *High School Journal* 20 (November 1937), 270–71.

own businesses. "Boys and girls," said one reporter, "have been making money in the school at Norris." As part of the Norris School Cooperative, they pooled their labor, with five hours of work equaling one share in the enterprise. They made loans, sold insurance, ran the school store, the cafeteria, the bank, and the gardens. Lilienthal's daughter, Nancy, became one of the leaders in the cooperative, and the general impression was that "these youngsters get more than theory in business training—they get actual experience."[13]

Another fascinating experiment in Norris was its library. The school was, of course, equipped with a library, and it served the community as well, but the Morganites knew that there were thousands of men clearing land out in the boondocks. What a shame it was that they were unable to indulge their tremendous desire for sound reading material. Morgan, as far back as his Colorado experience, had hoped that the common workingman could be raised to a higher level. Many of the people he hired to work for the Authority shared that vision. An article in the 1935 *Library Journal*, entitled "Saw-Filers and Book Boxes," describes one gem of New Deal idealism.[14]

After diligent speculation, if not research, it has been determined that a "saw-filer" is one who sharpens saws, and that somehow the New Dealers asked him to have something to do with book boxes. In fact, Morgan's TVA asked him to become a librarian. While the crews working in the immediate Norris area could be adequately served with books from a mobile unit, there were other crews, especially the men cutting the timber on the land that would become the reservoir, who were so far away and in such bad terrain that van service was impossible. Those mountaineers who had hired on to cut timber for the TVA surely were dying for books, just as the Colorado miners had been in the 1890s.

Each clearing crew consisted of sixty men to do the cutting, plus a saw-filer to maintain the toolbox and to sharpen the cutters' saws and axes. No bulldozers here, and no chain saws. This land was being cleared the hard way. So the answer came to the Utopians of Norris: "Why not place a box of books beside the tool box and make the saw-filer its custodian?"[15] For the fourteen cutting crews were made fourteen water-

---

13. Warner Ogden, "A School Co-operative," *School Activities* 9 (December 1937), 150–60, 185; Ralph M. Hogan, "The Norris School Cooperative," *Curriculum Journal* 8 (February 1937), 59–63; Glenn Kendall, "The Norris Community Program," *ibid.* 10 (March 1939), 108–10; Kendall, "Experience in Developing a Community Program of Education," *Social Forces* 19 (October 1940), 48–51.

14. R. Russell Munn, "Saw-Filers and Book Boxes," *Library Journal* 60 (Sept. 15, 1935), 720.

15. *Ibid.*

proof boxes, each with sixty books, one for each member of the crew.

The Authority's estimate that the reading level of these mountain men was at the seventh grade may have been on the enthusiastic side, as were the reports of book usage: "Some of the foremen constantly encourage the men to read while some of the saw-filers appear to take genuine pride in their added responsibility for lending the books." Beginning in February 1935, this library project carefully divided the sixty books equally into nonfiction, fiction, and children's works. These last had the highest circulation, which the TVA interpreted positively, in that it meant that books were getting into the homes of the workers. If not this generation, the next, so say all Utopians. After Norris Dam was finished and the workers moved on, their books were folded back into the school library, but it must have been grand in 1935 and 1936 to be a TVA librarian and help bring about the new order.

There is so much Morgan here, so much Antioch. It may very well be that, in addition to the fine engineers and other personnel whom he enlisted, Morgan's greatest and longest lasting impact was the town of Norris, with its unique features. Although Norris received wide, and generally positive, reviews in the nation's print media, not all liked it. To the conservative community it was just another example of New Deal socialism, and to a prominent Chicago minister it was "Godless Norris." Morgan, the preacher charged, had built the town "without provision for religious worship." The *Christian Century* undertook to examine this serious allegation.[16]

What the editors found in Norris were healthy signs mixed with some bothersome tendencies. There was little doubt, for example, that "what the TVA is driving toward is little less than a social revolution." On the other hand, they discovered that God had not been completely eliminated from Norris. The residents had voted to avoid the ruthless competition between denominations and had elected to hold interdenominational services in the schoolhouse. While the *Christian Century* would have preferred more religious diversity, its elitist attitude toward the typical mountain church, which it described as "a hotbed of holy rollerism and similar forms of religious obscurantism," led the journal to appreciate what the TVA had done. Better a state religion than those snake-handlers and pew-jumpers: "The *Christian Century* has no desire to see Protestantism represented in Norris by the Holy Rollers." It concluded: "Instead of being without regular religious provisions it is doubt-

16. " 'Churchless' Norris," *Christian Century* 51 (Nov. 14, 1934), 1448–89; A. D. Weage, "Churchless Norris; Reply," *ibid.* 51 (Dec. 5, 1934), 1565.

ful whether any similar construction job in recent times has had as full and intelligent religious service afforded it."

In December 1937 the magazine *Nation's Business* published a lengthy report on Norris. Despite a natural inclination to suspect that this journal would be biased against the socialism inherent in the Morgan program, one finds it both factual and analytical in sizing up Norris after four years. The homes, the editors noted somewhat approvingly, were not as pretentious as "the Ickes Subsistence Homesteads or the Resettlement Administration estates."[17] Despite this appreciation of Morgan's love of the simple and the economical, they found a number of failures in his plan for the town. For one thing, Norris had not attracted any industry, just as Yellow Springs had failed to do so to the extent Morgan desired. The planning, supposedly a central theme of the TVA, did not go "beyond pretty generalities," and the poor soil would never allow a strong agricultural base. Moreover, when Norris Dam was completed, the original population base—the workers—moved. They had to: Norris had no jobs for them. They started leaving in the spring of 1936 and were completely gone within a year. Even earlier, the magazine insisted, many of the grand schemes for Norris had been abandoned, and when, in July 1934, a new town manager took over, "he told the resettled folk [that] Norris would not be a Utopia after all."

The failure to attract industry was ascribed to high TVA wages that had ruined the labor market. The same wage scale made it very difficult for Norris's store, the creamery, and the demonstration farms to make a go of it. Prices in the food shop and drugstore were said to be very high. The administration of the town was actually in the hands of the Authority, which raked a whopping 12.5 percent off the top of the town's budget for overhead. The tourist business was, however, doing well. In August 1937 over 136,000 people visited the newly completed Norris Dam, and each visitor spent an average of eight cents at the TVA concession stands. Finding Norris "a far cry from what it was designed to be," the *Nation's Business* concluded that the resettlement experiment, which was to save submarginal farmers, "now appears about to be saved by shrewd business and the vacation-going public."

With the original workers gone and a housing shortage in Knoxville, Norris settled down as a bedroom community for commuters. After World War II and with Morgan's vision long faded, the TVA decided to

17. Stevenson, "A Contrast in 'Perfect' Towns," p. 114. For a discussion of other New Deal resettlement communities, see Paul K. Conkin, *Tomorrow a New World: The New Deal Community Program* (Ithaca, N.Y.: Cornell University Press, 1959).

get out of the housing business and announced that it would sell the town of Norris along with other sites. Fontana Village, in North Carolina, became a summer resort. Hiwassee Dam Village was merged into the North Carolina state park system. A combine of Philadelphia businessmen bought Norris lock, stock, and barrel. The Norris residents made a bid for the town, but the Philadelphians topped them at just over two million dollars. [18]

So ended Norris, and perhaps already knowing its future will diminish the reader's intensity in examining Morgan's vision of the Tennessee Valley Authority. But it should be clear by now that much of what he tried at TVA would not succeed. The fascinating aspect is that he tried to do so much. Beyond the ethical code and the Norris experiment, Morgan proceeded in 1933 and after to announce in the most public fashion the immense and varied social and economic changes he intended to bring to the valley. Like his writings at Antioch, Morgan's speeches and articles were often confusing, visionary, sometimes a bit whimsical, and given freely and openly as his considered truths without regard for any negative political or public relations repercussions. After all, he was Arthur Morgan.

The TVA gave Morgan a national platform from which to express his ideas on reform and planning. As chairman, he received hundreds of invitations to speak, and it is from his speeches and writings that a picture of the agency he envisioned unfolds. [19] His first national address set the tone for the rest of his public messages. On August 15, 1933, over the NBC radio network, he informed the nation of the progress of the Tennessee Valley Authority. If he lacked any charisma whatever over the

18. On the sale of Norris, see *Business Week*: "For Sale," (March 13, 1948), 56–57, and "Syndicate Gets Norris, Tenn.," (June 26, 1948), 28. See also *American City*: "Norris to be Sold by TVA," 62 (August 1947), 101; "Norris Now on Auction Block," 63 (May 1948), 107; and "Sold for $2,107,500," 63 (July 1948), 7.

19. In his tenure at TVA, Morgan wrote a great number of articles appearing in a wide variety of periodicals. In addition to those listed elsewhere, significant pieces include a series under the title "Bench-Marks in the Tennessee Valley," *Survey Graphic* 23 (January 1934), 5ff.; 23 (March 1934), 105ff.; 23 (May 1934), 233ff.; 23 (November 1934), 548ff.; 24 (March 1935), 112ff.; 24 (November 1935), 529ff.; 25 (April 1936), 236ff.; 26 (February 1937), 73ff.; "Planning in the Tennessee Valley," *Current History* 38 (September 1933), 663–68; "Tennessee Valley Authority," *Scientific Monthly* 38 (January 1934), 64–72; "Social Methods of the TVA," *Journal of Educational Sociology* 8 (January 1935), 261–65; "Social and Economic Implications of TVA," *Civil Engineering* 5 (December 1935), 754–57; "Next Four Years in the TVA," *New Republic* 89 (Jan. 6, 1936), 290–94; "Intelligent Reasonableness and the Utilities; Democratic Decency or Chronic Bitterness?" *Vital Speeches* (Feb. 1, 1937), 5–7, 77–81.

electric medium, he could still be fascinating simply because of the unconventional activities that he considered proper in the social and economic development of a region. He called for careful planning, for the encouragement of cooperatives and the rejuvenation of small businesses, for changes in the basis of land tenure so that destructive use of the soil would not be tolerated, for alterations in the structure of local government, and for elimination of real-estate speculation.[20]

With planning and the elimination of waste, Morgan believed that the United States could realize its great possibilities in the production and distribution of wealth. He still hated waste wherever he found it, and its destruction was a vital part of the new social order he prophesied. His criterion remained that old, peculiar clairvoyance: "The primary and controlling characteristics of such an order is that it will be government by policies which are desirable in the light of their total consequences."[21]

Morgan's plans for a brave new world depended greatly on two developments: the building of an "enlightened character" in the American people and the use of his long view of "total consequences" in treating social ills. For him, and for many others in 1933, the depression was clear evidence of the failure of a ruthless, competitive society, and an indication that the country needed another kind of foundation. The very survival of modern society seemed to him to require a new system. He summed up the answer to the problem in the expression "enlightened, socially-minded character." He had the idea that such character would allow "the infinitely varied capacities of men" to be released and would result in great strides of social progress.[22] This belief is an example of the Utopian strain in Morgan's thought. His presupposition was that people can develop such an enlightened character, and that with the exercise of discipline all men and women can be good. If society could only apply the discipline to itself that he had used in his own life, he seemed to say, then society would be reborn spiritually. If Morgan depended on charac-

20. NBC radio address, in Arthur Morgan, "Speeches and Remarks, 1933–1937" (2 vols., Knoxville, 1940), typewritten and mimeographed collection, vol. 1, no page. These and other basic ideas occur throughout his speeches.

21. Address before the Tennessee Valley Institute, University of Chattanooga, Chattanooga, Tenn., April 20, 1934, "Social and Economic Planning," in Morgan, "Speeches and Writings," vol. 1, 94.

22. Morgan, *The Long Road* (Washington: National Home Library Foundation, 1936), p. 29. Reprinted by Community Service, Inc., Yellow Springs, Ohio, in 1962, this work provides great insight into Morgan's general attitudes on ethics, business, government, social and economic planning, and the possibilities of human progress. An extension of topics developed in *Antioch Notes*, the three main chapters of *The Long Road* were delivered as lectures at the Chicago Theological Seminary in 1936. It is impossible to understand Morgan's view of the TVA without reading this particular work.

ter and his demanding emphasis on consequences (for everyone for all time) as the basis and approach for his new social order, the overriding concept remained what had come to be called "social and economic planning." Whether or not this term was any more than an important New Deal contribution to our treasure trove of sacred symbols and images shall be decided shortly. For the moment it is necessary to use Morgan's speech on NBC in 1933 as an outline, allowing the tracing of the components of his "plan" for the Tennessee Valley.

As with his original goal for Antioch College, Morgan wanted for the Tennessee Valley (indeed, for all of society) the development of a spirit of professionalism in business. Professionalism meant the creation of standards, codes, and guidelines, with the professional receiving only a modest salary, instead of extracting all that the traffic would bear. One's ability and resources should be used to promote the best industrial conditions.[23] On November 9, 1933, Morgan made a speech about business in the valley that was later cited as one of his wildest schemes. He had gone into Knoxville to the campus of the University of Tennessee to address a group of county farm and home demonstration agents attending the Third Conference on the Companionship of Agriculture and Industry. Having no time to prepare an address, he could not resist an extemporaneous examination of a subject so dear to him. His comments were taken down by a stenographer, and the university later published them in mimeographed form.[24]

In his speech he discussed the possibility of a region setting up its own economy. His point was that if the undertaking were made, the region should attempt to build a complete and unified economy, not just a fragment. Maintaining a high level of speculation, Morgan launched into a discussion of how he would handle this hypothetical problem. After noting that he would create a cooperative system for central purchasing and distribution, a socialistic but fairly safe view in 1933, he went on to make a major blunder: "I think I'd have that cooperative organization have its own tokens of credit—a sort of local money." It did not matter that local script was already being tried in some places around the country, because in the depression money was in desperately short supply. It did not matter that Morgan's idea might have stimulated local buying of local products and thus have decreased the flow of money out of the region. It did not matter that the local exchange of goods and

23. Morgan, "Vitality and Formalism in Government," *Social Forces* 13 (October 1934), 5.
24. *TVA Hearings*, p. 331. Address before the Third Conference on the Companionship of Agriculture and Industry, University of Tennessee, Knoxville, Tenn., Nov. 9, 1933, in "Speeches and Remarks," vol. 1, 15.

services might have increased. What did matter was that the phrase "a sort of local money" would haunt Morgan for years; he appeared to have advocated a separate coinage system for the Tennessee Valley.

Another unpopular suggestion frequently made by Morgan concerned the number of counties in the area. In the historical growth of the county system in the United States, he maintained, counties were originally laid out in small units because of the slow transportation of the day. With modern travel conditions, this seemed to him a ridiculous situation. "If we can make six or eight counties into one, and make other changes, we may cut in two the cost of local government. . . ."[25] He went so far as to suggest that the TVA initiate a study on the possibility of combining counties. It took the politically astute Harcourt Morgan only a few minutes to tell the chairman just how hopelessly impractical his idea was.[26]

Morgan offered a similarly Utopian solution, which proved equally unsatisfactory to the rest of the TVA board, in the matter of soil erosion. Because so much soil washed into the river channel and because the TVA had a mission to develop the Tennessee River, the Authority had a legitimate interest in soil care. Here Morgan again exhibited an authoritarian streak when he suggested that the TVA confiscate the land of farmers who refused to treat it wisely. To him, the farmer was merely the custodian of the land, which he held in trusteeship for future generations. If a farmer managed his land poorly, Morgan argued, a part of it should be taken away and put in forestry or even given to those who would care for it properly. In short, he wanted the laws of property changed to prohibit people from owning and occupying land unless they managed it in an enlightened manner, in the interest of a permanent agriculture, for everyone for all time. As he correctly noted, "Such a legal change would constitute one element of a social revolution." Land zoning was not a visionary concept when Morgan discussed it in the valley. FDR, for example, had surveyed all of the state of New York to determine which land was best suited for what purpose. But Morgan was far too casual in moving to the notion that recalcitrant farmers should have their land confiscated. And the way he presented it was frightening. No doubt about it; he would have started a revolution.[27]

25. Address before the Ohio Society, New York, Nov. 13, 1933, "Social and Economic Planning," in "Speeches and Writings," vol. 1, 12.

26. TVA Minutes, Aug. 30, 1933.

27. An appeal of this sort appeared in most of Morgan's speeches; a typical statement is contained in his address before the National Academy of Sciences, Boston, Nov. 20, 1933, "Speeches and Writings," vol. 1, 37.

What is to be made of all this? Was Morgan a failure so early in the New Deal? There is some evidence that suggests failure. His fellow board members had rejected his ethical code and other ideas important to him, and they had asserted their own power and limited his. He had made a number of politicians angry with his determined stand against political patronage, and a few journalists were beginning to zero in on his Utopianism. The code, for example, fell into the hands of Drew Pearson and Robert S. Allen, who had a field day poking fun at it in their "Washington Merry-Go-Round" column.[28]

It is, however, only a foreknowledge of the dramatic conclusion in 1938 that highlights the setbacks of 1933 and 1934. In fact, there was considerable enthusiasm over much of what Morgan was doing with the Authority. The bulk of the substantial attention given to the model town of Norris, for example, was extremely positive. A young TVA stenographer called it "a town which has no past, and whose future is a matter of breathlessness and wonder."[29] The *New Republic* heralded it as "the first example in the United States of what genuine, coordinated planning can accomplish."[30] Even *Fortune* found Norris "scrupulously planned and managed," concluding that "the way good work is done by a democratic government in the fourth decade of the twentieth century is the way TVA is doing it."[31] Morgan must have been vastly encouraged with the early success of Norris.

And there were the dams: Norris completed ahead of schedule, followed by Wheeler in northern Alabama and Pickwick in West Tennessee. Some forty thousand workers had been tested for TVA suitability, tested by Morgan's handpicked staff. Those deemed eligible were being trained in an elaborate, free program, with one training center in Norris, another in Muscle Shoals, and a special one for blacks at Wheeler Dam. When the TVA hired, wrote the director of training, it wanted people who were not only qualified for labor but who could benefit from training. Morgan's dream of eugenic selectivity was being fulfilled in the Tennessee Valley.[32] One of the ways Morgan's TVA did not break ground, however, was in race relations. Blacks lived in separate construction camps, and the only training available to them was in the one camp at Wheeler.

Morgan's labor policy was working well, and the Tennessee Valley

28. *Memphis Commercial Appeal*, Aug. 20, 1933.
29. Gwennie James, "I Live in Norris," *Independent Woman*, no vol. (October 1936), 315.
30. John T. Moutoux, "The T.V.A. Builds a Town," *New Republic* 77 (Jan. 31, 1934), 330.
31. "TVA I: Work in the Valley," *Fortune* 11 (May 1935), 92–98ff.
32. Floyd W. Reeves, "T.V.A. Training," *Adult Education* 7 (January 1935), 48–52.

Workers' Council represented both union and nonunion laborers. There were numerous examples to which Morgan could point as steps in his progress toward a new order. Cooperatives, for instance. The Norris Cooperative Credit Union was functioning smoothly, and Morgan went to great lengths to assist other cooperatives. He established the Tennessee Valley Associated Cooperatives, Inc. (TVAC), an agency that provided loans and guided the development of cooperatives.[33] Morgan is credited with having founded the Spruce Pine Cooperative in North Carolina, which specialized in farm produce. Similarly, his agency boosted the cannery cooperative at Lees-MacRae College in Banner Elk, North Carolina, and another one at Campbell Folk School.

By late 1934 the TVAC seems to have backed some half-a-dozen cooperatives, with thousands of members. Thereafter, others were founded, including the Land O' the Sky Mutual Association in Waynesville, North Carolina; a cooperative milling company at Newport, Tennessee; a dairy cooperative at Brasstown, North Carolina; and the Southern Highlanders, Inc., in Norris to assist handicraft producers. Technically, the TVAC was not part of the Authority, but in fact the two were inseparable until 1937, and Morgan's relationship with TVAC continued after his departure from TVA in 1938.[34]

The country was desperate in 1933, and if Americans tolerated Franklin Roosevelt in the White House because he promised to do something, they must have had a similar tolerance for Morgan's talk of a new social order. It is difficult to understand today the extent to which people were disappointed with capitalism during the Great Depression. Those years were particularly strange, and in being so they may have made Morgan and his ideas seem less bizarre. FDR certainly expressed no early reluctance concerning Morgan's wide-ranging activities. It was a time when any idea could be entertained, from the far left or the far right, but none were so popular as those subsumed under the sobriquet "social and economic planning."

33. Myer, "Tennessee Valley Looks to the Future," p. 245.
34. Joseph G. Knapp, *The Advance of American Cooperative Enterprise: 1920–1945* (Danville, Ill.: Interstate Printers & Pub., Inc., 1973), pp. 317–30.

CHAPTER 7

Planning and Power

It should be obvious by now that one concept is vital to this
narrative, that being the concept of planning, that vague and
sacred term that permeated so much New Deal talk. Both
Roosevelt and Morgan used the expression—the latter generally expand-
ing it to "social and economic planning"—often and loosely. Consider
Roosevelt's words in describing the Tennessee Valley Authority to Congress:

> . . . service to the people . . . transcends mere power development . . . leads
> logically to national planning . . . touches and gives life to all forms of human
> concerns . . . a corporation clothed with the power of government but pos-
> sessed of the flexibility and initiative of a private enterprise . . . charged with
> the broadest duty of planning . . . for the general social and economic welfare
> of the Nation. . . . It is time to extend planning to a wider field. . . .

These lines are probably the most often quoted about the TVA. They
appear in virtually every book on the Authority and in many works on
the New Deal. They also appear in a 1934 volume by Roosevelt himself:
On Our Way.[1] This fascinating work is more than a political document; it
is that of a reassuring president reporting in a most positive fashion on his
first year in office, and he included a separate section on the TVA. "No
parallel in our history," was his description of the agency, and he kept
using the line he had stolen from Uncle Tom's Cabin—the country, like
Topsy, had just grown. He loved that analogy, and he used it twice in this
section on the TVA. No planning, you see. Now, with the depression,
planning must begin. The Tennessee Valley Authority was an example
of how to go about such an activity, and Roosevelt again expressed his
hope that this experiment in regional planning would lead to a national
effort.

Almost everybody agreed that the TVA was a planning agency.
Secretary of Interior Ickes called it "a magnificent experiment in regional
planning," and he too looked forward to the day when "national planning
will become a major governmental activity."[2] Ickes could use words like

1. Franklin D. Roosevelt, On Our Way (New York: John Day Co., 1934), pp. 53–56.
2. Harold L. Ickes, The New Democracy (New York: W. W. Norton & C., 1934), pp.
117–21.

"social order" as easily as Arthur Morgan, although he stressed economic improvement and opportunity for people without the heavy emphasis on morality. One 1934 study claimed that, "In the Tennessee Valley Authority, the New Deal finds its most complete expression" and called the TVA "the greatest experiment in regional planning the world has seen outside of Soviet Russia."[3]

Morgan was enthusiastic about the wide range of missions assigned to the Tennessee Valley Authority, and the independent, decentralized nature of the agency was equally appealing. But nothing impressed him more than the fact that the president wanted the TVA to be, as Morgan put it, a "project in social and economic planning."[4] So quickly caught up in the significance of the Authority, he attributed the same feeling to Roosevelt. "The purpose of President Roosevelt," Morgan wrote early in 1934, "was to provide a limited area in which various elements of social and economic planning might be worked out before being applied to the United States as a whole."[5] If the several dimensions of the different TVA missions made their characterization awkward, they could essentially be summed up in one term: *planning*. The TVA was to be a planning agency. It was to be a regional planning agency with the practical job of helping people in the Tennessee Valley, but its really important task was to be a laboratory in which models could be developed and tested for adoption nationally. There is no doubt about this, and here Roosevelt and Morgan shared the same view. The planning and modeling mentality had been there at least since the Progressive Era, and both of them were imbued with it.[6]

With the enormous dislocation associated with the Great Depression, not just in the homeless and the unemployed, but in the very fabric of society itself, any number of bizarre groups appeared to suggest extravagant remedies for the disaster facing America. There was Kingfish Huey

3. Unofficial Observer (John Franklin Carter), *The New Dealers* (New York: The Literary Guild, 1934), pp. 190–91.
4. Morgan, "The Tennessee River Valley Project as a Great National Experiment," in National Conference on City Planning, *Planning and National Recovery* (Boston: no pub., 1934), pp. 103–9. Available in the Morgan Papers.
5. Morgan, "Conserving Natural Resources," *Civil Engineering* 4 (March 1934), 150.
6. The predilection for organizing people into perfectly planned societies has a rich tradition which includes the Fourierists at Brook Farm, the Christian communists at Oneida, and Bellamy's Nationalist Clubs. In the late 1960s and early 1970s, communes such as Twin Oaks continued this tradition with their devotion to the principles B. F. Skinner expressed in his Utopian *Walden Two* (New York: Macmillan Co., 1948). For a listing of the numerous and predominantly short-lived communitarian attempts of this period, see the "Special Commune Directory Issue" of *Communities*, no. 1 (December 1972).

Long, senator from Louisiana, promising to take from the rich and give to the poor. There was the End Poverty in California movement, the Townsendites, the Technocrats, the Social Creditors, and various "self-help cooperators," seeking a new basis for social and economic organization.[7] The Utopian Society of the thirties, which claimed to have hundreds of thousands of members, stressed planning and tried desperately to get FDR's endorsement.[8] In the New Order, no person would suffer unjustly, poverty and its associated evils would be only bitter memories, and all people would work together toward the perfection of the human race.

For many critics of the existing order, planning emerged as the obvious solution. Richard T. Ely, an old opponent of laissez faire, in *Hard Times— The Way in and the Way Out*, had urged as early as 1931 the creation of an industrial army to occupy the unemployed in public service.[9] George Soule called outright for a "planned society," stressing ever so vaguely the benefits of social and economic planning, while recognizing with little hesitation that such a shift involved at the least a mild form of socialism.[10] In a wonderful 1932 volume entitled *Can We Escape? Only by Bold Thinking Can Industry and Finance Be Lifted from the Bog in Which They Have Been Mired Since 1930*, the number-one remedy suggested was "planning." The author, Guy Mallon, was quick to reject Soviet-type planning because "we are not ready to surrender our individualism," but he did urge increased government control of public utilities and natural resources, as well as of banking and finance. That Mallon was a bit of a Utopian himself is clear, especially when he sounded so much like Morgan in claiming that "ruthless competition should give place in time to intelligent cooperation. . . ."[11]

So drastic was the situation in the 1930s that the United States had its own fascist movement. In *The Coming American Fascism*, Lawrence Den-

7. For a strong reminder of the effect of these lunatic fringe groups on planning, see George B. Galloway, *Planning for America* (New York: Henry Holt and Co., 1941).

8. The Roosevelt Papers contain a fascinating collection of materials on the Utopian Society, most having to do with the president's attempt to disassociate himself from the organization and its leaders' insistence that he had endorsed it. Checked out by the Secret Service, the Utopian Society seems to have been a harmless group of social and economic planning advocates.

9. Richard T. Ely, *Hard Times—The Way In and the Way Out* (New York: Macmillan Co., 1931).

10. George Soule, *A Planned Society* (New York: Macmillan Co., 1935).

11. Guy Mallon, *Can We Escape? Only by Bold Thinking Can Industry and Finance Be Lifted from the Bog in Which They Have Been Mired Since 1930* (Cincinnati: Ruter Press, 1932). This work is also a plea for the federal government to start spending for reflation through loans to states for public works. Mallon's last footnote cites John Maynard Keynes.

nis saw no hope for old-style American capitalism in a frontierless society. For him the "liberal capitalist system" no longer functioned, and planning was his answer. Even though he attempted to distinguish between his definition of fascism and that of Der Fuhrer and Il Duce, his argument remained a vacillating attempt to justify the use of force, since "any new scheme of planning has to be pursued with the power of the state."[12]

The real leader of the planning movement emerging in the 1930s was George B. Galloway, who had no doubts about the enormity of the changes wrought by the depression: "The old order is now ending in a revolution that is political, economic, and moral in character and world-wide in scope." He saw four basic sources for the planning idea in America: the city planners, the conservationists, the scientific managers of Taylorism, and the "contribution of the social sciences to an understanding of human institutions, values, and activities." Galloway took social and economic planning seriously, recognizing its inherent regimentation and social control. Underlying his thinking was the basically Utopian assumption of the possibility of cooperation and coordination.[13]

Galloway was essentially correct in his analysis of the development of the planning concept in the United States. In producing results the most prominent of the sources he mentioned were city planning and scientific engineering. It is also important to note the impact of the World War I experience on American thought. The involvement of the federal government in coordinating the use of the nation's resources and in controlling the lives of its people was unprecedented. Time and again, serious analysts suggested that the planning and coordination that had produced victory could be used as a model for action against the depression. It is equally significant that Roosevelt had played a considerable role in the war effort, which doubtless contributed to his appreciation of the concept of planning. In the Navy Department he had witnessed the tremendous effort it took to design and install the world's largest mine barricade in the North Sea. It was an immense undertaking, just the kind that required the most careful and integrated planning.[14]

In post–World War II society, planning remains sacrosanct. It has been taken so much to heart that we now stress "pre-planning," a wonderfully

12. Lawrence Dennis, *The Coming American Fascism* (New York: Harper & Brothers Pubs., 1936).
13. Galloway, *Planning for America*, p. 5.
14. David E. Wilson, *The National Planning Idea in U.S. Public Policy: Five Alternative Approaches* (Boulder: Westview Press, 1980), pp. 25–40, is an excellent overview of the development of the planning idea since 1900.

meaningless word for a technical era. If planning is one of the most important symbols of our time, it was in a fascinating and predictably vague state in the 1930s. In the first place, the so-called New Deal planners had no firm idea as to what they meant by the concept. For them, and to a large extent for us, the term was valuable primarily as a symbol.

Certainly the image of planning was firmly rooted in the public mind by 1933. "The substance and practice of economic, social, environmental, and strategic planning," a recent study asserts, "constituted a creative and critical political and intellectual experience during the administration of Franklin Delano Roosevelt."[15] Back in 1931 Roosevelt had insisted that planning "is the way of the future . . . planning that affects also the economic and social life of a community, then of a county, then of a state. . . ." Roosevelt predicted that "the day is not far distant when planning will become a part of the national policy of this country."[16]

While still a governor, Roosevelt had met the southern planners, including Howard W. Odum, when he keynoted a conference on regionalism in Charlottesville, Virginia, in 1931. Governor Roosevelt was deeply committed to the regional planning required to retire submarginal lands into reforestation and otherwise to improve the land, and he considered his New York techniques readily replicable in other areas, particularly in a South impoverished by soil erosion, devastating floods, and desperate poverty. He knew the South was the nation's number one economic problem.[17] The Tennessee Valley Authority was his great hope for a solution. When the president outlined his goals for the Authority before the National Emergency Council, he termed the selling of electricity only a "side function." In the real TVA:

> . . . We are conducting a social experiment that is the first of its kind in the world. . . . [The "forgotten man"] never had a chance, never sees twenty-five or fifty dollars in cash a year. . . . [We] are going to see that the farm he is using is classified, and if it is not proper for him to farm it, we are going to give him a chance on better land. . . . We are going to try to bring him some of the things he needs, like schools, electric lights, and so on. We are going to try to prevent soil erosion, and grow trees, and try to bring in industries. It is a tremendous effort with a very great objective.[18]

15. Albert Lepawsky, "Planning," in Graham and Wander (eds.), *Franklin D. Roosevelt, His Life and Times: An Encyclopedic View*, p. 329.
16. Quoted in *ibid.*
17. Michel J. McDonald and John Muldowny, *TVA and the Dispossessed: The Resettlement of Population in the Norris Dam Area* (Knoxville: University of Tennessee Press, 1982), p. 10.
18. Quoted in *ibid.*, pp. 263–64.

When Roosevelt visited Alabama and committed himself to Muscle Shoals, he promised "an example of planning not just for ourselves but for the generations to come, tying in industry and agriculture and forestry and flood prevention, tying them all into a unified whole. . . ."[19]

As powerful a symbol as planning was, many of the New Dealers themselves knew it was eyewash. Secretary of Labor Frances Perkins stated categorically that "there was no central unified plan." Aspirations, to be sure, but there was no single New Deal plan. The New Deal was born in crisis, and for all the fierceness with which Roosevelt clung to the image of planning, he never went beyond the operational level. A sympathetic study of the development of the planning idea since the New Deal finds that under Roosevelt it was "plastic and flexible, and fuzzy at the edges always."[20] Galloway himself concluded:

> From the viewpoint of national planning, the New Deal has been like Don Quixote who mounted his horse and rode off in all directions at once. Its "planning" has been sectional, restrictive, and uncoordinated; it has been piecemeal, empirical, and interventionist. It has consisted of a series of stopgaps designed, as Mrs. Roosevelt once said, "to give us time to think."[21]

Given the fact that planning seems to have been the most obvious common denominator in the Morgan-Roosevelt relationship, it remains a fact that neither one of them ever explained very definitively what he meant by it, but each relied on examples of good planning. Morgan's view, like that of most of his contemporaries, included several kinds of planning. There was the planning for the construction of his dams. There was town planning, the sort he had attempted with the construction camps of the Miami Conservancy, and the most evidently successful aspect of the town of Norris. Of course there was educational planning, involving the kind of curriculum design he had attempted at Moraine Park School and at Antioch College. And there was agricultural planning, forestry planning, navigation planning, and indeed plans for all the divisions of the Tennessee Valley Authority.

As important as these planning activities were, however, they were essentially operational. What was the central thread that tied them all together and gave them meaning? For Morgan, it must have been the development of a plan for morality. It was no accident that one of his

19. Quoted in *ibid.*, p. 12.

20. Otis L. Graham, Jr., *Toward a Planned Society: From Roosevelt to Nixon* (New York: Oxford University Press, 1976), p. 14.

21. Galloway, *Planning for America*, p. 46.

earliest proposals for the Tennessee Valley Authority was the adoption of a moral code. As he said repeatedly, no activity, no matter how well intended, could have desirable results unless it rested on a moral foundation. A second theme for Morgan involved the possibility of modeling—not in the technical, computerized sense in which it is now understood, but in the Utopian, perfectionist notion that rational people would adopt a model once it had demonstrated its success. To that end, Morgan's most important plan was to build models. Generally Morgan shied away from suggesting that people be forced to accept a proper plan, and so he failed to solve the Utopian dilemma.

What of this business of "social and economic" planning and development? Did Morgan and Roosevelt reach some specific agreement on this ill-defined term? FDR used it only in the most general sense, usually tucked safely within a reference to the welfare of the nation. He never spoke in the specific terms of codes of morality, ethics, or behavior, as Morgan loved to. In fact, most of the time Roosevelt talked about only one kind of planning—land planning. He was extremely proud of his efforts in that regard in New York, and he indicated that his first thoughts about the Tennessee Valley involved its being "an ideal location for a land use experiment on a regional scale embracing many States." At the same time, he said the mission of the TVA was "planning for a highly civilized use of the land."[22]

The closest Roosevelt got to "real" planning was with the establishment of the National Resources Planning Board, which had its roots in the 1933 National Planning Board. That office gathered a great deal of data and made a number of studies, but it was a frustrated effort, for it managed to create congressional opposition to the planning cult and to get itself killed off in 1943.[23] Indeed, the Utopian town of Norris lasted longer than the national planning agency.

President Roosevelt used the term *economic and social planning* in its symbolic sense. He might plan to get reelected, or plan to restore confidence, or plan to treat the land more wisely and efficiently, but he never had an overall plan to remake human life. Here lies the major difference between Roosevelt and Morgan. FDR lived and died in the political arena. Compromise was a basic tool of survival for him, and he did not share all the vision with Morgan. As much as Roosevelt gen-

22. Roosevelt, *On Our Way*, p. 54.
23. Philip W. Warken, *A History of the National Resources Planning Board, 1933–1943* (New York: Garland Pub., Inc., 1979), a photostatic copy of Warken's 1969 Ph.D. diss. at Ohio State University. See also Marion Clawson, *New Deal Planning: The National Resources Planning Board* (Baltimore: Johns Hopkins University Press, 1981).

uinely cared for the downtrodden, he was not ready for Bellamy's Industrial Army. As much as Roosevelt knew that soil erosion, power, fighting floods and malaria, making fertilizer, and building industry were all important parts of the TVA, he never talked about the introduction of a new moral order. Morgan did. They miscommunicated in some fundamental way. To say that Morgan and Roosevelt differed on the meaning and ultimate aims of planning is not to say that Morgan was altogether out of touch with the times. There was the Utopian Society and the Technocrats, and there was Galloway, and Morgan had as much in common with them as anyone. Roosevelt did not.

This is not to say that Roosevelt had no vision of the Tennessee Valley Authority. He did, borne out of his own vigorous progressive, World War I, and gubernatorial background, and as president his view of the comprehensive nature of the TVA was extraordinary. Roosevelt's world included political realities—in fact he loved politics—whereas Morgan hated it. Morgan's professional engineer's creed demanded autonomy, which meant in part complete freedom from political interference. Morgan the Utopian heard the president agree, but Roosevelt the politician had committed himself only to limit political patronage and attempt to make the TVA bipartisan. When Morgan heard FDR pledge no politics and speak of planning, he heard something entirely different from what Roosevelt meant.

Where is planning today? Despite the continued absence of any definite national plan, the idea of planning is firmly rooted in the national imagery. In a way it has been institutionalized and rendered harmless. We instinctively know that planning is desirable, but we still do not know what we mean by it. As early as 1947, one student of the subject observed that "national planning today simply means careful management in reviewing and timing government activity as a whole." The same author asserted that "national planning is synonymous with Presidential management."[24] Essentially, we plan when we say we are planning. Planning has become a way of life, but it is certainly not the kind of revolutionary social and economic planning for which Morgan and so many others hoped in the 1930s.

If social and economic planning was a vague and uncertain mission for the Tennessee Valley Authority, there was little disagreement about its other major task: the TVA would produce electricity. This narrative left

24. John D. Millett, *The Process and Organization of Government Planning* (New York: Columbia University Press, 1947), p. 179.

off on the story of power with the passage of Norris's bill in 1933, the one creating the Authority, the one springing from his long fight to save Muscle Shoals. The story resumes at that very first meeting of the TVA board of directors on June 16, 1933, when they met in the Willard Hotel, where Arthur Morgan had them plow through those stacks of mail, asking for decisions right and left.

As has been seen, the other two directors, Harcourt Morgan and David Lilienthal, were nonplussed by that meeting, and eventually they moved to curtail the chairman's authority. One of the letters in those stacks signaled the beginning of a major fight, within and without the TVA, over electricity. The missive was from Wendell L. Willkie, president of the Commonwealth and Southern Corporation, the holding company that controlled practically all the utility operations in the Southeast—the holding company with which the TVA would have to deal. Willkie's letter was addressed to the chairman of the board, and in it he requested a meeting with Arthur Morgan to discuss the relationship between the Authority and his corporation. Noting "problems of mutual interest," Willkie called for "our early and continued cooperative efforts."[25] Lilienthal recorded the effect of Willkie's letter:

> Then followed a considerable discussion as to what attitude the Board should take toward the private utilities, etc. While fundamentally we may be in agreement, there was some difference of opinion as to tactics and strategy expressed as between myself and Chairman Morgan, with Harcourt Morgan acting as a mediator. This will require a good deal of working out.[26]

Lilienthal did not appreciate his prophesy. The TVA board established itself, and the Authority was well on its way to becoming an actuality. That first meeting, however, produced a note of discontent and a dichotomy in philosophy of great significance; in short, it brought to the front the major question of the TVA's attitude toward private utilities. What was to be the Authority's power policy?

The Commonwealth and Southern had been created in May 1929 by a combination of J. P. Morgan's United Corporation and the American Superpower Company, owned by the Bonbright and Company banking house. The two Wall Street offices formed the giant Commonwealth and Southern by acquiring or exchanging stock in three already existing holding companies: the Commonwealth Power Company and the Penn-

---

25. Quoted in Thomas K. McCraw, *TVA and the Power Fight, 1933–1939* (New York: J. B. Lippincott Co., 1971), p. 47.
26. Lilienthal, *Journals*, vol. 1, 39.

Ohio Edison Company in the North, and the Southeastern Power and Light Company, which through its large holdings controlled the utilities near the Tennessee River. By the end of 1932, the total assets of the Commonwealth and Southern and its subsidiaries amounted to $1.13 billion, which made it one of the largest holding companies in the United States, serving more than five million customers. Willkie, who voted for Roosevelt in 1932, became president of this company on January 4, 1933.[27]

The TVA board authorized Arthur Morgan to meet with Willkie, and the chairman scheduled the session for the following week in New York. On June 28 he and Willkie met for dinner in a private room at the University Club. After eating, they discussed the common interest of the Commonwealth and Southern and the TVA. Morgan explained to Willkie that his board had existed for only a short time, and that it had not yet formulated a specific power policy, but that if the matter were approached in a direct and straightforward manner, there should be certain fundamentals on which they could agree. Morgan's attitude was that the law committed the Authority to the generation and distribution of electric power. Willkie disagreed, observing that the act allowed the TVA only to generate and transmit power, and that distribution should be left in the hands of private utilities, which is to say that the agency would be a wholesale supplier to the already existing private companies, which would distribute it retail. Passing over for the time being this significant question of who would market the power, the conversation ended on the friendly note that the problems could be solved satisfactorily for both parties.[28]

Morgan had given some limited thought to the question of public versus private power since the 1920s. From his correspondence with Morris L. Cooke, he had picked up the term *yardstick*, the notion that at least a few public endeavors were justified so as to set a standard by which to gauge the performance and rates of the private companies. Morgan had insisted to Cooke that such a yardstick should be an accurate test. As he put it, "I am in favor of public ownership wherever it can compete in fact with private ownership. In that I think we are agreed." This attitude must be understood in the context of the conservative 1920s, before the depression changed the rules. Even Cooke was cautious enough to respond, "I personally will be quite content to let private

27. Barnes, *Willkie*, pp. 49–60.
28. Morgan, "Memorandum of a Talk between Arthur E. Morgan and Mr. Willkie," June 28, 1933, Morgan Papers.

companies now performing public functions continue in most instances if they will do a reasonably good job."[29]

The depression after 1929 and the collapse of the Insull pyramid induced Morgan and others to believe that the time had come for government to go into the electric power business. For Morgan, however, this was to be more than a fight over power. He demanded that both sides rise above the old methods of strategy, intrigue, deceit, and subterfuge. As he said only a week after the passage of the TVA act:

> It is time for both the managers of private utilities and for the proponents of public ownership and operation to play the game openly and fairly like mature, self-respecting and dignified men and women. Such a change would add to the self-respect and decency of American life, and would greatly help to relieve us of prejudice and confusion.[30]

As far as Morgan could tell, things were going swimmingly with Willkie. He had met the man face to face and had judged him to be a person of sound character with whom he could work honestly. He put his relationship to the test a few weeks after their meeting when he wrote Willkie that a certain Dr. Samuel S. Wyer of Columbus, Ohio, was making virulent attacks on the new TVA, and, in the interest of coopera- tion, Morgan asked Willkie to intercede and have Wyer hold his peace so that the negotiations could proceed without an atmosphere of hysteria. Willkie did! On July 15 he wrote Morgan: "I like the directness of your style—it leads to clarity and I shall accordingly adopt it. . . ."[31] Willkie hooked Morgan early.

The relationship between Morgan and Lilienthal, the director with the most experience on power questions, was not going at all well. From their disagreement at the first board meeting, matters continued to deteriorate. The fundamental question was probably more one of style, with Lilienthal's knowledge of the nature of the power fight on the TVA's hands making him much more aggressive than Morgan, who was content to wait on goodwill to carry the day. Lilienthal already had been through

29. See the Morgan-Cooke correspondence of March 1928 in the Cooke Papers at the Roosevelt Library; on microfilm in the Morgan Papers.

30. Morgan, "Government and Business," May 25, 1933, "Speeches and Remarks," vol. 1, 10.

31. See the July 1933 correspondence between Morgan and Willkie in the David E. Lilienthal Papers, Seeley G. Mudd Manuscript Library, Princeton University, Princeton, N.J.; subsequently referred to as Lilienthal Papers. After the August 5 division of respon- sibilities and the ensuing fight over power policy, Morgan apparently turned over his files on the subject to Lilienthal. For more on Wyer, a consulting engineer with a long history of diatribes against public power, see Lowitt, *Norris*, pp. 260–62.

the wars with the utilities, and his Wisconsin experience had not been altogether a happy one. Beyond style and personality, however, the question boiled down to whether the Authority should build duplicate power lines beside those of the private utilities and actively compete with them, or whether a contract should be concluded that would give each party a monopoly in a given area. To Morgan, duplicating lines would be an unprogressive waste, and consequently he supported a division of territory. To Lilienthal, it was essential that the TVA begin selling power to the people as soon as possible. Wilson Dam down at Muscle Shoals already produced electricity, and the Authority could move into that market very quickly.

In less than a month after the first board meeting, Morgan could endure the divisiveness no longer. Sometime between July 10 and 15, 1933, he dispatched what came to be called "the penciled memorandum" to Lilienthal with the following points. "I think that we should assume reasonableness, fair play and good will on the part of the utilities," he said in his didactic way, "unless experience in *our own* [Morgan's emphasis] relations with them demonstrates the contrary." First, the TVA should decide on the area in which it planned to distribute power, "and then ask the utilities to cooperate with us in transferring that territory to us on fair terms." This test site was important: "until that matter is settled or has had fair opportunity to be settled, we should not go into the market for contracts."[32]

The penciled memorandum was Morgan at his best, and because it signaled the beginning of a bitter feud between him and Lilienthal it is worth scrutiny. When typed—and both men had their offices type a copy—the memorandum was only five single-spaced paragraphs totaling thirty-one lines, rather short for Morgan. Moreover, the document had the tone, if not the form, of a code, of a statement of fundamental principles. Morgan used the expressions "I think" or "I believe" seven times. The memorandum was also Utopian. Its author used "reasonable" twice and "reasonableness" once; "fair terms" twice, along with one usage each for "fair play," "fair opportunity," "good faith," and "cooperate." The enemy was waste: "wasteful form of competition" and "competitive activity which will destroy invested values." Also present is the tendency toward Utopian modeling so frequently evident in Morgan's work and writings. He wanted to take a small area, selected as scientifically as possible, and set up a demonstration of the TVA public

32. Morgan, "Copy of a Penciled Memorandum from A.E.M. to D.E.L. about July 10 or 15, 1933," Morgan Papers; another copy, undated, is in the Lilienthal Papers.

power program. Morgan was deeply committed to the "yardstick," a powerful image of the times that called for public programs to serve as standards for private efforts.

Most public power activists, and certainly Lilienthal, saw the yardstick idea as a fairly general one and in rather negative terms. It was the stick part they liked because they knew in their hearts that the big power companies were overcharging the American public, and now they were going to prove it. It is difficult to exaggerate the significance of the issue of the cost of electricity in the 1930s. Since the revelations of the Federal Trade Commission and the collapse of the Insull pyramid, there had been widespread animosity toward the private interests, which for their part were downright hysterical and paranoid. Both sides watched the TVA experiment intensely because it was widely understood that Roosevelt hoped to extend it nationally. Media coverage of the TVA, in all its aspects, was particularly heavy during the New Deal, and the agency found itself in a series of court fights and legislative battles. For Lilienthal the yardstick was a weapon to be used in that fight. Details, such as rate schedules and the intricacies of cost allocation, did not matter nearly so much as winning the hearts and minds of the people for public power. A tough political strategy that would produce victory was the single immediate essential. It is crucial here to emphasize that the details did matter to Morgan. His yardstick had a Utopian characteristic: it was pure, mathematically and morally. Not only would the TVA's strategies be guileless, but the accounting procedures for establishing rates and value would be unimpeachable. With that sort of yardstick, Morgan would then compare the public approach versus the private. And let the most efficient win.

Lilienthal responded to the penciled memorandum on July 21, and his letter reads like a legal brief; in it he reviewed the development of his disagreement with the chairman. Morgan, it said, had met with Willkie to work for cooperation, and he had given the other two directors a copy of his minutes of that session. In a later board meeting Morgan had proposed the idea of a division of territory, recommending that requests from municipalities around Muscle Shoals not be considered until negotiations were completed with the private utilities. Lilienthal thought then that such a decision to delay seeking markets was premature, "because we had not had a survey made of our available market; that until we had the facts in our possession we should make no commitments at all about our market," especially not a commitment to stay out of certain areas.

The board had again faced the question of power policy, Lilienthal noted in his lengthy response to Morgan, at its meeting on July 12, when

Morgan urged that the TVA write Willkie stating that it had not sought markets. "We have therefore," the chairman wanted to say, "not taken any steps to secure customers for Muscle Shoals power." H. A. Morgan had not been present at that meeting, and Lilienthal had secured a postponement of the matter until Morgan's penciled memorandum arrived. Then Lilienthal undertook to respond to that document. He embraced Morgan's warning against wasteful competition; after all, who could favor it?

Lilienthal, however, could not agree to wait, and he expressed his "deeply felt disagreement" with a policy to delay service until the negotiations on territory were completed with Willkie. Noting his "prayerful reconsideration of the entire subject," Lilienthal urged that they get on with the "program which Congress has directed us to carry out." Territorial divisions represented "far-reaching commitments the consequences of which we cannot foresee." Lilienthal wanted action, and he proposed that the TVA begin as soon as possible to serve as many towns near Wilson Dam as it could. While this was being accomplished, the Authority would have time to survey other areas for expansion.

Lilienthal's plan was to delay Willkie, make no commitments to him, and use the time to get into the power business. That was a matter of strategy. What disturbed Lilienthal most about Morgan's plan was its presumption of fairness and cooperation on the part of the private utilities. Lilienthal was "skeptical" of this approach, which he found "running counter to every reasonable expectation under the circumstances" and one that exposed the TVA "to the gravest hazards."[33] When Arthur Morgan spoke of cooperation, goodwill, and resisting the destruction of "invested values," it sounded very much to public power advocates such as Lilienthal that Morgan was sympathetic to Willkie, who spoke constantly of the unfairness of government-sponsored power and the grief it would bring to millions of widows and orphans—the sole possessors, it seems, of private power stock. Eventually, of all the charges hurled at the Utopian, the accusation that Morgan was pro–private power would be the most damaging.

The debate over power policy in July 1933 occurred at the same time that Morgan wrote his ethical code, which with other musings revealed his enormously wide definition of the TVA's mission. All of these positions brought Lilienthal and Harcourt Morgan together in their move to assign each board member responsibility for certain areas. Essentially, Harcourt Morgan combined with Lilienthal, and each took

33. Lilienthal to Morgan, July 21, 1933, Lilienthal Papers.

the area he most wanted. Lilienthal got power policy. That meeting of August 5 was an ordeal for Arthur Morgan. Not only had Morgan learned that Lilienthal intended to engage in a bitter political fight with Willkie, but there was now political intrigue on the board itself. In a fortnight, however, the chairman renewed the discussion on power policy in yet another memorandum, and he began to show some of the pettiness under pressure he had exhibited at Antioch.

Regarding electricity, he asserted, the TVA had two missions: to create a "laboratory of planned development" and to provide the yardstick "to measure the relative effectiveness and economy of public and private ownership." The Authority's purpose was not to begin "a contest for the general substitution" of public for private power. Investors had bought Willkie's stock in good faith, and it was incumbent upon the TVA not to be wasteful. Morgan was particularly detailed in citing the unknown results of the yardstick experiment: "If, all things considered, private operation is more satisfactory, then an extension of government operation would not be indicated. If government operation should fail to compete successfully for a long period, say twenty-five years, it probably should be given up."[34]

This second document on Morgan's power policy is especially fascinating. Morgan claimed that President Roosevelt supported his version, bringing once again to the fore the question of the nature of the relationship between the two men. He was extremely direct in criticizing Lilienthal's plan, which Morgan believed to involve selling power to "all inquirers" prior to an agreement with Willkie. "The present course," he said, "is equal to a declaration of war . . . [which] if persisted in will surely result in an attitude of strife and antagonism." Moreover, Morgan found himself "embarrassed" by the course of events. He had met with Willkie, and he had promised "to deal directly and in a straight forward manner with him." Lilienthal's plan, however, was not straightforward, and it would make Willkie feel "uncertainty, misgiving, and perplexity." This was an ethical problem for Morgan, and he felt "put in a position of either having made false representations, or of having been irresponsible." Either is agony for a Utopian. To solve his dilemma, Morgan proposed notifying Willkie that, following the August 5 division of responsibility, Lilienthal was now in charge of power and hence was the proper contact at TVA. Morgan wanted to disassociate himself from Lilienthal and his low road.

Lilienthal, for his part, was not about to take these charges without a

34. Morgan to H. A. Morgan and David Lilienthal, Aug. 14, 1933, Lilienthal Papers.

response. Two days later he submitted a "Memorandum in Opposition." Lilienthal was mad, and in a carefully reasoned argument on legal-sized paper he called Morgan's ideas unscientific, impractical, without the public interest, a danger to the TVA, and opposed by "time-tested public men." Mostly, he said, Morgan was impractical. Who but a visionary would suggest, given all the evidence of the evils of the private utilities, that reasonable men could cooperate with them? Their "antagonistic and litigious attitude" was a matter of "history and fact." They were the "enemies" of the Authority and of the president. Who were these time-tested men who opposed Morgan's proposal? Lilienthal had contacted a number, among them Senators Norris and La Follette, Morris L. Cooke, E. F. Scattergood, and his old Harvard mentor, Felix Frankfurter. "All of these men took the position that it would be a grave mistake" to negotiate with Willkie. He quoted Cooke, who found his position "thoroughly sound" and called Morgan a "layman." Cooke was adamant: "Go ahead and do Uncle Sam's job without promising any private interest anything." Morgan's policy would bring "failure and essential disgrace." Lilienthal also quoted Frankfurter, who judged Morgan's proposal "fraught with every kind of danger" and guaranteed to produce "a first-class row."[35]

If Lilienthal had these men on his side, who supported Morgan? Roosevelt did, or at least so the chairman believed. Upon giving his last memorandum to Lilienthal, Morgan informed him that he had scheduled a meeting of the board with Roosevelt. This conference would decide the issue. Somewhat rattled by the prospect of taking the matter so quickly to the president, Lilienthal wrote Senator Norris.[36] He told the senator that he had arranged for Harcourt Morgan to wire the chairman that the president should know that the meeting with him was really Morgan's appeal of a decision already made by the board. Harcourt dutifully telegraphed Morgan and threatened that if he did not so inform the president "it will be necessary to place a copy of this telegram in the hands of his secretary to that effect."[37] Now Morgan was rattled, and he wound up going to see the president alone, where he showed him H. A. Morgan's threatening telegram.[38]

When Morgan returned to Knoxville, Lilienthal greeted him not only

35. Lilienthal, "Memorandum in Opposition to Proposal of Chairman A. E. Morgan for Territorial Division Agreement and 'Cooperation' between Tennessee Valley Authority and Private Utilities," Aug. 16, 1933, Lilienthal Papers.

36. Lilienthal to Norris, Aug. 17, 1933, Lilienthal Papers.

37. H. A. Morgan to A. E. Morgan, Aug. 16, 1933, Morgan Papers and TVA Files.

38. A. E. Morgan to H. A. Morgan, Aug. 17, 1933, TVA Files.

with his devastating memorandum in opposition to his conciliatory attitude toward Willkie, but as well with a full-fledged power policy that expressed his views.[39] Because Harcourt Morgan agreed with Lilienthal, Morgan was beaten, and he made unanimous (more goodwill) the board's decision to establish Lilienthal's declarations as the official TVA power policy. On August 21, Lilienthal telegraphed Cooke: "Power Policy Developments Satisfactory."[40]

Necessity intervened and dictated a solution to this first bout on power policy. The White House conference did eventually occur, and Roosevelt seemed to back Morgan, who must have been encouraged with the apparent support of the president in opposition to Lilienthal. It was to be his only victory in appealing to FDR to resolve his conflict with Lilienthal. The president took the view that because the old Army Corps of Engineers' contract for the sale of Wilson Dam power to one of Willkie's subordinate companies was due to expire shortly, and because the TVA had no other market ready for its power, it seemed wise to conclude some agreement with Willkie. At the same time, Roosevelt went over the power policy developed by Lilienthal, and after the meeting Morgan and Lilienthal repaired to the Cosmos Club, where they hammered out a document with which both could live. This policy outlined the geographic areas the TVA would serve, as Morgan had demanded, but it left the option open for expansion, as Lilienthal desired.[41]

On January 4, 1934, Willkie and Lilienthal signed a contract, in which the former promised to continue purchasing electric power from Wilson Dam and to sell sufficient properties to the TVA to enable it to create the yardstick area. In February the Authority got its first client, the city of Tupelo, Mississippi, which had a municipal power company. From his perspective, Willkie had contained the socialistic experiment of the federal government to a small area. Lilienthal might be unhappy with the territorial restrictions he had fought so bitterly to avoid, but at least the TVA was selling power, and for the moment the animosity between him and the chairman subsided into a simple avoidance pattern.[42] With each

39. Lilienthal, "Principles for a Power Policy for the Tennessee Valley Authority," Aug. 16, 1933, Morgan Papers.
40. Lilienthal to Cooke, Aug. 21, 1933, TVA Files.
41. The development of the disagreement between Lilienthal and Morgan has been admirably treated by Thomas K. McCraw in *Morgan vs. Lilienthal: The Feud Within the TVA* (Chicago: Loyola University Press, 1970). The power aspect is further amplified in his *TVA and the Power Fight*.
42. McCraw, *TVA and the Power Fight*, pp. 65–66.

in control of specific areas and with the power question resolved, they had no further need to speak to each other, and rarely do they appear to have done so.

Lilienthal now focused his attention on Tupelo and the other tiny towns the TVA was allowed to serve. Tupelo fascinated Americans, and there Lilienthal earned his stripes as a proponent of the people's right to power. In doing so, he took a major gamble. Lilienthal believed that the cause of high electrical rates was low demand, and that as long as rates remained high the demand could certainly not grow during a depression. He wanted to take the risk of introducing very low rates, hoping that consumption would increase to a point where the cheaper rates were justified. It took a while to build such a demand. For one thing, many of the homes in Tupelo were not wired for electricity. At prevailing costs, it took about five 1934 dollars to have this done. Furthermore, to reach the farmers outside of town, lines had to be built.

Fortune magazine called the argument over power policy "a burning political and social issue, particularly in these New Deal days."[43] As one might expect, *Fortune* was not particularly pro–public power, but the magazine did note the great difficulty the private industry had gotten itself into, citing Insull's crash and the recently completed Federal Trade Commission hearings, "featuring the seamy side of boomtime high finance." If the article was wishy-washy, and if it found the TVA "strong medicine," and if it did not buy the yardstick idea, *Fortune* did at least state fairly Lilienthal's argument that cheap power would increase demand. The Authority nearly met defeat in the courts, and for the victory Lilienthal must receive credit, but beyond the legal issue was the question of whether or not Lilienthal's gamble on low rates would succeed. Here the youngest member of the board surpassed the chairman in his willingness to take risks, and in his triumph he doubtless produced more social results than Morgan ever imagined. In his methods, oddly enough, Lilienthal aped Morgan.

Lilienthal adopted two of Morgan's favorite ideas: he used cooperatives and he embraced simplicity. By November 1933 he was as much of a whirlwind as Morgan, and the job applications alone threatened to overwhelm both their offices. The paperwork and the endless meetings required of men in their high positions deterred neither from pursuing his dreams. A careful review of their papers presents the definite impression of an incredible amount of activity. Such intensity is a general characteristic of the early New Deal period, but on following these two

43. "TVA II: The Power Issue," *Fortune* 11 (May 1935), 98ff.

men through it on a personal level (we are, after all, reading their mail and peeking into their desk drawers), one literally feels the enormous pressure they were under, as well as the excitement, the commitment, and even the joy of it.

One difference easily noticeable between the two is that Lilienthal focused on the New Deal as a crusade far more than did Morgan, who had, after all, been calling for a new moral order for years. Maybe their commitment was different. Morgan was never ideologically committed to the New Deal, although until the last he fantasized about some special relationship with FDR. Lilienthal, however, was head over heels in love with the New Deal. For Morgan, the TVA was just another experiment, one that he probably expected to fail as had his others. For all his Utopianism, Morgan was essentially pessimistic, perhaps because of that very Utopianism. For Lilienthal the New Deal was Armageddon. The sort of youthful enthusiasm expressed by Lilienthal did not reappear in American politics until John F. Kennedy's New Frontier, and in a way the young lawyers of the New Deal, of whom Lilienthal was one of hundreds, saw it as Camelot. Lilienthal cared in a profound way about the New Deal. In his own manner he was as well-meaning and as innovative as Morgan.

While Morgan built Norris (which one observer called the TVA's "Exhibit A"), Lilienthal set out to create a new demand for electricity in small towns and rural areas.[44] The agency would never sell power directly to individual households, but it would wholesale it to municipalities and cooperatives set up to distribute electricity. That was the first of his great innovations. David Lilienthal probably helped develop more cooperatives than did Arthur Morgan, but while the latter stressed vegetables, Lilienthal built power companies.[45]

Just as Morgan had set up a semi-independent agency to foster his cooperatives, so Lilienthal established the Electric Home and Farm Authority (EHFA). He was, of course, president, and in what was probably an attempt to gloss over the differences of August 1933, he listed Morgan as vice-president. This agency assisted in the establishment of electric cooperatives to distribute TVA power, and it developed cheap appliances for the electrified public to purchase. In Lilienthal's papers are several examples of the stationery he designed for the EHFA,

44. Katherine Palmer, "The Tennessee Valley Experiment," *Review of Reviews* 89 (April 1934), 47.
45. Joseph G. Knapp, *The Advance of American Cooperative Enterprise: 1920–1945* (Danville, Ill.: Interstate Printers & Pub., Inc., 1973), covers both Morgan's and Lilienthal's cooperative endeavors, pp. 317ff.

his brainchild. At the bottom right of the page appeared in bold black ink a fist holding a lightning bolt and the block letters "TVA." Beneath that powerful image were the words "Electricity for All." This logo was obviously a copy from the famous National Recovery Administration, where his close friend Donald Richberg worked, with its well-known Blue Eagle and slogan "We Do Our Part."[46]

Developing the municipal and rural cooperatives to deliver TVA power was actually one of Lilienthal's easier tasks. After all, there was plenty of federal public works money available to get them into operation. The real problem was low demand for electric power. Lilienthal had a number of strategies. It was relatively easy for him to set up the private utilities as the enemy, since the public was predisposed to hate them. Having a target, he launched a vigorous campaign on behalf of electricity as a natural right for all Americans. This was all well and good, but in the depths of the depression, especially in the South, and even with cheap TVA rates, there remained the problem that people could simply not afford the electrical appliances that would use the power. Here Lilienthal was little short of a genius. He worked out a deal with appliance manufacturers, even getting Willkie's blessing, to make a cheap, no-frills line of ranges and refrigerators that bore the TVA stamp of approval and were far more affordable for the average family. That was the heart of Lilienthal's gamble: cheap appliances and cheap rates would yield great demand.

By June of 1934 there were six companies in Tupelo, population six thousand, selling electrical appliances, including the cheaper models authorized by the TVA. In just over two weeks after the introduction of that new line, 137 refrigerators and 17 ranges were sold, eighty dollars each. This was even before the wiring of the houses had been completed; at that time only one mile of wire had been strung in Tupelo. "But," reported one of Harry L. Hopkins's informants, "dealers say they are taking orders from farmers right along." Hopkins, Roosevelt's chief relief administrator, got his intelligence from a former journalist whom he had hired to travel around the country and provide reports on grass-roots feeling. She found TVA land in good shape:

> I carry away the impression that all over the area, from Knoxville, Tennessee, to Tupelo, Mississippi, and on up to Memphis and Nashville, people are in a pretty contented, optimistic frame of mind. They just aren't thinking about the depression any more. They feel that we are on our way out and toward any

46. For a sample of the symbol on Lilienthal's Electric Home and Farm Authority, Inc., stationery, see Lilienthal to FDR, Dec. 3, 1934, Lilienthal Papers.

problems that have to be solved before we get out their attitude seems to be, "Let Roosevelt do it."[47]

Not only did Lilienthal's Electric Home and Farm Authority provide those cheap and simplistic appliances that people were buying even before they had electricity, but he arranged for them to get the credit to do so. The EHFA, in another innovative program, provided low-rate loans directly to the consumer to make these purchases. Just as the program was getting under way, one observer called it "instalment [*sic*] buying on a grand scale with the Government holding the IOU."[48] Lilienthal's gamble paid off in a big way. Never mind that he picked his low TVA rates right out of thin air. Never mind that the accounting procedure was "quick and dirty," instead of the moral and scientific approach desired by Morgan. Where Morgan had wanted to wait, Lilienthal had forged ahead. He started selling power to Tupelo on February 4, 1934, and the reduction in the electric rates was more than matched by a drastic increase in power usage. As one authority on the electrical issue of the 1930s concluded:

> By demonstrating that a rigorous program of rate reduction, publicity, and appliance saturation would increase consumption and thus raise the standard of living, TVA performed an exceedingly valuable service for the private tradition and for the country. It had demonstrated that elasticity of demand vastly exceeded private operators' estimates.[49]

Lilienthal's success in promoting public power was clear by the end of 1934, at least as far as consumers were concerned. The court cases would drag on, and they provided the backdrop for the last eruption of the feud between Lilienthal and Morgan. For all the early interest that Morgan's town of Norris aroused, the real human drama was expressed in refrigerators and electric cooking stoves. In terms of establishing himself as a vital part of the New Deal, Lilienthal had won and had won early.

It is impressive, moreover, that examination of his papers indicates that Lilienthal showed patience in dealing with Arthur Morgan. With so

47. Lorena A. Hickok to H. L. Hopkins, June 11, 1934, Hopkins Papers in the Roosevelt Library. Hickok was a reporter for the Associated Press who felt she had become so friendly with Eleanor Roosevelt that she could no longer report on her, hence, the job with Hopkins. Hickok's recollections are in *Reluctant First Lady* (New York: Dodd, Mead, & Co., 1962), while her biography is in Doris Faber, *The Life of Lorena Hickok: Eleanor Roosevelt's Friend* (New York: Morrow & Co., Inc., 1980); her papers are in the Roosevelt Library.
48. Palmer, "The Tennessee Valley Experiment," pp. 46–47.
49. McCraw, *TVA and the Power Fight*, p. 74. McCraw provides ample evidence that Lilienthal's accounting methods in establishing TVA rates were not only sloppy but a deliberate gamble.

much at stake—indeed, the future of public power—the younger man was easily frustrated by the ramblings of the Utopian chairman. But in 1934 and 1935, Lilienthal's long suffering attitude is striking. He wrote endlessly to Frankfurter, La Follette, Richberg, and Norris. They listened sympathetically, for they were as committed as he, and they counseled endurance, that the battle was obviously being won. It seems clear from the record that in these early years Lilienthal was willing to work with Morgan, as long as he had a free hand in the power fight. Had Morgan been at all politically inclined, Lilienthal could have dealt with him. The division of board responsibilities, from Lilienthal's perspective, represented a compromise. Morgan, however, hated compromise and was both ignorant of and antagonistic toward politics. Lilienthal was a professional. In this matter, Morgan, as Morris Cooke said, was a layman.

CHAPTER 8

Morgan and Lilienthal

The Tennessee Valley Authority became a nightmare for Arthur Morgan, and it was David Lilienthal who haunted him. It was Lilienthal, the chairman came to believe, who had conspired to limit his power and who had brought politics into the board of directors. It was Lilienthal who was lying to the public about the economics of TVA power and making a caricature of the yardstick. It was Lilienthal who was manipulating crass politicians by participating in patronage. Morgan came to hate Lilienthal with an incredible passion, and he hated him that way for years. Such intensity of feeling, and particularly its effect on the early Tennessee Valley Authority, demands attention.

From the first moments of official TVA history, Morgan differed with his fellow directors about administrative style. He believed that the agency was supposed to be revolutionary, even, and perhaps most of all, in the area of management. For his purposes Morgan had long ago adopted the method of conducting business common to the Quakers, with whom, because of his wife's connection, he had developed close ties. Quakers did not take formal votes on questions; they reached something called consensus. Morgan explained his conception of this procedure:

> Consensus of judgment would not mean taking formal votes on the "one man, one vote" principle. Consensus of judgment may be arrived at by the deference of the many who do not know to the superior judgment of the few who do. The balance of competence to judge may shift endlessly as different subjects for judgment arise.[1]

The reader has already seen that Morgan felt himself competent in a great many areas. He knew his judgment would usually be "superior," for such had been the case in the past. Moreover, he was accustomed to being in control as an engineer and as a college president. Sharing authority was something new and no doubt threatening to him. Not only had Lilienthal and Harcourt Morgan stripped him of control, but they had instituted the hated "one man, one vote" process. It further seemed to Morgan that Lilienthal had recognized this situation immediately and

1. Morgan, *The Long Road*, p. 1.

had begun a campaign from the beginning to win the support of the third director. Years later Morgan recalled, "The process of Mr. Lilienthal, of assiduously cultivating H. A. Morgan, was so obvious that anyone could see it."[2]

For all that we have come to appreciate Morgan's naïveté, he was not so stupid as to fail to expect some difference of opinion on the board regarding policy. Indeed, his approved method of consensus allowed for such. In fact, for three years every official board vote was unanimous, and when that unanimity, if not consensus, ended, it would be Morgan's negative that broke the tradition. Morgan's problem with the TVA's decision-making procedure was essentially that he found Lilienthal habitually acting in a manner that was less than straightforward. For Morgan, such deviousness was dishonest. He also began receiving disturbing reports from other TVA staff members. After the August 5, 1933, meeting that delimited each director's responsibilities, Director of Personnel Floyd Reeves came to him, Morgan recollected four years later, and told him point-blank that Lilienthal was creating division and discontent within the Authority.[3] Reeves advised Morgan to resign, saying that most of the staff would follow him, thus forcing the president to intervene in what was a hopeless situation. Morgan, however, felt obliged to keep the matter within the TVA because, he said, he did not want to let such adverse publicity damage Roosevelt's attempt to rebuild the nation.

Morgan's defeat on the separation of responsibility and, later, on power policy certainly gave him misgivings, and another prick came in the form of confidential reports from a low-level staff member in the Authority's Washington office. Arnold Kruckman, hired in the early days of TVA before the other directors were selected, worked as an assistant in the information division. With a good ear for office gossip and being a bit on the paranoid side himself, he began in September 1933 to send Morgan confidential letters dealing with intrigue in the TVA and with the chairman's image in the valley. Kruckman informed Morgan that his emphasis on planning and creating a new social order was beginning to sound a bit spooky to the plain folk of the South. What they wanted, he

2. Morgan to Albert Lepawsky, November 1966, Morgan Papers. Philip Selznick refers to the possibility of an H. A. Morgan–Lilienthal bloc whereby "Lilienthal received support for the electric power program in exchange for his support of the fertilizer program," *TVA and the Grass Roots: A Study in the Sociology of Formal Organization* (Berkeley: University of California Press, 1949), p. 92.

3. Morgan, "A Statement by Arthur E. Morgan of Conditions in the TVA, Intended to Supply a Basis for Understanding the Situation," April 1937, Morgan Papers.

said, was cheap electricity and jobs. No doubt the Utopian overlooked entirely the essential truth in Kruckman's report, but he certainly would have keyed on another datum: Lilienthal, Kruckman related, had made arrangements with congressional leaders to bypass Morgan in matters of political appointments. This alleged patronage railroad twisted through the TVA's Washington representative, Marguerite Owen, and Lilienthal's assistant, V. D. L. Robinson. According to Kruckman, the politicians "feel welcome in those quarters; even more than welcome. As for approaching AEM again, they say they are through." In addition to this serious allegation, Kruckman charged that Lilienthal was behind a concerted effort against Morgan involving business leaders, newspapers, and public officials in the Tennessee Valley. "The major point of attack," Kruckman said, "is AEM, his ideas, ideals, purposes. They regard him as a fanatical sentimentalist. They call him a snob. He is to be discredited—if possible."[4]

Whether or not there was, at this early date, an overt conspiracy against Morgan, he was doing a superb job of discrediting himself in the valley. His constant harping on the need to revitalize the area obviously suggested that something was terribly wrong with it, something beyond the depression, some fatal flaw in the people's character. Naturally, they resented that accusation. For all their poverty, Southerners were immensely proud, and they tended to take Morgan's criticisms of their area as personal insults. Their sentiments were no doubt admirably expressed by Tennessee Sen. Nathan L. Bachman in an angry letter to Morgan:

> Finally, I do resent, on behalf of my people, and for myself, the suggestion that we are in need of a new cultural civilization, which you continuously advocate in your addresses. A people whose forbears went with Sevier to Kings Mountain, destroyed Ferguson and forever broke the hope of British domination in this country, and later under Jackson annihilated Packenham at New Orleans are surely in no need of intellectual or sociological admonitions in the pursuance of their welfare. They are of a breed that helped make these United States and will help save them in their hour of travail.[5]

Of all the places for Morgan to attempt Utopia, he could hardly have found more barren ground than the hills of Tennessee.

A split in the leadership of an organization seems mysteriously to permeate the entire body, and it happened in the TVA. This occurred

---

4. Arnold Kruckman to Arthur Morgan, Sept. 5, 1933, Morgan Papers; author's interview with Morgan, Aug. 15, 1966.
5. Bachman to Morgan, Oct. 19, 1933, TVA files.

despite the fact that Morgan made no attempt—for it would not have been straightforward conduct—to build up his own body of devoted followers. It is true that he had brought in several old associates and young Antiochians, people who shared his vision and who often stuck fiercely by his side, but when the chips were down their numbers were few. Lilienthal, a gregarious and friendly person, contrasted sharply with the austere chairman, and he appears to have attracted quite a coterie. To some observers, however, it seemed that Lilienthal developed his clique by determined effort. Kruckman recalled that very soon after the TVA started up, "the word came down the grapevine that Mr. Lilienthal had made it clear one would either have to be for him or against him."[6] The polarization of staff members into Morgan and Lilienthal camps originated, as Kruckman later told Morgan, because "everyone seemed to know that Lilienthal was at odds with you."[7] The really curious thing about Kruckman's reports is what Morgan did with them. He locked them away and told Kruckman not to write him further. Morgan was so high-minded, so committed to the inevitable triumph of goodwill!

As a matter of fact, the tension between Morgan and Lilienthal lessened after the dramatic summer of 1933. Both men had their hands full, and Morgan for the time being at least had opted out of the fight over power policy. There was Norris to build. The issue was rejoined in the summer of 1935 when Morgan received definite proof that Lilienthal had hired TVA employees based solely on their political merits. The reader has already seen Morgan's 1933 encounter with Postmaster General Farley over patronage, and we know that politics were anathema to the chairman; they represented all that he was against. For this crime, he would never forgive Lilienthal. For his part, Lilienthal could never understand why Morgan got so excited over a few concessions that yielded desperately needed political support.

Lilienthal had obviously given considerable attention to the connections of his chief assistants. He knew his battles were fought in the political arena. Marguerite Owen had worked for Senator Norris before Lilienthal made her the TVA Washington lobbyist.[8] V. D. L. Robinson

6. Kruckman to Morgan, March 28, 1938, Morgan Papers. Also available in this writer's "The Human Engineer: Arthur E. Morgan and the Launching of the Tennessee Valley Authority," M.A. thesis, Vanderbilt University, 1967.

7. Kruckman to Morgan, May 31, 1938, Morgan Papers.

8. Gordon R. Clapp, TVA office memorandum, July 23, 1935. Hereinafter cited as Clapp Report. This document and others relating to it were so important to Morgan that he kept them in his safe for the rest of his life. They are reproduced in this writer's "The

was attached to the office of Senator Bachman at the time he became TVA Chattanooga representative of the information division and a personal assistant to Lilienthal. He seems to have been responsible for obtaining jobs for Bachman's deserving constituents.[9] The conditions under which Robinson himself came to TVA are obscure. The personnel division reported, "There is nothing in the application of the negotiations leading up to his appointment. . . . There is no correspondence in the file between Mr. V. D. L. Robinson and Mr. Lilienthal."[10]

In the summer of 1935 Floyd Reeves, secured by Arthur Morgan from the University of Chicago to head the TVA's personnel division, directed his assistant Gordon R. Clapp, himself later a TVA chairman, to investigate the number and occasion of political appointments in TVA. Clapp's thorough report, even including Arthur Morgan's hiring of Eleanor Roosevelt's crippled friend, R. Harold Denton, cited several appointments made by Lilienthal that could be considered as nothing less than political. A case in point is that of George D. Brew, about whose appointment Clapp concluded:

> The fact of the matter is, however, that if Mr. Lilienthal, through Mr. Robinson, did not prevail upon a division head to recommend the appointment of Mr. Brew, the examiners probably would not have reached Mr. Brew for appointment. . . . It seems clear, therefore, that the appointment of Mr. Brew was brought about because of the interest shown in him by Speaker [of the house Joseph] Byrns. . . . The fundamentally decisive factor, therefore, seems to be one of a political character.[11]

An equally disquieting case concerned Claude P. McReynolds, nephew of Rep. Samuel D. McReynolds of Tennessee. In this matter Lilienthal and James W. Cooper (the TVA land commissioner) began in August 1933 to channel the appointment around the proper personnel selection process. Lilienthal took it upon himself to promise the repre-

---

Human Engineer." Owen later wrote her own account of the TVA in *The Tennessee Valley Authority* (New York: Praeger Pub., 1973).

9. Clapp Report. See also Nathan Bachman to Floyd Reeves, Aug. 10, 1933, TVA Files.

10. Clapp, office memorandum, July 25, 1935, TVA Files. Surely Lilienthal corresponded with the man who became his personal assistant, but it seems likely that he failed to file the letters. John F. Pierce, in charge of the TVA Files in 1933, informed this writer on July 15, 1966, that Lilienthal's departments never sent material to the central files. Clapp stated further in his report that "I recall that at the time Mr. Robinson was appointed, there was considerable conjecture from certain circles in Washington as to why the appointment was made. There are no records available to the personnel division to throw any light on the matter."

11. Clapp Report.

sentative a job for his nephew. Floyd Reeves rebelled at this extraordinary behavior and angrily wrote the power director: "It is my sincere belief that since your commitment to the Congressman was made on the basis of insufficient if not misleading information, it would be an act of bad faith on my part to effectuate this commitment. . . . I prefer not to sign a letter appointing Mr. Claude McReynolds unless requested to do so by the Board."[12] Robinson intercepted Reeves's memorandum to Lilienthal and returned it to him with the excuse that he thought it unwise to disturb the director with such a problem at that time. The personnel officers still refused action until Robinson assured them that Lilienthal had formally requested them to do so. In 1935, however, Clapp passed judgment:

> It is difficult for the Personnel Division to construe this appointment as anything other than a violation of section 6 [prohibiting political appointments] of the Act. It would seem that the qualifications of Mr. McReynolds were such as to make it quite improbable that he would have received appointment had it not been for the fact that his uncle brought his influence to bear upon Mr. Cooper and Mr. Lilienthal to the effect that the appointment be made.[13]

There is no room for doubt here. Lilienthal had been caught with his hand in the till. As early as August 1933 Lilienthal was subject to dismissal from the TVA for violating the antipatronage clause in the law creating the TVA. Section six of the Tennessee Valley Authority Act specifically stated that "no political test or qualification shall be permitted or given consideration," and any board member who committed a violation could be removed by the president.[14] But wait a minute! This was the depression. Times were hard. As Kruckman himself noted, "Those were the days when every place that remotely offered a chance for employment was besieged by the newly poor."[15] Outside of Arthur Morgan, Senator Norris, and a few other old-line progressives, nobody would have given these few instances of political patronage a second thought. If anything, by comparison to other federal agencies, the TVA's record was remarkably clean.

That is, of course, just the point—nobody but Morgan and Norris cared. They were both great antagonists toward the awarding of jobs

12. Floyd Reeves to Lilienthal, Feb. 2, 1934. This letter is among those retained in Morgan's safe.
13. Clapp Report.
14. United States, *Statutes at Large* 48, p. 63.
15. Kruckman to Morgan, May 31, 1938, Morgan Papers.

based on politics. Although Lilienthal's sins may have been minor, as one student of the subject observed, "any departure at all was major."[16] Morgan had what he needed. He could confront Norris and use his support to get the president to dispose of Lilienthal. Morgan could go for the jugular. If he moved swiftly in the summer of 1935, he could destroy Lilienthal. All that was required was decisiveness and an instinct for the political kill. Morgan had neither.

Lilienthal was unaware that Morgan was weighing his future in the balance. It is, moreover, highly instructive to view the TVA situation from Lilienthal's perspective. Arthur Morgan was becoming a great problem. The chairman had an incredible knack for alienating politicians, without any regard to the hard political facts that the TVA had to have an appropriation each year and that its enabling legislation could be amended or even ended altogether. With all his Utopian chatter about building a new moral order, Morgan seemed almost unaware that the Authority was in a fight for its life with the private utilities, led by the eloquent and brilliant Wendell Willkie. What plagued Lilienthal more than anything else about Morgan was that the latter continued to insist that Willkie was a reasonable man, even while castigating Lilienthal for his overly militant attitude toward private power. Morgan had rejected the concept of a war between the TVA and Willkie. He wanted cooperation. Lilienthal knew just how desperate was the Authority's struggle as well as the strength of the enemy. Beyond that, Morgan had already demonstrated that he was not wholeheartedly in support of public power: if it did not work, he could say so casually, then he would do away with it. Neither electric power nor politics was important to Morgan.

There were also the court cases, not just the fairly routine matters of land condemnation, grave removal, and sometimes actual eviction from land needed by the TVA, but two extremely important cases that threatened to rip out its very soul. These cases proved restrictive just at the time that Lilienthal was desperate to demonstrate that he could sell power far cheaper than Willkie had ever thought possible.

In the meantime, Willkie was making considerable progress with what appeared at first blush to be a sound attack on the yardstick idea. "The yardstick," he said, "is rubber from the first inch to the last." Beyond that, the TVA had a grossly unfair advantage over his free enterprise companies: "TVA enjoys privileges and exemptions which are denied to the private utility, which conceal the true cost of TVA power, and the cost of which comes out of the pockets of you and me as taxpayers."

16. McCraw, *Morgan vs. Lilienthal*, p. 50.

When Willkie totaled up these privileges they seemed considerable: the Tennessee Valley Authority paid no taxes; it did not have to account for depreciation; it was built largely by interest-bearing government bonds, but its books did not have to account for that interest as a cost; and the municipalities that bought TVA power were able to build their delivery systems with federal loans. Given these same special advantages, Willkie claimed, the private companies could produce power cheaper than the Authority.[17]

Altogether the TVA faced some thirty-four separate lawsuits instigated by the private power companies. The first major challenge came on September 13, 1934, when stockholders of the Alabama Power Company, one of Willkie's holdings, sued to keep the Authority from moving into what had been Alabama Power territory, a move sanctioned by the January 4 Willkie-Lilienthal contract. For all that one might wish that the courts had called this the First Major TVA Case, it was known, in typical legal jargon, as the Ashwander case, from the name of the first plaintiff. Another fascinating aspect of the case is that Willkie's holding company, along with the TVA, was a defendant, on the basis that Willkie had signed the contract giving the Authority some of his territory in return for staying clear of his other areas. The plaintiffs held that such a deal could not be allowed because the TVA itself was unconstitutional. From the outset it was by no means clear that the agency would win this case. In fact, the Authority lost round one, and as it went on to the appeal process, the suit must have been central to Lilienthal's thinking in 1935. If they lost the Ashwander decision, the TVA was over.

Lilienthal survived round two, and the trial proceeded to the U.S. Supreme Court. There, in early 1936, and even though Lilienthal had expected the worst, the TVA was vindicated. As he said, "I had completely resigned myself to a bad decision, only holding out hope that we would have some crumb of comfort in that unlike AAA and NRA [the Agricultural Adjustment Administration and the National Recovery Administration, both killed by the courts] we would not be swept completely out to sea, bag and baggage."[18] No sooner had this victory been secured, however, than the Authority found itself with a second major challenge, this one known as either the "nineteen companies" or

17. Willkie's best piece on the TVA, and from which this material is taken, is his "Political Power: The Tennessee Valley Authority," *Atlantic Monthly*, 155 (August 1937), 210–18; reprinted in *This is Wendell Willlkie: A Collection of Speeches and Writings on Present-Day Issues* (New York: Dodd, Mead & Co., 1940).

18. Quoted in McCraw, *TVA and the Power Fight*, an excellent account of these involved court cases.

the "eighteen companies" case, depending on when one counted the plaintiffs. The suit began on May 29, 1936, and by December it resulted in a sweeping injunction against the agency that halted all new construction and extension of services. Although the injunction soon was lifted by a higher court, this suit was not decided, in the TVA's favor, until early 1938.

This overview of what were enormously important and complex legal issues is offered here as background to the fight between Morgan and Lilienthal that renewed itself, after a cease-fire of about two years, in late 1935. Although the focus here is on the battle within the board, it is important to understand that the whole issue of the TVA was in doubt throughout the period. While Morgan had come to see Lilienthal as an unscrupulous manipulator, an immoral compromiser, a political opportunist, and a vile patronage dispenser, Lilienthal saw the chairman as a major threat within the TVA itself, as a collaborator with the enemy, as a simpleminded, naïve, do-gooder, whose Utopian mouthings were doing actual harm to a great enterprise on behalf of the American people. As early as December 13, 1934, Lilienthal's close friend Donald Richberg had written McIntyre in the White House that "there had been some feeling on the part of the legal staff of the TVA [read Lilienthal] that the public emphasis given to the TVA [by Morgan] as a social experiment provided fuel for a legal attack upon its activities."[19] By the time he won the Ashwander case, Lilienthal must have thought his position secure, and his problem with Morgan was largely one of containment and damage control. It did not occur to him that, far from being tenured at TVA, he was actually quite vulnerable. As the junior member of the board, Lilienthal's term was due to expire on May 18, 1936, only months after his success with Ashwander. He had every reason to believe that Roosevelt would reappoint him. Morgan felt otherwise. He knew Lilienthal had to go.

From late 1935 into the spring of 1936 Arthur Morgan's usually complete records are strangely silent. Little is known about the specific manner in which he made the decision to move against Lilienthal. After the accusations started flying the record is somewhat clearer, but it was not until July 1938, by which time the war was over, that the Utopian set down a brief sketch of his thinking and methods.[20] What is most

19. Richberg to McIntyre, Dec. 13, 1934, Roosevelt Papers.
20. Morgan's longest account of his dealings with both Lilienthal and Roosevelt is his "A Statement of My Relations with the President," July 1, 1938, in his papers and in *TVA Hearings*.

remarkable about his decision to fight Lilienthal is that having made it, he executed so weakly and ineffectively. The bare facts are these: late in 1935 Morgan went to Roosevelt and asked that Lilienthal not be reappointed. "So far as I could see," Morgan later recalled, "he entirely agreed with me. . . ."[21] Some months later, fearing that additional pressure might be required, he took his case to Senator Norris, whose word carried a great deal of weight in TVA matters and who followed the project carefully.

Morgan seemed to feel that, as chairman of the board, it was sufficient for him to tell the president and Norris that he lacked personal confidence in Lilienthal and no longer desired him on the board, and that if Lilienthal stayed he would resign. They were both reasonable men whom he admired, and surely they respected his judgment and would comply. Both men did seem to have a genuine liking for Morgan, but they also appreciated Lilienthal's talent and his victories. In addition to the life-and-death situation for the TVA in the courts, the year 1936 was also important for another reason. Both Roosevelt and Norris were up for reelection, and each regarded November with substantial trepidation. Neither wanted to see anything embarrassing happen within the Tennessee Valley Authority. The solution for each was to smooth over the situation and to keep both Lilienthal and Morgan in the TVA and relatively calm. Adverse publicity was to be avoided.

What Morgan did not do was to launch a carefully coordinated, no-holds-barred campaign to oust Lilienthal. It would have taken a master at infighting to defeat the younger man, who had worked so diligently to entrench himself in the New Deal establishment. Morgan was limited by his very philosophy of high-mindedness, and the fact that a rough-and-tumble, eye-gouging contest was his only chance for success doomed him from the start. As a matter of fact, he really did not begin to fight until the battle was over. There is some evidence that he attempted to undercut Lilienthal with Norris by showing the venerable senator the documents proving political patronage, but the accounts differ here and reinforce an impression of Morgan's futility. Actually, Morgan had only a relatively small amount of real dirt on his enemy, yet he failed to use even that. He never revealed the internal report about Lilienthal's political dealings. Years later the only excuse Morgan could offer for such a lame offensive was that he had a profound admiration for the investigator who had compiled the report that could have hurt Lilienthal, and he decided not to use it because it might have damaged that person's career. (Fifty

21. Morgan, "Relations with the President."

years later, here is the crowd at ringside trying to shout as much encouragement to our protagonist as we can, and he will not throw a single stinging punch. This Utopian quality is not precisely cowardice, but it does make for a losing strategy.)

Lilienthal had no inkling that Morgan was "actively opposing my reappointment" until less than a month before his term expired. If Morgan's efforts were lackluster, Lilienthal's were brilliant. He saw immediately that Morgan's charges about personal incompatibility could be written off as a mere personality clash, which did not sound high-minded at all. While thus defusing Morgan's ammunition, Lilienthal wrapped himself in the nobility of the TVA project, while at the same time painting Morgan as a threat to those aspirations. After Morgan went to see Norris, the latter informed Lilienthal, who immediately girded up his loins.

It was not a matter of personality, nor of his own career, Lilienthal wrote Norris, "The responsibility which rests upon us as trustees of a great public issue makes personalities irrelevant." The problem was Morgan's attitude toward the Willkie gang, an attitude fraught with "grave hazards to the project," representing "grave danger that the objectives of the law and the policies of the President will be frustrated." Lilienthal became at this moment, and the public would eventually fully accept him as, Mr. Tennessee Valley Authority. "As I view the matter," he continued to Norris, "the life of the project in which I believe with all my heart is at stake."[22]

Lilienthal then proceeded to give his version of the real differences between him and Arthur Morgan, and he produced another dazzling legal brief that again summarized, starting back in the summer of 1933, his argument with the chairman over power policy. Morgan wanted to "cooperate" with Willkie when any practical man of affairs would have seen the perils of such a course. "TVA now knows from . . . actual experience . . . ," Lilienthal told Norris, "how naïve and unwise it is to risk our electricity program on the promises of the utilities, or to assume we have their good will." But the Utopian Morgan, he charged, "continues to express confidence in . . . the cooperation of the utilities," which were in actuality "a ruthless and well-financed antagonist." Lilienthal reminded Norris that he had compromised with Morgan back in early 1934 by entering into a contract with Willkie to provide the territorial restrictions Morgan wanted so badly, but Willkie had conspired against the TVA even while serving as a codefendant in the Ashwander case.

22. Lilienthal to Norris, May 4, 1936, Roosevelt Papers.

The argument over his reappointment, Lilienthal concluded, involved "matters of principle, not of personality."

The fight over Lilienthal's status made newspaper headlines, as Roosevelt waited until the last minute to announce his decision. Rumors varied from declaring Morgan's imminent resignation, if the reappointment occurred, to having the power director shifted to the Rural Electrification Authority, about to be greatly expanded by another Norris bill that gave preference for REA loans to cooperatives. Lilienthal's Electric Home and Farm Authority had already been folded into the REA, created in May 1935. The *Knoxville Journal* called the problem over Lilienthal's continuation "one of the strangest situations that has arisen under the many-sided New Deal."[23]

The round ended with a decision for Lilienthal. Roosevelt informed Morgan that in "the national interest" he had to reappoint Lilienthal. Failure to do so, he said, would be regarded by the enemies of the New Deal as a change in policy and "the first victory against your fundamental beliefs and mine."[24] Then FDR put in the hooks:

> I ask you, my dear Arthur, to consider not only the big fundamentals involved, but also, two other considerations: First, that the TVA is the first of, I hope, many similar organizations and that we are in the formative period of developing administrative methods for a new type of government agency; second, my own personal problems. In regard to the latter, I have told you of the somewhat heavy load which is on my shoulders at the present time. I ask your sympathetic consideration.
>
> If you are to be here next week, come and lunch with me.

What Utopian could resist such a call for understanding from Franklin D. Roosevelt? Morgan took his bitter pill, at least for the moment, but he was immensely unhappy. Not that he gave up completely. On May 18, 1936, the day FDR announced Lilienthal's reappointment, Morgan attempted to get the president's permission to limit the power director. He wanted the TVA to hire a permanent general manager who would take operations away from the board, and he renewed his old progressive notion that an outside board of consultants be called in to evaluate the TVA's power policy, but most of all he wanted to limit Lilienthal's scope of authority by leaving him only power sales.[25] This gambit was doomed, and even if he did not know it Morgan had lost. On the

23. The Lilienthal Papers have numerous newspaper clippings concerning his reappointment. The material from the *Knoxville Journal* is in the May 18, 1935, issue, with the headline "FDR Trying to Untangle TVA Discord."
24. Roosevelt to Morgan, May 15, 1936, Roosevelt Papers.
25. Morgan to Roosevelt, May 18, 1933, *ibid.*

162 · *Morgan and Lilienthal*

following day, Roosevelt received a telegram from Felix Frankfurter praising him for having made the right decision: "Knowing some of the difficulties [I] congratulate you all the more warmly on Lilienthal reappointment."[26]

It may be sufficient to cite only Roosevelt's political concerns in supporting Lilienthal, but the record indicates that the president gave the matter considerable thought and took unusual steps to see that Morgan himself did not cause an equally large problem by resigning. Roosevelt had to keep the TVA boat reasonably steady, even if that meant intimating to Morgan that after the election he would move Lilienthal to another government agency.[27] He was not entirely successful in containing the issue, and after Lilienthal's second term was confirmed by the Senate, the press continued to report that Morgan and Lilienthal were at each other's throats.[28]

Roosevelt used his patented charm on Morgan, writing another "My dear Arthur" letter in July, asking the chairman very nicely to visit him some time, obliquely referring to the yardstick problem, and discussing in the most visionary terms his plans for other TVAs throughout the country.[29] What is especially illuminating about FDR's file copy of this letter is that in his papers it is clipped to a message from Morris L. Cooke, over in the REA:

> Perhaps you already know [Cooke told Roosevelt] that Dr. Arthur E. Morgan remains quite upset about the T.V.A. situation and especially as to Lilienthal. At the moment he is in Yellow Springs rusticating and trying to make up his mind what he ought to do, write a series of letters to the *New York Times*, resign or do something else which will absolve him from responsibility for what he believes to be misleading "yardsticks" etc.[30]

Morgan, said Cooke, was "a tired and overwrought man who should have a long rest." Shades of Antioch. At the same time that this shows a Morgan deeply depressed by Lilienthal's victory, it provides a wonderful example of Roosevelt as a manager. One subordinate reports that another is unhappy, and the leader dispatches a warm, reassuring, stroking note. Roosevelt did that and went even further. Cooke mentioned that FDR and Morgan shared a common supporter in Samuel S. Fels, the wealthy soap manufacturer, who not only was loyal to Roosevelt but was an old

---

26. Frankfurter to Roosevelt, May 19, 1936, *ibid.*
27. McCraw, *Morgan vs. Lilienthal*, pp. 52–57.
28. For examples of the controversy in the press, see *Knoxville News-Sentinel*, July 14, 1936; *Chattanooga Times*, July 31, 1936; and *Memphis Press-Scimitar*, July 20, 1936.
29. Roosevelt to Morgan, July 11, 1936, Roosevelt Papers.
30. Cooke to Roosevelt, July 7, 1936, *ibid.*

and substantial contributor to Antioch. On the very same day that he wrote the "My dear Arthur" letter, Roosevelt sent a "private and confidential" missive to Fels:

> I know that you have a good deal of influence with Arthur Morgan [note FDR's ingenious use of Morgan's simplified name, always preferred by his ardent followers]. He is in a somewhat unhappy frame of mind in regard to the so-called "yardstick" for electricity which is to be applied in the TVA area. Please read, in great confidence, [a] copy of this letter I have sent to him. If the opportunity offers it would be a great service to me if you would advise Arthur "to keep both feet on the ground."[31]

Here is FDR charming Morgan and at the same time sending word indirectly to him to shape up. Moreover, Cooke was right; Morgan was within a hair's breadth of resigning, and all through June and July of 1936 he sulked in Yellow Springs. Had he resigned, one can well imagine the attendant publicity, the vague and emotional statements he would have made, and the damage he might have done to Roosevelt. Morgan was a definite problem for the president, and insofar as his goal was to contain the worst of the crisis until after the 1936 election, FDR managed him perfectly.[32]

Morgan actually believed that Roosevelt intended to move Lilienthal after November, which is no doubt precisely what Roosevelt wanted him to believe. On July 25, Morgan wrote FDR a particularly defensive letter, in which he accused Lilienthal of being in league with George Fort Milton, editor of the *Chattanooga News*. Milton was a New Deal supporter and clearly allied with Lilienthal, but Morgan saw some dark conspiracy. "I have carefully refrained," he said, "from any public expression and have refused all newspaper comment." He promised to continue his silence because, "In view of your assurance to me that our present power director will be replaced at a later date, I think that is the best course to pursue."[33]

Morgan was not well, and his vacation had not helped. When he returned to the Authority in late July, he was in a very bad mood, and it was at this moment that he cast the first negative vote in board history. Lilienthal had been quiet after his reappointment, as he told his Harvard mentor, "pursuant to the earlier Frankfurter-LaFollette strategy." In his letter to Frankfurter, he described in detail the events subsequent to the

31. Roosevelt to Fels, July 11, 1936, *ibid.*
32. For the view that Morgan nearly resigned after Lilienthal's term was renewed, see McCraw, *Morgan vs. Lilienthal*, and James Douglas Lorenz, "Arthur Morgan and the Tennessee Valley Authority," senior honors thesis, Harvard College, April 1, 1960.
33. Morgan to Roosevelt, July 25, 1936, Roosevelt Papers.

renewal of his position, including the president's handling of Arthur Morgan's demands. The failure of the latter's desire for external consultants, said Lilienthal, "went down very hard." When Roosevelt had covered all the points, deciding against Morgan in each case, he asked "Now, is that satisfactory[?]" Lilienthal said that Morgan's response "from a gray face was [a] scarcely audible 'I understand your views.' " The power director also described to Frankfurter Morgan's appearance upon his return to duty:

> He looks like the wrath of God—dark bags under his eyes, nervously tight as a drum, thin. Been brooding and planning all that time. I think he is sick. He came into a conference attended by perhaps ten of the principal managers, after an absence of 6 weeks, and didn't pass a word of greeting, not a handshake, not a *word*: just walked in, sat down, with a dead pan face. The chilling effect on normal men is awful.[34]

The situation remained tense throughout the summer of 1936. Not only was there the pressure of the elections coming up in November, but there was the problem of the lawsuits. All three directors engaged in considerable correspondence with FDR, primarily concerning the matter of territorial restrictions brought on by the injunction of the nineteen (or eighteen) companies suit. In addition, Lilienthal had gotten FDR excited about the prospects of what came to be called the "power pool" concept. Based on the British grid system, this actually was the forerunner of our modern national power structure whereby electric utilities, public and private, buy power from each other depending on supply and demand. In early August the TVA directors requested a meeting with Roosevelt on these several matters. Morgan told Stephen T. Early, the president's press secretary, that he wanted a few minutes alone with Roosevelt before the other directors arrived. "Dr. Morgan," Early faithfully recorded, "wants the President to be assured that he is going along, will make no trouble and that reports to the contrary need not be of any concern. . . ."[35] Obviously Fels had spoken to Morgan, and, as difficult as it was for the Utopian, he did try to keep his mouth shut, at least until the election.

The press, especially in Tennessee, continued to publicize the TVA feud, with much speculation about Morgan's possible resignation. The

34. Lilienthal to Frankfurter, Aug. 2, 1936, Lilienthal Papers.
35. Stephen Early's note, Aug. 6, 1936, and Lilienthal and H. A. Morgan to Roosevelt, Aug. 5, 1936, Roosevelt Papers. For more on the board's request for a conference with the president, and the typically petty bickering it occasioned, see Lilienthal to Norris, Aug. 7, 1936, Lilienthal Papers.

Knoxville News-Sentinel and Milton's *Chattanooga News* were the most vociferous in opposing Morgan. The *Memphis Press-Scimitar* was his best supporter, claiming:

> We cannot do without Arthur Morgan in the TVA. . . . Arthur Morgan is the wise statesman and executive who assembled the splendid TVA personnel— and kept politics out. It was Arthur Morgan who built Norris Dam and the town of Norris—the two achievements which have most captured public imagination. . . . So we say to Chairman Morgan: "Whatever the opposition to you in the TVA, stay in there and fight!"[36]

The struggle to gain Norris's favor, a contest that Morgan did not know was already over, continued into August. Morgan was on especially good terms with Norris's secretary and son-in-law, John P. Robertson, who lobbied unsuccessfully for the Utopian. For his part, Lilienthal kept up his correspondence with Norris and Frankfurter in an unbridled attempt to prove that Morgan was "soft" on Willkie and the private utilities. Now that Morgan had tried to take his job away from him, Lilienthal took off his gloves.[37] The young attorney had been following fairly well Frankfurter's advice that he be patient with Morgan, but now the Utopian had threatened him. Morgan, for his part, had botched what little scheme he had formulated regarding Lilienthal. Far from routing the menace, he had only made him mad. Lilienthal turned on him with a ferociousness unimaginable to anyone with the slightest of Utopian tendencies. The youthful director started to build his case, and when he was ready Arthur Morgan never knew what hit him. From Lilienthal's perspective, the feud did not even begin until Morgan tried to keep him from being reappointed.

The situation did not improve for Morgan. In September an old ghost rose to haunt him. E. F. Scattergood, whom Morgan had originally rejected as a director in favor of Lilienthal because Morgan felt he was too militant toward the private power companies, turned out to be an old acquaintance of FDR. They had carried on an occasional correspondence since before the creation of the TVA, and Roosevelt had asked Scattergood's advice on the Muscle Shoals project shortly after his election.[38] Later Lilienthal had hired Scattergood, and Morgan had

36. Quoted in McCraw, *Morgan vs. Lilienthal*, p. 64.

37. Robertson to Norris, Aug. 6, 1936, and Dec. 12, 1936, Norris Papers; Morgan to Norris, Aug. 13, 1936, Morgan Papers. See also Lilienthal to Frankfurter, Aug. 20, 1936, Frankfurter Papers; and Lilienthal to Norris, Jan. 21, 1937, Norris Papers.

38. Roosevelt to Scattergood, Aug. 19, 1933; Morgan to Roosevelt, Nov. 21, 1933; Scattergood to Roosevelt, Sept. 29, 1936; all Roosevelt Papers.

expressed considerable discontent at that, but Roosevelt had protected Scattergood and appeared to have confidence in his opinion. In September 1936, Scattergood wrote FDR a letter that was as positive about Lilienthal as it was negative toward Morgan. "It is self-evident," Scattergood concluded, "that [success] cannot be accomplished by anyone through the policies expressed by the Chairman of the Board. . . ." That FDR was treating Morgan fairly at this point is obvious by the fact that he forwarded this damaging letter to Morgan. Perhaps it was another way he attempted to put pressure on his now clearly irascible TVA chairman, but Roosevelt does seem to have been enormously patient with the Utopian.

It is equally obvious that the president saw the Morgan matter as serious. About the same time as the Scattergood letter, and perhaps because of it, Roosevelt brought in his own external consultant for an evaluation of the Morgan-Lilienthal dilemma. His candidate for this role was another stroke of Roosevelt genius. Oswald Garrison Villard's reputation as a liberal, pro–public power man was unimpeachable and now, at the end of a great career, he was sufficiently self-confident to be able to tell a president the truth, not what he wanted to hear.

Villard's background is fascinating. His father, Henry Villard, was a Bavarian immigrant who came to this country in 1853 and made a fortune in publishing, railroads, and finance. He was among the first to spot the potential of electricity, not only backing Edison's experiments, but founding the company that became General Electric. In the process he also gained control of two New York newspapers, the *Evening Post* and the *Nation*. Villard's mother was equally interesting. The daughter of the great abolitionist William Lloyd Garrison, she assisted the National Association for the Advancement of Colored People and also founded the Women's Peace Society. Oswald Garrison Villard became a distinguished publisher, owning and editing the liberal weekly the *Nation* from 1918 to 1932. In the 1920s he had been, despite his father's connections with the private electrical industry, a firm supporter of public power, including the Muscle Shoals idea and Governor Roosevelt's effort to bring public power to the state of New York.[39] His relationship with Roosevelt went back to before World War I, and he was one of those special people who had easy access to him when he became president. His file at the Roosevelt Library shows that while Roosevelt and he talked about a wide variety of subjects, he never tried to ingratiate himself. The

39. D. Joy Humes, *Oswald Garrison Villard: Liberal of the 1920s* (Syracuse, N.Y.: Syracuse University Press, 1960).

president would invite him to lunch, and it might be months before Villard felt he had anything of importance to say again. He was, altogether, an intriguing character.

In the late summer of 1936 Roosevelt asked Villard to interest himself "in the situation of Mr. Arthur Morgan and the TVA."[40] His report came in just before Christmas:

> I have kept in touch with Mr. Morgan and with others in the organization, and I now write to tell you that the situation there has reached such a crisis that I feel that no time should be lost by you in grappling with it. As you requested, I have done my best in urging Mr. Morgan to stay, but the friction between him and Mr. Lilienthal has now become so serious that one or the other must go, and I say this by authority of Mr. Morgan. That his leaving would have a most serious effect upon the engineering portion of the work seems to me certain.[41]

Even as Roosevelt mulled over the TVA problem in the fall of 1936, Morgan made another mistake. Roosevelt was still keen on the power pooling concept, and he had scheduled a world power conference for the last of September. Morgan made a complete fool of himself. Not only did he seek advice from an electrical consultant who had ties to the old Insull pyramid, but his contribution to the conference was a rambling memorandum calling again for cooperation and what anybody could see was a go-easy approach with the private utilities. The problem for Morgan was that somehow his memorandum was leaked to the *New York Times*, which gave it ample space.[42] Although Morgan denied releasing the report and apologized profusely to the president, the damage had been done.[43] Lilienthal used this occasion to unleash a barrage of criticism against his nemesis. He lined up his troops, which by now included powerful senators, editors, and senior officials in other New Deal agencies, and had them all write letters to the president, accusing Morgan, as Norris said, of having "gone over to the enemy."[44]

Why did Roosevelt not take advantage of Morgan's inclination to resign in 1936? The trusted Villard had appraised the situation as hopeless, but at the same time he had observed that Morgan was essential to "the engineering portion of the project." Maybe Roosevelt felt him essential

40. This line comes from Villard's report to Roosevelt on Dec. 21, 1936, but a brief letter of Sept. 25 indicates that the president had given him the task shortly before; Roosevelt Papers.
41. Villard to Roosevelt, Dec. 21, 1936, *ibid.*
42. *New York Times*, Oct. 1, 1936.
43. Morgan to Roosevelt, Oct. 1, 1936, Roosevelt Papers.
44. Quoted in McCraw, *Morgan vs. Lilienthal*, p. 73. The power conference, and the idea of a power pool, for reasons associated with the suits against TVA, never got off the ground.

168 · *Morgan and Lilienthal*

for another reason, somehow related to Utopia. FDR liked Arthur Morgan; he went out of his way to be gentle with him. It is certain that he read, or at least received, *Antioch Notes:* the last one in his files is dated March 15, 1938. He also shared Morgan's misgivings about Lilienthal's yardstick. In late 1935 he said to one of Lilienthal's friends, "I want it to be a real yardstick that actually has the cost items in it. . . ."[45] Roosevelt wanted to keep Morgan. Even after the disaster of the power conference in the fall of 1936, he kept Villard working on a solution that would allow both Morgan and Lilienthal to stay. He told Villard he thought he could handle each man, and bring them together in some unspecified feat of magic. Villard finally agreed that it was worth one more shot, but that the president had better move quickly to get them up to the White House immediately after the inaguration.

Was it possible that Roosevelt could charm and cajole these two men out of what was now a deep-seated bitterness on both their parts? Morgan had hated Lilienthal since August 1933, and Lilienthal had in the summer of 1936 vowed to smash his enemy. Morgan was virtually helpless, except for this strange vacillation on the part of the president. Lilienthal could not understand what the president saw in Morgan. As George Fort Milton said to him in late 1936, "Morgan would not proclaim and broadcast the way he is doing, without having some White House background."[46] Roosevelt had to make up his mind. But not now. He had just overwhelmed his political opposition, and for him the tension, at least in terms of establishing the New Deal, was over. He had won, and as long as Morgan and Lilienthal kept relatively quiet he could afford to wait. If push came to shove, all he had to do was accept Morgan's resignation, which as far as he could tell was always in the offing.

45. Quoted in *ibid.*, p. 52.
46. Milton to Lilienthal, Nov. 28, 1936, quoted in *ibid.*, p. 83.

CHAPTER 9

Farewell to Utopia

Villard had urged Roosevelt to act shortly after his inauguration, which was to take place, as a result of the twentieth amendment, on January 20, 1937. This was the logical time for the New Deal president to make some move regarding the TVA, but the fact of the matter is that he soon became embroiled in one of the biggest and most memorable fights of his long tenure—the famous court-packing plan, which he announced on February 5. Most analysts agree that this attempt to enlarge the membership of the Supreme Court (which had set a new record during his first term in declaring legislation unconstitutional and which was clearly a major thorn in the president's side) was his worst political blunder.

At the same time, Roosevelt was involved in a bitter debate with Congress over his proposed legislation to reorganize the executive branch, a concept he had submitted to Capitol Hill in January. The myriad of agencies created by the New Deal, many of which reported directly to the White House, had demonstrated that this traditionally poorly staffed branch had to expand. Roosevelt also wanted to consolidate his effort for national planning and to move ahead with his goal of creating additional TVA-type organizations around the country. Together, the court-packing plan and the reorganization scheme created a major headache for FDR. He was accused of attempting to become a dictator like Hitler, Stalin, and Mussolini. Although the Supreme Court did become more accommodating, and Roosevelt did get a compromise measure through on reorganization that pretty much created the executive branch as we know it today, these fights spelled the end of New Deal innovation.[1] For the purposes of the story about the Tennessee Valley Authority, the point here is that in early 1937 Roosevelt was obviously too preoccupied to deal with the Tennessee situation. Eventually he resorted to a time-honored administrative technique for wishing problems away: he created a special committee to study TVA administration.

1. William E. Leuchtenburg's entry on "Court-Packing Plan" and Charles Schlike's on "Reorganization Act of 1939" in Graham and Wander (eds.), *Franklin D. Roosevelt, His Life and Times: An Encyclopedic View*, are excellent analyses with good bibliographies.

During the years of his controversial New Deal, Roosevelt faced any number of agonizing personnel decisions. He had problems with General Hugh Johnson, first head of the National Recovery Administration, whom he was able to ease out. There was George Peek, first administrator of the Agricultural Adjustment Administration, who resigned in December 1933, and labor secretary Frances Perkins, who got into difficulty in 1939, but whom Roosevelt backed strongly. Given the nature of the tumultuous New Deal, dramatic crises over personnel and policy were to be expected. What is illuminating is how Roosevelt handled them. Rexford G. Tugwell maintained that the president never fired anyone. When faced with someone as unhappy as Arthur Morgan had become, the New Deal president handled the situation in a series of stages:

> He called [said Tugwell] its homeopathetic phase "holding hands"; and when this proved insufficient he resorted to promotion. He devoted an unconscionable amount of time and thought to these affairs, although the victims could never be persuaded that he cared in the least, and often went away complaining bitterly about him. . . . His failure [to resolve a personnel dispute amicably] always rested on his conscience, making the sight of one of the defectors most unpleasant.[2]

Roosevelt had already used the hand-holding method with Morgan in numerous letters with invitations to lunch in the White House, and as early as 1936 there were rumors flying that either Morgan or Lilienthal would be "promoted" to another agency. These were standard Roosevelt tactics in dealing with conflicts between his subordinates. When hand holding and promotion failed, he resorted to a tougher measure known as "the squeeze," where, as another student has observed, "a presidential shift in policy, subtle acts of presidential hostility, or a presidential reorganization of authorities and responsibilities would leave the individual affected no alternative but to resign."[3] "The squeeze," noted Tugwell, "was permitted to go on until the tortured victim cried out in pain— meaning that he made a speech or a statement attacking his competitor or detractor—and presently even he could perceive the impossibility of his position."[4] Tugwell also observed that the one single episode where the Roosevelt treatment did not work was in the strange case of Arthur E. Morgan.

2. Rexford G. Tugwell, *In Search of Roosevelt* (Cambridge, Mass.: Harvard University Press, 1973), pp. 291–92.
3. Charles E. Jacob, *Leadership in the New Deal: The Administrative Challenge* (Englewood Cliffs, N.J.: Prentice-Hall, Inc., 1967), p. 30.
4. Tugwell, *In Search of Roosevelt*, p. 293.

How about Morgan? How did he act when he found himself in a bitter contest? His handling of the crisis at Antioch just a few years earlier was something less than brilliant, and by 1937 the situation in the TVA made the Antioch imbroglio seem more like a picnic. Morgan was clearly under a great deal of stress and was totally frustrated over being unable to deal with Lilienthal. After the power director's reappointment in the spring of 1936, a growing sense of hopelessness, anxiety, and loneliness overcame the Utopian. In the early 1950s, in an unsuccessful attempt to write an autobiography, Morgan gave this description of himself in times of emotional tension:

> When I have been under heavy stress for too long a time, the front part of my head, just back of my eyes, feels as though it were in a high fever, and in that limited area there is a sense of extreme physical discomfort. I find difficulty in controlling the course of my thoughts. That is, I cannot dismiss a subject from my mind, but it "runs away with me," keeping me awake at night. There is a lack of control which inclines me to lose my temper or to talk too much. . . . I become incapable of consistent mental effort. . . . Sometimes I would sit through business meetings, going through the motions of participating, when I was in no condition to take part in what was going on.[5]

Morgan believed that his problem resulted from nerve damage stemming from spinal meningitis suffered as a small child. Whether or not this was the case, the old hypochondriac felt that he was the victim of a brain disorder that sometimes incapacitated his normal mental effort. The bizarre actions of the late 1930s certainly seem to support his belief that at times his mental ability was diminished.

Roosevelt's personnel strategies were often hard on all parties to a squabble within his administration. As Tugwell put it, in his typically perceptive way, "Even those closest to him were sometimes confused about his maneuvers."[6] The aggressive Lilienthal had to wait several agonizing months before he could be sure that he understood Roosevelt's position, and even longer before he or the president had any ideas on a particular method for handling the recalcitrant Morgan. After the fight over his reappointment, Lilienthal was out for Morgan's blood. He complained to Frankfurter that he had been "attacked from within the Authority. Sabotage is the word commonly applied to the practice." Initially he stayed away from a personal attack on Morgan, seldom mentioning him by name. Instead, he spoke in terms of saving the TVA and even of protecting the president. "This thing can't continue," he told

---

5. Morgan, "Early Memories," undated typed manuscript, Morgan Papers.
6. Tugwell, *In Search of Roosevelt*, p. 293.

his Harvard mentor, "without adversely affecting him." The danger to the electricity mission was so great that Lilienthal wanted to take his complaints to Roosevelt: "I expect to make it strong—and plenty strong."[7]

On Frankfurter's advice, Lilienthal decided to delay confronting the president, but he kept up his campaign, hoping that Morgan would self-destruct. "As to the situation here," the power director told Senator La Follette, "it grows progressively worse and therefore progressively better, if you follow me." Morgan's fiasco at the power-pooling conference in the fall of 1936 had produced additional ammunition for his adversary, who continued writing vigorously to the son of the old fighting liberal from Wisconsin. Now he felt sufficiently confident to attack Morgan directly. The chairman's attitude of trying to cooperate with Willkie, Lilienthal said, was "really an amazing thing and brings the whole problem of TVA's power policy to a crisis which cannot be ignored or evaded." Two weeks later he accused Morgan of favoring "concessions by the public to private interests." He quickly added, "The President, of course, has no knowledge of what has been going on, so far as I know." On December 18, 1936, he gave La Follette his summary of the situation:

> The evidence is now overwhelming that A. E. Morgan has gone over to the power boys, hook, line and sinker. I hear indirectly that Senator Norris has taken a strong position as to the Chairman in a letter to the President. If the President takes positive action promptly to clear up the situation, TVA can be saved. If he lets it rock along, complete disintegration of morale and purpose will follow.[8]

Lilienthal was wrong that Norris had demanded Morgan's resignation, and he was wrong that FDR had any real intention of acting early in 1937. What amazed Lilienthal during the next three seasons was just how much the president would take before acting. The best thing the power director had going for him was Morgan, who had begun plying the rope with which to hang himself. If the Roosevelt treatment was disconcerting and almost terrifying to Lilienthal, it was the undoing of Arthur Morgan.

Morgan had to write the *New York Times*. He had to. When he finally realized that he was in a tough fight, he automatically resorted to the same methods he had used successfully in the Everglades dispute back in 1912 and the very same techniques his hero had employed in *Seed Man*:

7. Lilienthal to Frankfurter, Sept. 8, 1936, Lilienthal Papers.
8. Lilienthal to La Follette, Sept. 6, Oct. 19, Nov. 4, and Dec. 18, 1936, *ibid.*

appeal to the public through the press. His lengthy article appeared on the front page of the January 17, 1937, *Times*. There had been less opportunity for the president to act than Villard had feared.

"This is an effort," Morgan began, "to state my personal views on the electric power issue." The TVA was there to protect the consumer, he said. No doubt about that. And the abuse of special privilege had to cease. But beyond those admirable and progressive goals, there was the matter of going about it in the right way, in the moral way. "Aggressive action in the public interest," he insisted, must be taken "in a spirit of open dealing and of honest regard for legitimate interest, both public and private. In the long run sharp practice and arbitrary methods will not be helpful" to either side. The question was simply whether or not public officials were going to be reasonable and efficient, or whether they were to "drift into an attitude of a fight to the finish against the private power companies. . . ." Such militancy might turn the people altogether against the idea of public power. Why fight, when it could be handled "on the basis of mutual confidence and goodwill. . . "? It is true, he stated categorically, that the private companies had abused their power, and he cited his record of opposition to their "misleading propaganda." Such abuses, he noted, in what seemed a defensive statement, were "great though not universal." Nevertheless, some of the private utilities had been "ruthless," and he credited Senator Norris with having given of himself selflessly in fighting those evil forces. Not every public power proponent, however, could be as noble as the old progressive from Nebraska. Some would inevitably show "various mixtures of public interest and self-interest, and they tend to complicate the problem." Enter Lilienthal. Morgan never mentioned him by name in the article, which ran nine full columns, but he lurked everywhere.

Were it not for these people consumed with self-interest, Morgan said, some compromise could be worked out with the private companies. Enter Willkie, also unmentioned, but equally present: "I believe that some leading utility executives are today in a mood to desire a reasonable working arrangement. . . ." Such an agreement might avoid an adverse reaction to "aggressively liberal governments," which "seldom have remained in power for long at a time." Better to consolidate what gains had been made on behalf of the public while "the electric power interests are on the defensive" rather than risk the whole ballgame. Moreover, a new generation of private power leaders had taken over (Willkie again), and they were "public-spirited, forward-looking men," if only because they saw "the handwriting on the wall. . . ." In the meantime, the government could begin to prepare itself for running the power industry. As long as the public interest was enmeshed in "graft, incompetence, bureaucracy, red tape, and patronage," government was unsuited for wholesale ownership of utilities.

Such talk was hardly what the liberals wanted to hear, but Morgan was absolutely right when he observed that "our government has little experience in handling large operating businesses, and we have not yet developed effective methods. With all the good will in the world, it will take time to evolve them." Those who saw the issue only as a political fight were naïve. All that was needed at the present was a yardstick area to serve as a laboratory and a model. Anything else was premature. "The people have a right to actual examples of public ownership to supply a basis for coming to long-time conclusions on the subject." Hardly a resounding statement of support of Roosevelt's frequently expressed desire to create more TVAs.

There was another, even more important, reason to cooperate with Willkie:

> By the manner in which this conflict and others like it are handled, America is deciding little by little whether, in the great social readjustments that are taking place, there shall be a strengthening of democratic methods, reasonableness, fair play, and open dealing; or whether we shall drift into bitter class controversies which lead to violent and arbitrary action, so prevalent today in several other countries.

To guard against becoming either a Germany or a Soviet Union, "a spirit of tolerance and reasonableness on both sides is a public obligation." That was precisely why methods concerned Morgan. If reasonableness triumphed, "there would be an advance in the quality of public life." He was absolutely eloquent as a Utopian when he insisted: "At some time or other such vicious cycles must be broken." What the TVA and the public power movement did not need, he said, in what every student of the issue knew was a direct slap at Lilienthal, were "people who are ruled by a Napoleonic complex, which leads them to use any method at hand, including intrigue, arbitrary force and appeal to class hatred."[9]

Nothing happened as a result of this amazing article. Roosevelt was caught up in the court-packing fight, and Lilienthal must have been in shock. Morgan followed up the piece with a telegram to the president stating that the TVA was more than dams and electric power—it was navigation, flood control, and many other matters. The president, however, was still in his hand-holding phase. "You are right," he replied,

9. *New York Times*, Jan. 17, 1937.

"about the coordination of the problem of a river as a whole. I hope you will run in to see me very soon."[10] Lilienthal must have been confounded by the president's lack of action, and Morgan seems to have been encouraged. He pressed Lilienthal directly in a memorandum, accusing him personally of creating a "very inaccurate impression of the situation [with Willkie] . . . misleading to Congress, the President, and the public." He called the younger director's attitude at a recent meeting "very definitely to be that of endeavoring to prevent any basis for agreement from being found, and to force Mr. Willkie into an apparently unreasonable position."[11] There it was, a matter of record: Morgan opposed Lilienthal and supported Willkie.

Lilienthal now had all the evidence he needed. He wrote quickly to Norris:

> There has just been handed to me the enclosed memorandum from Dr. Arthur E. Morgan, dated February 24. I hope you will read this amazing statement at your earliest opportunity. It is further confirmation of the close team-play, both open and covert, which exists between the Chairman of this Board and the utilities.
>
> How in God's name we can be expected to make any progress, or even to hold our ground, under these circumstances, is beyond my understanding. The situation is intolerable, and to think that it has been going on for over a year is almost incredible. . . .
>
> I want again to go on record as saying that the consequences of permitting this situation to go on without official corrective action are grave in the extreme and will be disastrous.[12]

In a similar letter to La Follette written the same day, Lilienthal referred to "the close and skillful team-play" between "the Chairman of this Board and Mr. Willkie" and the fact that "for over a year now, on many fronts, we have been sabotaged."[13]

One week later Lilienthal got Harcourt Morgan to co-sign a letter taking the issue to the president. "We have come to you," they told Roosevelt, "for your counsel." They cited both Morgan's article in the *New York Times* and the more recent inflammatory memorandum to Lilienthal. The power policy and the position regarding Willkie had been set by the majority of the board, they said, and by his public

10. Morgan to Roosevelt, Jan. 27, and Roosevelt to Morgan, Jan. 29, 1937, Roosevelt Papers.

11. Morgan to Lilienthal, Feb. 24, 1937, Lilienthal Papers.

12. Lilienthal to Norris, Feb. 26, 1937, *ibid.*

13. Lilienthal to La Follette, Feb. 26, 1937, *ibid.*

challenge to it Morgan had demonstrated his unwillingness "to abide by a decision of the Board, and on the contrary is actively collaborating with Mr. Willkie in opposition to the Board's action. . . ." They earnestly requested the president's advice in dealing with a situation that "handicaps if it does not indeed tie the Authority's hands in working out its electric problems."[14]

Nothing happened. Roosevelt took no action, and Lilienthal showed his impatience when he wrote Frankfurter: "The trouble is that the decision to clear the matter up is, I fear, going to be taken too late. It is being delayed, I think, in the hope of an eleventh-hour miracle of some kind."[15] The wise old Frankfurter repeated his advice: Be patient. On April 3, 1937, Roosevelt acted. He appointed a fairly low-level committee to study the question of TVA administration. Not power policy, not the feud between Lilienthal and Morgan, but the general question of management. To this not-so-blue-ribbon panel, he appointed Assistant Secretary of Commerce Ernest G. Draper, Rear Adm. Archibald Parsons, and Herbert Emmerich, the deputy governor of the Farm Credit Administration. The committee visited Authority headquarters and interviewed many members of the staff. Lilienthal followed his oral presentation with a written memorandum to the presidential investigators. The problems of organization and management in the TVA, he told them, were the result of nothing less than "the mental state of Dr. A. E. Morgan." He cited "an unreasoning obsession" against Harcourt Morgan and himself, particularly the latter. "This obsession and its accompanying personal ill-will and fantastic suspiciousness," Lilienthal said, "directly affect almost every relation with the Board and the staff." The committee had apparently indicated to Lilienthal that some people, such as Villard, feared that Morgan's exit would be followed by "wholesale resignations among construction engineers." Lilienthal countered by calling these reports idle threats and by citing the fact that in the fight over his reappointment the same challenge had been made with no action. He suggested that a reorganization that limited Morgan's authority would produce no mass exodus. The committee proved reluctant to intervene in the bad blood between Lilienthal and Morgan. It stuck to studying organizational charts. Its mild report was not completed for months, by which time it had been overtaken by events.[16]

14. Harcourt Morgan and Lilienthal to Roosevelt, March 5, 1937, *ibid.*
15. Lilienthal to Frankfurter, March 25, 1937, *ibid.*
16. The evidence concerning FDR's appointment of a committee to study the Authority is found in his own statement during the formal inquiry he conducted into the TVA situation in March 1938. The report itself is in the Roosevelt Papers, as is a complete

For the moment, at least, Morgan seems to have believed that his effort to state his case fairly and honestly before the public was having some success. In August 1937 he wrote a long piece for the *Saturday Evening Post* that was upbeat about the multipurposes of the TVA, the need for a unified plan required by such an agency with its several missions, and a continuation of his argument on power pooling. Aside from mentioning "people who are committed to fighting to the bitter end against the utilities" and who might wish such a fight "to ride to political precedence or to personal power," there was no specific reference to Lilienthal.[17] This fairly stable view and balance of temperament was not to last. Events were fast getting out of hand. The source of the final explosion was Morgan's conviction that Lilienthal was involved with a group of conspirators determined to perpetrate a gigantic real estate swindle against the U.S. government. It was 1912 all over again. Duty, morality, and a typical dash of paranoia sent Arthur Morgan over the edge. The issue came to be called "the Berry marble claims."

George L. Berry was a retired army major, a prominent Tennessean, and a great supporter of Franklin D. Roosevelt, who had appointed him to a minor post (coordinator of the remains of the defunct National Recovery Administration) in 1935. The year before, Berry and two others had obtained the mineral rights to certain properties required by the Tennessee Valley Authority for the reservoir behind Norris Dam. They had developed a marble quarrying operation, and when the TVA approached them to purchase the land, the Berry group claimed that the valuable marble deposits made it worth some millions of dollars. A series of geologists, both inside and external to the Authority, disagreed, and they along with Arthur Morgan came to believe that the commercial operation was nothing less than a fake, designed simply to defraud the government. The other directors were initially inclined to make a settlement with Berry in order to expedite the agency's construction program (and no doubt to avoid alienating a strong Roosevelt man), but Morgan was able to delay any favorable decision because he believed Berry should receive absolutely nothing. The Berry matter had become a point of disagreement about the same time that the fight over Lilienthal's reappointment occurred, but it dragged on into 1937. By the spring of

---

transcript of the presidential hearings, hereinafter referred to as FDR's TVA Hearings; also available in U.S. Senate, *Removal of a Member of the Tennessee Valley Authority*, Senate Document no. 155, 75th Cong., 3rd sess., 1938. Lilienthal's memorandum to the president's committee is dated May 10, 1937, and is in his papers.

17. Morgan, "Yardstick and What Else?" *Saturday Evening Post* 210 (Aug. 7, 1937), 5–7ff.

that year the rest of the board, faced with the geologists' reports, agreed with Morgan to enter into legal proceedings to have Berry's land condemned. In the meantime, the case was further complicated by the fact that Berry had been appointed to fill out the unexpired term of U.S. Sen. Nathan Bachman, who died in April 1937. Berry later failed in his attempt at election in his own right.

By the fall of 1937 Morgan had become obsessed with the Berry case, convinced that both Lilienthal and Harcourt Morgan were conspiring to help this immoral politician. The situation within the TVA was pretty much as Lilienthal had described it to the president's committee back in the spring. The board simply no longer functioned. Morgan voted nay on every motion made by Lilienthal, and his own motions invariably died for lack of a second. Hostility, suspicion, backbiting, and intrigue were the order of the day. It is important to understand that within this unstable internal environment the Authority was still fighting for its life in the courts.

The famous eighteen (previously nineteen) companies case was coming to court just at this moment. As chief legal officer, Lilienthal was rightly concerned about what Morgan might say if called to testify. In pretrial briefings conducted by a recently augmented TVA legal staff, Morgan had actually inquired as to whether or not the courts could invalidate part of the Authority while leaving the rest of it intact. Presumably he had in mind eliminating electricity, as he had done with the Miami Conservancy, and retaining Utopia. Morgan was now totally unpredictable, and the TVA attorneys had to regard him as a hostile witness. One of them recalled that Morgan "was under apparently great strain and very greatly overwrought":

> He said he had been conspired against and that he had been ignored; he had been humiliated; he was deeply resentful. He was not just angry in this conference, he was deeply moved, and he intimated that the attorneys were in conspiracy to keep him out of the case.[18]

In August of 1937 Wendell Willkie presented his attack on the yardstick idea in the *Atlantic Monthly*.[19] It was a thoughtful, well-reasoned argument, citing the problems of a private company competing against the power of the federal government. He had only one good thing to say about the TVA, and that was the responsible attitude expressed by Arthur E. Morgan. Such a compliment was the last thing Morgan

18. Quoted in McCraw, *Morgan vs. Lilienthal*, p. 94, an excellent examination of the details of both the Berry marble case and the several legal battles of the TVA.
19. Wendell L. Willkie, "Political Power," *Atlantic Monthly* 160 (August 1937), 210–18.

needed. This endorsement by the hated Willkie could only be regarded as the kiss of death by public power advocates. Without a doubt they knew that Morgan had gone over to the enemy, just as Lilienthal had been telling them. To make matters worse, at the end of the article the editors noted that in the September issue Morgan would offer his own "conclusions about public ownership of the utility industry." In the familiar territory of the *Atlantic*, a supporter of his for nearly twenty years, the Utopian committed political suicide.

Morgan's article began calmly enough, much like his earlier writings on power policy: he endorsed power pooling, called for a proper yardstick, and stuck to his plea for honest and open negotiations. His condemnation of public officials who used improper tactics grew stronger as the article came to a close: "I have no confidence in the supposed liberalism of people who use such methods. Whoever will use unfair methods for the public probably will use unfair methods against the public for his own advantage." Still, Morgan did not mention Lilienthal by name, but there was really no question about it when, on the last page, he declared that he was "a minority member" of the TVA board and that in "important respects" he was at odds with the "actual power policy" of the other directors, policies which he said contained "improprieties," not further defined.[20]

Here was an open attack against his fellow board members. Morgan had gone public first, the fundamental error when the president's squeeze was on, and the move left him vulnerable to the charge that he had challenged his codirectors' integrity with vague inferences. On August 31, just after the *Atlantic*'s September issue reached the stands, the majority of the board voted to censor Arthur Morgan for his article, and Harcourt Morgan wrote the president to that effect, noting that the piece "might not have given the Board quite so much concern if it had not been published so shortly before the trial of the 17-utility [!] suit against TVA. . . ."[21] Three days later, while aboard the *U.S.S. Potomac*, Roosevelt came down hard on Arthur Morgan, citing Harcourt's letter:

> Naturally, I am concerned by this and do not think that the matter can properly rest where it is. May I suggest, therefore, that there is a very definite obligation on you either to withdraw what your colleagues believe to be an impugning of their integrity or that you present whatever specific facts you may have, if any, to justify your statements.[22]

20. Morgan, "Public Ownership of Power," *Atlantic Monthly* 160 (September 1937), 339–46.
21. Harcourt Morgan to Roosevelt, Aug. 31, 1937, Lilienthal Papers.
22. Roosevelt to "My dear Arthur," Sept. 3, 1937, *ibid*.

This time there was no invitation to lunch. Roosevelt sent a copy of his letter to Harcourt Morgan, who responded: "I note your recognition of the serious consequences of such a situation upon the Board's administrative responsibility."[23]

Here the record once again breaks down. No evidence has been found that Roosevelt called Arthur Morgan in, as he had promised Harcourt Morgan he would do, or that the Utopian responded to the president's request that he substantiate his charges against his associates on the board. Indeed, what is revealing about the fall of 1937 is Morgan's absence from the TVA scene. On October 9, the president received the report from his committee investigating the Authority's administration; he forwarded it, not to Arthur Morgan, but to Harcourt Morgan, suggesting: "You can, of course, talk with Lilienthal about it and I should much like to have your thought." No mention of the chairman of the board. The committee's product was a document entitled "Report on Administrative Organization of TVA," and it was in no way a direct attack on the Utopian. The report itself was routine, suggesting basically nonthreatening structural changes, such as the appointment of a permanent general manager. The vice-chairman appears to have taken it in that spirit, informing the president that the agency had already implemented most of the recommended changes. No mention of Arthur Morgan or of the board's problems. Morgan seems to have been deliberately cut out by the president. In early November it was again Harcourt Morgan who wrote the president regarding power policy, and still there was no mention of Arthur Morgan. It seems as if "H.A." was running the TVA, and Roosevelt, as part of the squeeze, was sending a fairly blunt message that he was unhappy with "A.E." by failing to include him in the discussion. Not until November 12 do the records show the chairman, who had obviously been away on another vacation, writing the president, a mundane letter on land leases.[24]

Morgan must have been going through hell in the fall of 1937. It was at this time that he came up with the off-the-wall idea that Lilienthal's power part of the project might be declared unconstitutional, and his own Utopian part salvaged. This position was characterized by his fellow board members, when they reported it to the president, as "almost incredible."[25] For the most part, however, after the appearance of his *Atlantic* article, Morgan was unusually quiet. No doubt he was sick, for

23. Harcourt Morgan to Roosevelt, Sept. 7, 1937, *ibid.*
24. Roosevelt to Harcourt Morgan, Oct. 9, 1937; Harcourt Morgan to Roosevelt, Oct. 16, 1937; Arthur Morgan to Roosevelt, Nov. 12, 1937; all Roosevelt Papers.
25. Harcourt Morgan and Lilienthal to Roosevelt, Nov. 19, 1937, Lilienthal Papers.

surely he had fallen back on that lifelong excuse of poor health. The *Atlantic* piece had not been exactly a Letter from Portugal or a *Seed Man*, but somehow one senses that something very much like that is coming, that the man is about to succumb to his paranoia. It was the Berry marble case that finally did it.

On December 20, 1937, Morgan made a surprise appearance before the Berry condemnation hearings. He told the three-member commission that the claims were nothing more than an attempt "to defraud the government." Here he finally made all too public the rift in the TVA board. He accused Lilienthal and Harcourt Morgan of having agreed to settle with Berry, even though they knew his claims to be worthless. Two days later what the *New York Times* called the TVA's "family quarrel" got another thorough airing, when the majority directors publicly insisted that Morgan's charges were "false and malicious." They accused Morgan of attempting to discredit his agency's own attorneys and of "giving a prejudicial account of an agreement by a majority of the directors to conciliate the Berry claims in 1936."[26] Meanwhile, the chief counsel for the private utility corporations suing the TVA became ill, and the case was recessed for two weeks. It was a tough time for the Authority.

The student of these events has to ask why Morgan chose to make such a major case of the Berry claims. To be sure, nearly two years earlier his opposition on the board had appeared willing to settle with Berry, and Morgan had rightly, as it turned out, opposed any payment. Soon enough, however, when the geologists proved that Berry's marble was totally worthless, the other two directors agreed with Morgan and eventually went the whole legal route of condemnation. Why, then, did Morgan not settle for a simple, "I told you so," and wrap himself in his moral mantle? Why indeed? He appears to have become thoroughly irrational regarding Lilienthal, and the very fact that the latter even considered, however briefly, making a deal with a known politician, was too much for Morgan. No matter that Lilienthal had a clear trail showing that he had made the right decision about Berry. No matter that in fact Morgan had no case, beyond his paranoid belief that had he not stepped in Lilienthal would have sold the TVA for a mess of political pottage. Nothing mattered now. Morgan had crossed over the line.

Before and during the condemnation hearings, Berry and his fellow investors had made varying claims for the amount due them when their land was flooded by the Norris reservoir. The lowest appears to have been a measly million and a half, but the highest reached $87 million.

26. *New York Times*, Dec. 21 and 22, 1937.

When the final decision by the federal commission came on March 1, 1938, Berry said he had been robbed. The commission awarded him nothing for his marble.[27] Morgan felt vindicated. The day after the commission's decision, he issued a press release that made page one of the *New York Times*. That newspaper reported his claim that the Berry case represented "the kind of difficulty with which, as chairman of the TVA Board, he had been faced in the effort 'to maintain good standards of public service.' " Morgan called for a joint congressional inquiry, saying that "the real difficulty has been in the effort to secure honesty, openness, decency, and fairness in government. The Berry marble case is an instance of this difficulty." The *Times* concluded that the "long-standing breach" between Morgan and Lilienthal "had reached a point where healing appeared utterly impossible."[28]

After his startling appearance at the Berry hearing, Morgan took a long vacation in Florida. Just as he had done at Antioch, when the pressure overwhelmed him, he retreated. This time the stress was intense, and Morgan was so disturbed that he had little appreciation of any reasonable course of action he might take. Eventually, all he could do was engage in a recalcitrance and insubordination virtually unparalleled in New Deal history. It is problematical as to what precisely was the last straw that brought Roosevelt and Lilienthal together in a determined effort to oust Morgan. Most likely it was the *Atlantic* article in September 1937, but his testimony in the Berry case, and then his outrageous statements upon its conclusion, clearly pushed matters to a rapid finale.

On January 18, 1938, the majority members of the board sent a long statement to the president listing Morgan's crimes against public power. "Since the spring of 1936," they said, noting correctly that the real fight began over Lilienthal's reappointment, "the Authority's work has been accomplished in spite of the repeated failure of Arthur E. Morgan to accept and cooperate in carrying out provisions of law and Board decisions." Although this indictment was signed by both Harcourt Morgan and Lilienthal, the latter's legal hand became evident as the case against the Utopian developed. He was guilty of "continued efforts to obstruct Board decisions with which he disagreed." Five paragraphs began with the phrase "It is not permissible":

. . . to attack the personal motives and good faith and impugn the integrity of his associates on the Board, not upon the basis of direct charges but by innuendo, indirection, and aspersion.

27. *Ibid.*, March 1, 1938.　　　28. *Ibid.*, March 3, 1938.

. . . to engage in unsupported attacks upon the integrity, professional ethics, and competence of key members of the staff, and to harass and interfere with them. . . .

. . . to fail and refuse to carry out explicit action taken by the Board.

. . . to cooperate with a utility executive. . . .

. . . to collaborate with the former Chief Engineer of the Insull utility system. . . .[29]

Morgan, they suggested, somewhat obliquely, should retire. Morris L. Cooke, long a supporter of Lilienthal, had already made a public call for Morgan's dismissal. In the December 29 issue of the *New Republic* he had criticized Morgan by name, called him an enemy of public power, and suggested that "there should be strenuous objection to anyone remaining in office and opposing national policy. . . ."[30]

After his behavior in the Berry case in late December, Morgan suffered what appears to have been a fairly substantial physical, and probably emotional, breakdown. The trip to Florida was made to recuperate, and there he stayed for six weeks. It was not until St. Valentine's Day that he felt strong enough to begin the second phase of his patented progressive program for the triumph of good over evil: after appealing to the public via the press, one takes the issue through the legislative investigative process. He wrote a long letter to U.S. Rep. Maury Maverick of Texas. This document was clearly another Letter from Portugal. In the TVA, Morgan told the congressman, he faced "a menace to good government." He further stated that the other two directors met privately to make decisions, that he was not allowed to know in advance what issues would be presented to the board, and that his minority views were not placed in the minutes of board meetings. Of Lilienthal, in particular he claimed:

> There is a practice of evasion, intrigue and sharp strategy, with remarkable skill in alibi and the habit of avoiding direct responsibility, which makes Machiavelli seem open and candid. It took me a year or more of close associa-tion to be convinced that the attitude of boyish open candor and man-to-man directness was a mask for hard boiled selfish intrigue; so I am not surprised that Congressmen do not quickly see the situation from a distance.[31]

Harcourt Morgan did not escape the chairman's wrath. He charged that the vice-chairman had become, through control of Authority sup-

29. Harcourt Morgan and Lilienthal to Roosevelt, Jan. 18, 1938, Roosevelt Papers.

30. Morris L. Cooke, "Eddies in National Power Policy," *New Republic* 93 (Dec. 29, 1937), 217-20. McCraw, in *Morgan vs. Lilienthal* (p. 96), quotes Roosevelt, in giving Cooke permission to print this article, as saying: "Go the whole hog—and the quicker the better."

31. Morgan to Maury Maverick, Feb. 14, 1938, Norris Papers; also available in the *New York Times*, March 7, 1938.

184 · *Farewell to Utopia*

port to land grant colleges and county farm agents, "one of the most powerful figures of the South, though he nearly always chooses to be behind the scenes." Morgan reported a conspiracy on the part of the other directors that had them voting together on all matters and allowing each other a free hand in their respective programs. He wanted a congressional investigation, which he promised would disclose "disorder, waste, confusion and lack of planning to a startling degree."

It appears that Roosevelt had put his famous squeeze on Morgan since at least the summer of 1937. Back in October 1936 the president had sent Morgan the letter from E. F. Scattergood that had been so critical of the chairman. Morgan, for reasons forever lost to us, never responded to FDR's kindness in sharing with him this damaging report from a subordinate. Not, that is, until August 1937, when he wrote the president asking for permission to take the matter up directly with Scattergood "in order to learn the basis for a statement made in that letter." Roosevelt's response, when compared to others to his Utopian, seems cold and distant. Fine, said the president, go talk to Scattergood, "yet it seems to me rather a waste of time to do so now, as his letter is nearly a year old." Despite the closing, "I hope to see you one of these days soon," one senses, while sifting through FDR's papers, that he had had enough of Arthur Morgan.[32]

The events of the subsequent months certainly did not reassure the president, and the record shows that he began to isolate Morgan and deal directly, on matters crucial to the TVA, with Harcourt Morgan. Moreover, the fall of 1937 was full of public recriminations and desperate letters from the majority members of the board seeking Roosevelt's intervention. Normally, the squeeze worked, but Morgan was an entirely different animal, and when he was full of righteous indignation—as he surely was over the Berry claims—he became not only emotional and unpredictable but fully capable of refusing to play the presidential game. Morgan should have retired, probably as soon as he lost the bid to fire Lilienthal back in 1936. Roosevelt and Lilienthal most certainly would have arranged for an honorable exit, full of praise for his great engineering work. The president was even prepared to offer him some other, no doubt less sensitive, post. These were options that anyone with a modicum of political savvy would have taken. The handwriting, as Morgan had said about Willkie, was indeed on the wall, and it had been

32. Morgan to Roosevelt, Aug. 16, 1937; Roosevelt to Morgan, Aug. 21, 1937; both Roosevelt Papers.

for some time. The rules call for one in Morgan's position to cut his losses and to make the best of a bad deal. He had allowed himself to become the issue, and when that happens, the game is over.

Not so with Morgan. He would defy the president, remain in office until the bitter end, and continue to rely on his vindication before Congress. On March 3, 1938, in the aftermath of his "victory" over both Berry and Lilienthal, he issued another call for a joint congressional investigation into the TVA in the interest of "honesty, openness, decency and fairness in government." By this time a number of resolutions had been introduced in Congress calling for various sorts of inquiries into the problems in the Tennessee Valley Authority. Senator Norris had called for an investigation by the Federal Trade Commission. As the *New York Times* put it, in another page-one story on March 4, "Senator Norris and others close to the TVA operations were obviously concerned at the turn of affairs which saw Dr. Morgan take his case against the other two directors to the public."[33]

That was the problem: Morgan had gone public, and in a way it was one of the scenarios acceptable to the president—keep the squeeze on until one of the parties did something incredibly and openly stupid; then he had to resign. That was the way Roosevelt wanted the matter handled. Morgan would resign. Friends of the Authority, however, were worried about the political effects this bitter and public fight might have in Congress. Enemies of the New Deal were stronger than ever by 1938, and the Tennessee Valley Authority might well be in danger. Moreover, there was the immediate problem of the appropriation for the dam at Gilbertsville, Kentucky, termed "the very backbone of the TVA." At the very least funding would be held up pending the outcome of the crisis precipitated by Morgan.[34]

As much as Roosevelt wanted to avoid an embarrassing public airing of the dirty linen within the board of one of his favorite agencies, Morgan's increasingly vitriolic attacks on his fellow board members forced his hand. Following Morgan's outrageous statements at the conclusion of the Berry case, FDR complained before reporters about Morgan's lack of "good sportsmanship" and ordered the release of the January "it is not permissible" indictment from Lilienthal and Harcourt Morgan. The *New York Times* reprinted the incriminating memorandum to the president in its entirety, noting that it called for Morgan's resignation and concluding: "Washington observers were almost unanimous in placing President Roosevelt on the side of Dr. H. A. Morgan and Mr. Lilienthal

33. *New York Times*, March 4, 1938.   34. Quoted in *ibid.*

in the TVA dispute."[35] That should have done it. Morgan was now clearly unwelcome in the Roosevelt administration. Anyone but a Utopian would have resigned on the spot, yet Morgan remained adamant.

The following day, Senator Norris called for his resignation, and Morgan, still in Florida, promised that he would have a release soon "which presents my opinion."[36] He countered Roosevelt's disclosure of the "it is not permissible" memorandum by revealing his St. Valentine's Day letter to Representative Maverick. That document, also reprinted in full by the *Times*, made yet another front page with the headlines: "TVA Head Assails 'Intrigue,' Hinting Refusal to Resign. . . . Cites 'Waste,' 'Evasion,' Denunciation of Two Fellow-Directors Charges Tactics Outdo Machiavelli." The matter was now fully public and thoroughly dirty, and the ball was in Roosevelt's court. Morgan would not resign. As he told reporters:

> I am nearly 60 years old and many years ago deliberately gave up expectations of a public career. . . . I did not seek my present position in any way. It would be pleasanter to resign and do some of the many things I am anxious to get at. Yet to surrender the chance to make some contribution to decency and effectiveness in government does not seem to be the right course.[37]

In the days that followed, the president decided on an exceptionally bold strategy, daring and dangerous, but one that had worked well for him when he was governor of New York. Then he had found himself in a fight with the flamboyant mayor of New York City, James J. (Jimmy) Walker. The mayor had become notorious for his social and sexual affairs but, more important, his administration had been found to contain considerable corruption. Governor Roosevelt, a presidential candidate, intervened with a unique method to force Walker out. He held a special gubernatorial hearing, conducted it himself, publicly, and for days kept the mayor on the hot seat. Finally, on September 1, 1932, Walker had obliged the governor by resigning, which was, of course, what Roosevelt had wanted.[38] It was the ultimate squeeze. The process was, FDR told Lilienthal, "my own invention," and he suggested that they use it on Morgan.[39]

Roosevelt scheduled his special presidential hearing for Friday, March

35. *Ibid.*, March 5, 1938.
36. *Ibid.*, March 6, 1938.
37. Quoted in *ibid.*, March 7, 1938. The entire Morgan to Maverick letter of Feb. 14, 1938, is reprinted in this issue.
38. See George Walsh, *Gentleman Jimmy Walker* (New York: Praeger Pub., 1974).
39. Quoted in McCraw, *Morgan vs. Lilienthal*, p. 99.

11, 1938. For weeks Lilienthal had been preparing his case and forward-
ing a series of briefs to FDR. His papers at Princeton and Roosevelt's at
Hyde Park contain stacks of various legal analyses, mostly unsigned but
all undeniably Lilienthal's work, that sought to prove that Morgan had
not only conspired with the enemies of the TVA but had publicly and
unprofessionally attacked his associates. One of these documents, entitled "Confusion of Thinking Shown in his Concept of Dishonesty"
demonstrates how well Lilienthal had come to understand his nemesis:

> In the course of the hearing it will be interesting to note that, to the Chairman,
> disagreement with him is frequently considered evidence of dishonesty. Ex-
> perience has shown that unless he is compelled by specific demand to use the
> word dishonesty in its customary meaning, he will use it in the special AEM
> sense meaning departure from his judgment. . . . AEM typically turns a
> disagreement into evidence per se of improper motive or personal attack.[40]

For his part, Morgan simply refused to go to the hearing. He told the
president that he did not believe it would accomplish anything. Roosevelt
was furious and telegraphed the chairman:

> Meeting Friday is not called as you say to reconcile the differences between the
> board members but to enable me to get facts. You have made from time to time
> general charges against the majority members and they in turn have made
> counter charges against you. I want to get all of you together to substantiate
> these general charges factually. It is your duty as chairman and member of the
> authority to attend this meeting. Please advise.[41]

The press was keen on the prospect of a major scandal in Roosevelt's
administration. Morgan's letter to Maverick made it sound as though
there was significant corruption going on in the TVA. On the appointed
day the meeting was held in the president's oval office, and in an ante-
room the reporters waited anxiously for the conclusion of the hearing.
They waited a long time, some six hours, and in the end they were
disappointed. Not only did Morgan fail to produce the dirt they desired,
but he refused to participate in the proceedings. Just before the meeting
began, he had announced to the press: "I am an observer and not a
participant in this alleged process of fact finding."[42]

Roosevelt opened the session with a calm note that the purpose of the
hearing was to determine the facts about various charges that had been

40. "Confusion of Thinking Shown in His Concept of Dishonesty," unsigned, undated
typed manuscript, Roosevelt Papers.
    41. Roosevelt to Morgan, March 9, 1938, Roosevelt Papers.
    42. Quoted in *New York Times*, March 12, 1938.

bandied about. The investigation was an official one, with testimony taken by stenographers, and with the president acting as judge, ordering that various documents be entered into the record as exhibits. After referring to Morgan as "my dear old friend," and giving a lengthy overview of the development of the feud, he asked the chairman for his response. Hearing none, the president called Lilienthal to make his presentation. The power director went over a long list of the things that Morgan had done wrong, and when Roosevelt turned to Morgan and asked, "Is there anything you want to say about it?" Morgan replied:

> I do not feel I can say very much. They contain misstatements, misrepresenta-tions and omission in an extreme degree. One of them, the presenting of it in this case and at this time—I am not indicating what anybody's motives are but it is what would be done if there were a very grave failure to meet public responsibility, is what would be done if there had been a very grave failure to meet responsibility to the public and there was an effort to minimize that failure and cover it up by bringing it in under favorable circumstances. . . .

That confusing paragraph is precisely what Morgan said, and it was the extent of his defense. In what other few and brief comments he did make, he was rambling and vague. More than anything else his perform-ance at the hearing was a desperate cry for help. "I'm hurt," he seemed to say, "and they're bad." Roosevelt kept hammering at the chairman to give specifics, and Morgan continued to say that this forum was not the proper place, that only a congressional investigation would satisfy him. Roosevelt offered to give him another week to reconsider whether or not he could come in with specifics. The president summed up the day's absolute frustration:

> Frankly, I am disappointed that [Morgan] has not answered by giving any factual answers . . . but I hope that in the course of the next week [he] will realize that it is of the utmost importance to the continuation of the work that he should reply to very simple factual questions.

Morgan did get in the last word at that first hearing: "Mr. President, before I go I would like to make this statement: I personally want to thank the President for the fine consideration he has shown us."[43] What a statement for the Utopian. Here he was, going down with the flag of goodwill still flying. The hearing adjourned at six in the evening, and the reporters, who had received, page by page, mimeographed copies of the transcript taken down by a team of stenographers, had plenty of time to write up their amazing story. Not about scandal, but, as the *New York*

43. FDR's TVA Hearings.

Times page-one headline put it: "Morgan Defies President's Airing of TVA Board Row."[44] The *Times* was equally correct in calling the hearing "the most unusual meeting of its kind ever held in Washington." The paper also stresssed the fact that Roosevelt had told Morgan that if he could not produce the particulars behind his accusations against his colleagues, he should resign: "an ultimatum," the *Times* said, "to Chairman Morgan to drop or substantiate his statement by next Friday or quit."

During the ensuing week, various members of Congress continued to call for additional investigations, with Senator Norris still favoring one by the Federal Trade Commission, and Representative Maverick supporting Morgan by urging a joint congressional inquiry. Also during that week, Lilienthal met with Willkie, attempting to resolve the thorny problem of the division of territory between the public and private utilities.[45]

The hearing reconvened on Friday, March 18. With the president's permission, Morgan began by reading a prepared statement which did little more than cite his extremely vague charges against his fellow directors. The president kept interrupting, growing increasingly exasperated, asking for specifics. Finally, Morgan agreed to give an example and began discussing the Berry case. He noted, however, that to get into the matter seriously they needed "witnesses who may have to be subpoenaed and where there must be facilities for examination, cross-examination and arguments which are not available here." Morgan was trying, however ineptly, to beat the president at his own game. Roosevelt went off the record. When he returned:

> **The President:** You have used the Berry case, Chairman Morgan, as an illustration. You have used the word "illustration."
> **Chairman Morgan:** Yes.
> **The President:** The law gives me complete authority to investigate the Berry case.
> **Chairman Morgan:** Yes.
> **The President:** Are there any cases relating to the charges that you have made other than the Berry case which I could not investigate under that section?
> **Chairman Morgan:** I believe so.
> **The President:** What?
> **Chairman Morgan:** A vast number of them.
> **The President:** What?

44. *New York Times*, March 12, 1938.
45. *Ibid.*, March 13 and 18, 1938.

> **Chairman Morgan:** May I. . . .
> **The President:** Please specify.
> **Chairman Morgan:** I would like to make a statement of fact also.

At this point Morgan began complaining that FDR's secretary, Marvin McIntyre, had told him not to bring any statements or briefs, and there was considerable haggling over whether Morgan had been given sufficient time to prepare. The situation became increasingly frustrating for everyone. Morgan tried to finish his statement calling for "a full and impartial inquiry by the Congress." The president kept interrupting him. To continue:

> **Chairman Morgan:** I would like to finish my statement.
> **The President:** Please answer my question. I asked you a question.
> **Chairman Morgan:** I am not in a position to do so at the present moment. I was told by Secretary McIntyre that I should not bring papers and briefs.
> **The President:** Would you be ready tomorrow morning?
> **Chairman Morgan:** No.
> **The President:** Would you be ready Wednesday?[46]

And on it went. Everyone, as the official transcript shows, clearly was done in by the whole affair. Roosevelt called in his secretary and discussed the sensitive business of whether or not Morgan had been told not to bring any documents with him. McIntyre denied such involvement, but he appears to have felt some sympathy for Morgan. There is substantial evidence that McIntyre tried to intervene to help Morgan; the document is unsigned and undated, but it is typed just as McIntyre typed all his notes to the president. It was probably at just such a moment that he slipped the following message over to Roosevelt:

Mr. President:

> Would it not be well to ask Arthur Morgan to remain a few moments when the others leave. Then to tell him how sorry you are that he has refused to participate and has given the impression that he cannot receive from you a fair hearing. That you had honestly hoped he would help you to lay the basis for a review of TVA policies on their merits. Such a review can never be obtained when the opponents of the Administration are ready to seize the opportunity to condemn the TVA and all its works simply because Arthur Morgan thinks David Lilienthal is a scoundrel and David Lilienthal thinks Arthur Morgan won't play ball if he can't call the plays. Maybe you can make the poor old fellow feel that he has not only let you down, but has let down the sort of TVA he really wants.

46. FDR's TVA Hearings.

McIntyre typed this on legal-sized paper; it had to have been him, and the room had to have been filled with legal-sized paper. The note took up less than half the page. There was plenty of room for the president to scrawl his answer in the remaining space. And he did. There was no doubt about it. Despite McIntyre's clear understanding of the basic nature of the feud, Roosevelt was finished with Morgan, and he was in this fight to the bitter end. McIntyre's fainthearted attempt to help the Utopian was too little, too late. Roosevelt was adamant, as he made plain when he wrote and initialed the following response to Mac's plea for a last-minute reconciliation. The emphases are the president's:

> I *greatly* fear he would misquote it into a request from me to let bygones be bygones—be a good boy & stay on—& make it appear I had no case—& also that he would continue to give the idea he *still* had no confidence in my fairness & only the Congress would be fair.
>
> FDR[47]

At the end of the March 18 hearing, the president concluded that Morgan had failed to support his charges of dishonesty and want of integrity on the part of his fellow directors. On the other hand, judged Roosevelt, Lilienthal had substantiated his charges that "Chairman Morgan has obstructed and sabotaged" the work of the TVA. Because Morgan had refused to answer his questions, the president had no recourse but to observe that "on the record as it stands today he is guilty of contumacy in his refusal." Roosevelt, however, still was not ready to fire Morgan. He wanted that resignation. He tried to pin Morgan down on the question of whether or not he would prefer to continue the present investigation or for the president to appoint a special counsel as allowed in the TVA act. Morgan vacillated, as he had done throughout the hearing.

> **The President:** Can you give me some idea, Chairman Morgan, as to when you can give an answer to the last question I have asked you? I think, in fairness to myself, you owe it to me to tell me today when I will have that answer.

Morgan rattled on about a congressional investigation. Roosevelt repeated the question. Finally, the president gave up:

> I can give you only until Monday at 1:30. And, when you do it—when you give me this answer at 1:30 on Monday, I want you to say, "Yes" or "No." It has reached that point now.[48]

47. This document on legal-sized paper contains at the top the typed note that is suspected to be from McIntyre. The rest of the page is covered in Roosevelt's large hand and is initialed by him. Roosevelt Papers.
48. FDR's TVA Hearings.

Naturally this second session also made the *New York Times* front page: "Roosevelt Fixes Morgan Dead Line to End 'Contumacy.' " The reporters had to resort to the dictionary to discover that *contumacy* meant "pertinacious resistance to authority; willful disobedience to summons or orders of a court, or willful contempt of court." Now the press grew excited over whether or not Roosevelt could fire Morgan, with the *Times* claiming that "numerous legal authorities at the Capitol, including men close to the President, doubted that the terms of the TVA Act gave the Executive authority to remove a director."[49]

The administration was quick to respond that the president did in fact have such removal authority. The White House staff recognized that earlier Roosevelt had been foiled by the courts in an attempt to remove a member of the Federal Trade Commission because that agency was "quasi-judicial" and thus outside of executive control. They relied, however, on a 1928 Supreme Court decision that approved a president's authority to remove members within his own branch. Meanwhile, pressure continued to mount for a full-scale congressional investigation into the TVA, due at least in part to the obvious fact that Roosevelt had, as Arthur Krock of the *Times* said: "exploded in Chairman Morgan's face."[50]

Monday rolled around, and the third and final session convened. The president began by repeating the question about whether Morgan was prepared for the investigation to continue. The Utopian had made up his mind and was prepared to take his stand. He read a prepared statement:

> Mr. President, since Friday last I have given the deepest consideration to the question you put to me at the end of the session. For reasons which I have given in the two conferences already held, I cannot participate further in these proceedings.
>
> Assuring you of my deep respect,
>
> I am very truly yours,
>
> Arthur E. Morgan[51]

Roosevelt was prepared for this recalcitrant attitude, and he too had a statement. He reviewed the details of the TVA feud, starting with Morgan's articles in early 1937. Then the president made his findings, as the *New York Times* said, "in the role of a judge rendering a decision at the end of a trial."[52] He found Morgan guilty on all counts. In addition to having failed to sustain his grave and libelous charges against Lilienthal

---

49. *New York Times*, March 19, 1938.   50. *Ibid.*, March 20 and 21, 1938.
51. FDR's TVA Hearings.   52. *New York Times*, March 22, 1938.

and the other Morgan, the chairman had obstructed the work of the TVA and had injured its morale, and he was "guilty of insubordination and contumacy" in refusing to answer questions put to him by the president of the United States. Roosevelt still, however, stopped short of firing Morgan. He told his Utopian to withdraw his charges; if not, to resign. If Morgan did neither, said Roosevelt, "I will give him until tomorrow, Tuesday, 2:30 P.M. on March 22," to present any reasons why he should not be suspended or removed.[53]

Morgan continued his defiance. He would not resign, he said, because it was not in the public interest to do so. Furthermore, Roosevelt did not have the constitutional power to fire him. The conference adjourned at 2:40 in the afternoon of March 21. Morgan got on a train and headed back to Yellow Springs.[54] Two days later Roosevelt, faced with the fact that Morgan would never yield and resign like an ordinary man, finally fired him. In this way Morgan became the only case that Tugwell could recall as an exception to the Roosevelt treatment. As hard as he had tried to avoid it, in the end the president bit the bullet and sent his Utopian packing. McIntyre had wired the day before to let him know the axe was falling. "As a matter of courtesy," he told Morgan, "I wanted to inform you before the announcement [of your dismissal] is given to the press. The president again expressed his regret that this action has become necessary."[55] Whatever Roosevelt's feelings, in the end his plan to force Morgan's resignation failed, and he had to fire him.

Arthur Morgan was a first-class example of a man ultimately unsuited for public life. Although he never realized it, such life is found only in the political world, and in that environment he represented an endangered species. He was the progressive who hated politics. If Lilienthal had not gotten him, Willkie would, no doubt, have eaten him alive. At the very best, had Morgan somehow survived at the TVA, it would have been an Authority without an emphasis on electricity. The TVA we know today is Lilienthal's, and it is to him the standard textbooks give the credit. He deserves it, too, because he revolutionized the electrical industry with his gamble on cheap rates producing great demand.

Morgan's Tennessee Valley Authority never really had a chance, not

53. FDR's TVA Hearings.
54. *New York Times*, March 22, 1938. The extensive coverage the *Times* gave to FDR's hearings included lengthy extracts from each of the sessions. During the course of these White House proceedings, the *Times* awarded them as much space as it did to Hitler's takeover of Austria, which was occurring at the same time.
55. McIntyre to Morgan, March 22, 1938, Roosevelt Papers.

even in the strange days of the New Deal. His personal flaws were many, described by George Fort Milton as "the utter lack of focus to his thinking; his inability to get along with equals; his jealousies and suspicions; his Messiah complex, almost paranoiac in its growth. . . ."[56] He certainly could not share authority, but required the autonomy of the engineer. Give him a swamp to drain, a flood control system to build, a college to save, give him a problem and turn him loose—then he could be imaginative, extraordinarily creative, and amazingly energetic and productive. Tie him down with faculty rights, rules of procedure, or the political process, and he was doomed.

Over the years, especially as the TVA aged and came to be just another utility and the difference between public and private power became almost indistinguishable to the consumer, some historians asked if there had been another Tennessee Valley Authority, the Morgan version, that might somehow have avoided the problems with reform groups that the historic Authority began to face in the 1970s. The answer here must be in the negative. Not because of Morgan's personality. Not because of Lilienthal or Willkie. Eliminate all the practical aspects of his failure and give Morgan more than an even chance to succeed. Where would the TVA be? Nowhere. This is precisely the meaning of the word *Utopia*, as coined by Sir Thomas More. The TVA, as Morgan saw it, was another benchmark on the road to Utopia. Nothing more. Not expecting success, he fought simply to continue the tradition of Utopian experimentation. That was the way he viewed his contribution. Morgan's Tennessee Valley Authority existed in Morgan's mind. It was part of the long-term effort to remake human society, another seed planted by a seedman in a long line of seedmen. His TVA was only a model, an example. Given his limitations, the immensity of his dream, and the realities of the times, he went surprisingly far and probably accomplished more than he ever expected.

56. Milton to Norris, Nov. 4, 1936, Lilienthal Papers.

Epilogue

Morgan eventually got his congressional investigation. Congress obviously could not miss participating in such a comic-opera. Old friends from his Antioch and Miami Conservancy days rallied to his side, supplying funds and serving as his staff. This time, however, the progressive magic of such hearings was gone for Morgan. It was not 1912. The inquiry lasted from May to December 1938 and produced great amounts of testimony, but few hard facts. Once again he failed, as he had in the 1936 fight over Lilienthal's reappointment, to produce the documents proving that the power director had made appointments recommended by politicians when more qualified applicants were available.

Why he refused to use what little hard information he had is not known, except for his life-long explanation that he felt such revelations would have damaged the career of the man who conducted the original investigation into Lilienthal's patronage activities. One historian found Morgan's decision not to reveal his most damaging data "puzzling in view of [his] readiness to make other serious charges that he was unable to document at all."[1] The result of the joint committee's effort reflected partisan lines. The Democratic majority exonerated Lilienthal and Harcourt Morgan and praised the work of the Authority, while accusing Arthur Morgan of failing to cooperate. A minority report condemned the entire TVA program.[2]

Morgan finally admitted his defeat at the hands of Lilienthal, but when he returned to Yellow Springs he had no intention of retiring, even at the age of sixty. Antioch College had not been the answer to his dreams, and he had suffered a major setback in Tennessee, but his missionary zeal continued unabated. Although he was too old to conceive and direct personally major projects, he carved out a role for himself as philosopher

---

1. McCraw, *Morgan vs. Lilienthal*, p. 104.
2. U.S. Congress, Joint Committee on the Investigation of the Tennessee Valley Authority, *Hearings, May 25–December 21, 1938*. Pursuant to Public Resolution no. 83 (75th Cong., 3rd sess.) (14 parts; Washington: U.S. Government Printing Office, 1939); *Report, Together with the Minority Views of Mr. Davis, Mr. Jenkins, and Mr. Wolverton, and the Individual Views of Mr. Jenkins*. Senate Doc. no. 56 (76th Cong., 1st sess.) (3 parts; Washington: U.S. Government Printing Office, 1939).

and author. Most of his activity for the rest of his long life revolved around his connection, through his Quaker wife and children, with the American Friends Service Committee and an organization he founded in 1940 called Community Service, Inc. In 1939 he visited Mexico to inspect possible sites for settlement by Jewish and other European refugees, a project jointly sponsored by the Mexican government and the Friends.

Community Service carried its purpose prominently on its letterhead: "To promote the interests of the small community as a basic social institution, concerned with the economic, recreational, educational, cultural and spiritual development of its members." A more formal statement of his ideas came in 1942 with his publication of *The Small Community*.[3] In many ways what Morgan suggested was the creation of more communities like Norris, Tennessee. He wanted towns dedicated to planned, balanced living. As always, the thrust of his message was ethical, but in *The Small Community* his earlier moral rectitude was more subtle. He continued to believe that a community must operate on the basis of a generally accepted code of ethics, but he did not offer a code of his own, as he had done in the 1920s and 1930s. Instead, he urged that the first task for a community was to develop a code suited to its needs. While he insisted on the desirability of an end to harmful individualism and the rebirth of a spirit of cooperation and sacrifice for the general good, he gave equal attention to individual freedom.

While still with the Tennessee Valley Authority, Morgan had re-kindled a personal interest in Edward Bellamy, the author of *Looking Backward* and *Equality* who had influenced him so much in his youth. His return to the quiet of Yellow Springs gave him time to complete in 1944 a full-scale biography of Bellamy, using the private papers of the Utopian writer. Morgan was very much impressed with Bellamy, "one of the most ranging and penetrating minds America has produced." He called him "almost a modern Leonardo da Vinci," and ranked him with Freud, Emerson, Thoreau, Hawthorne, and Henry George.[4] In many ways Morgan respected traits in Bellamy that he had attempted to develop in himself or had determined to be valuable:

> Bellamy had [he said] a rare quality of freeing himself from prejudices, of keeping an open mind, and of letting his imagination play upon problems; and of trusting to intuition rather than to the carefully reasoned but treacherous *a*

---

3. Morgan, *The Small Community, Foundation of Democratic Life: What It Is and How to Achieve It* (New York: Harper and Brothers, 1942).
4. Morgan, *Edward Bellamy* (New York: Columbia University Press, 1944), pp. v–viii.

priori logic of the philosophical schools. As a result, in numerous fields, as in eugenics, socialism, economics, and religion, he arrived at conclusions which grow in men's respect as the years pass.[5]

The traditional subject of debate about Bellamy's Utopia is the matter of regimentation. Would his Industrial Army free or enslave mankind? Morgan concluded that it was impossible to escape regimentation under Bellamy's plan, but if the program were wisely administered, "it might be no more distasteful than some of the striking regimentation of present-day American life."[6]

In looking for origins of Edward Bellamy's ideas, Morgan became convinced of the importance of the Incan civilization on Western Utopian thought. In 1946 he published *Nowhere Was Somewhere*, setting forth the thesis that Sir Thomas More's 1516 *Utopia* was actually an account of Peru.[7] More had claimed that his classic was based on the story told to him by a sailor who had been stranded in South America, but scholars had unanimously accepted this as a standard "apology" to avoid censorship and punishment. Morgan took More at his word. He worked out a theory whereby the sailor used an Incan balsa sailing vessel to cross the Pacific and return to England to describe Peru.

Morgan's evidence on the possibility of a balsa crossing is fascinating, and he anticipated Thor Heyerdahl's experiments on the same subject, but his main concern was to show that More's *Utopia* had been based on a real civilization and thus to refute the notion that human nature was incapable of achieving an ideal society. He believed that there was a definite and continuing tradition of the idea of Utopia, in both Western and Eastern thought. In a sense he was defending his own life when he made a plea that the search for Utopia was not a single-minded, visionary nothingness, but a high-minded drive for progress. He urged the continuation of this Utopian tradition, and he added his own formula in words he had used for more than forty years: "refinement of the personal impulses and motivations," "ethical actions and social motives," and the "application of the science of eugenics."

During World War II, Morgan conducted a correspondence course on community for imprisoned conscientious objectors. In 1945 he served as

---

5. *Ibid.*, p. 169.

6. *Ibid.*, p. 331. Other shorter works by Morgan on Bellamy are *The Philosophy of Edward Bellamy* (Morningside Heights, N.Y.: King's Crown Press, 1945) and *Plagiarism in Utopia: A Study of the Continuity of the Utopian Tradition with Special Reference to Edward Bellamy's Looking Backward* (Yellow Springs, Ohio: published by the author, 1944).

7. Morgan, *Nowhere Was Somewhere: How History Makes Utopias and How Utopias Make History* (Chapel Hill: University of North Carolina Press, 1946), p. 150.

chairman of the Conservation Committee for the Ohio Postwar Program Commission. Another war-related activity originated with Lucy Morgan's idea of using whole grains as a relief cereal for Europe. Morgan sold the idea to the Ralston-Purina Company, and the result was the "Ralston Purina Special Relief Cereal" sent to Europe by the Friends Service Committee and other groups. In 1946 he published *A Business of My Own*, one of his few books with more facts than moralizing, suggesting ways to earn a living without undue competition or wastefulness.[8] In 1947 he went to Finland as a consultant to the Finnish government (which decorated both him and Lucy) on self-help rehabilitation and American markets for Finnish small businesses. The following year he was in India to study higher education possibilities in rural areas.[9] While there he collected books on ancient Hindu medicine, which he donated, along with his extensive collection of Bellamy material, to Harvard University.

In the next decade he continued to work, serving in 1950 as chairman of the Conciliation and Arbitration Board for U.S. Steel and the Congress of Industrial Organizations. In 1951 he published *The Miami Conservancy District*, a history of that project.[10] Two years later the American Society of Civil Engineers acknowledged its respect by making him an honorary member. In the same year he served as a consultant to Ghana on the Volta Dam project.

In 1955 Morgan's interest again focused on India and one last attempt at Utopia. Through his Quaker contacts he met an Indian named Viswan who had grand ideas for rebuilding his remote village of Mitraniketan (the Abode of Friends), in Kerala. From the spirit with which Morgan wrote of this effort in his Community Service newsletters, it was obvious that he hoped it would achieve the success he had missed at Antioch and TVA. Viswan and Mitraniketan were the subject of *It Can Be Done in Education*, written by Morgan in 1962.[11] In 1968, at the age of ninety, he returned to India to see Viswan's work.

In 1955, soon after meeting Viswan, Morgan published *Search for Purpose*, another attempt to explain his ideas, and in many ways it ranks as his best book. His staunch self-righteousness had mellowed with time into a sincere humility that insisted only on the possibility of goodness in man. His logic and definitions were tighter than before, and the book bore the stamp of much editorial work. As always, Morgan wrote in a

8. Morgan, *A Business of My Own* (Yellow Springs: Community Service, Inc., 1946).
9. Morgan, *The Rural University* (Sevagram, India: Hindustani Talimi Sangh, 1950).
10. Morgan, *The Miami Conservancy District* (New York: McGraw Hill, 1951).
11. Morgan, *It Can Be Done in Education* (Yellow Springs: Community Service, Inc., 1962).

largely autobiographical style, tracing the impact of fundamental Christianity and science on his life and attempting to show how over a span of seventy years he had come to believe in a definite purpose to life and the universe.

He did not find meaning in any supernatural power or in the existence of a natural order. On these points he could only acknowledge that he had incomplete evidence and could make no judgment. What he did see was humanity involved in a great adventure where there were unlimited possibilities, and purpose lay in the process of choosing between "various possibilities of excellence." Morgan hoped that people would accept the challenge and, through continued research and development, "achieve design which is large enough, intelligent enough, nearly enough universal, and enough in accord with reality, to include all values."[12] In speaking of the possibility of progress, he saw four major lines that had to be developed to increase human welfare and progress:

> They are (1) the mastery of the physical world; (2) education, or the increase of knowledge and understanding; (3) the refinement, enlargement and strengthening of purpose and attitude, largely by the contagion of association with desirable quality; and (4) eugenics, the science which deals with influences which improve the inborn qualities of men.[13]

On the matter of eugenics, Morgan was less rigid than he had been in the 1920s. He appreciated the complexities of human genetics that led most scientists to admit the impossibility of any meaningful eugenic reform. On the other hand, he still regarded eugenics as basically an ethical matter, and he held that properly motivated individuals would select mates with eugenic concern uppermost in their minds. "Man," he wrote, "must direct his own biological evolution."[14]

In 1957 the former TVA chairman entered his last public fight. This time he took up the cause of the Seneca Indian nation, whose lands in Pennsylvania were threatened by flooding through the construction of the Kinzua Dam. For three years Morgan worked to find alternatives to the Army Corps of Engineers' plan. He arrived at a solution (involving flooding the excess water into Lake Erie) and even appealed to the public through an appearance on a national television news show. He created no great public furor (the cycle of conservation enthusiasm was on a downturn at the time), and his fight was lost.

In terms of earlier comments about the racial views Morgan shared with most of his contemporaries in the 1920s, it is proper to note that in

12. Morgan, *Search for Purpose* (Yellow Springs: Antioch Press, 1955), p. 130.
13. *Ibid.*, p. 147.   14. *Ibid.*, p. 159.

1963 he appeared at the head of six hundred Antioch students, faculty, and townspeople in a protest march against a local barber who refused to serve blacks. In a memorandum Morgan recorded his mixed feelings about the demonstration. On the one hand, he knew that Yellow Springs should not have conditions that implied the inferiority of a particular race. "On the other hand," he added, "I am inclined to a process of gradual change within the borders of good will." He expressed equal concern that the Antiochians who instigated the march were "motivated by vague emotion, rather than by critical conviction."[15] In 1965, however, he participated in another walk in Yellow Springs in sympathy with a more dramatic one being held in Selma, Alabama, to promote black voter registration.

In his nineties, Morgan was afflicted with poor eyesight, loneliness, and generally failing health, which finally forced an end to hikes in his beloved Glen Helen. He continued to work with magnifying lenses attached to his typewriter and telephone, and he seemed to survive largely on will, refusing to accept the fact that his battle must finally come to an end. He published three more books. The first of these represented a compilation of extracts from his earlier writings, published in 1968.[16] The two others, however, took on his old enemies, the Army Corps of Engineers and David Lilienthal.

Morgan had argued with the corps about flood control since the 1920s, and he was especially disturbed when he lost the battle to save the Seneca Indian lands from flooding behind a corps dam. In *Dams and Other Disasters* (1971) he criticized the Corps for being a highly conservative, closed-minded society dominated by the West Point mentality.[17] Unfortunately, he lacked the aid of a good editor, as he did in so much of his writing, and the book was rambling, repetitious, and full of moral judgments. Morgan's last book, *The Making of the T.V.A.*, appeared the year before his death.[18] Certainly this kind of effort was amazing for a man of more than ninety-six years, and perhaps readers should bear his physical condition in mind when considering the mistakes and poor writing. The interesting aspect of the work concerns Morgan's attitude toward Lilienthal. He never could bring himself to forgive his antagonist of forty years, and it was only after great urging from his small staff that

15. Quoted in a letter from Ruth Bent to this writer, Sept. 26, 1969; original in Morgan Papers.
16. Morgan, *Observations* (Yellow Springs: Antioch Press, 1968).
17. Morgan, *Dams and Other Disasters: A Century of the Army Corps of Engineers in Civil Works* (Boston: Porter Sargent, 1971).
18. Morgan, *The Making of the T.V.A.* (Buffalo, N.Y.: Prometheus Books, 1974).

he included a line suggesting that in light of his later splendid career, perhaps Lilienthal was not so evil after all.

To his deathbed, on November 15, 1975, Morgan carried with him bitterness, agony, and a certain amount of astonishment over his failure with the Tennessee Valley Authority. He never really understood what happened to him. By all that he held to be true, he should have won. The TVA was his moment in history, and a crucial period in American history at that, yet he had failed, failed in spectacular fashion. The shambles of 1937–1938 should not, however, detract from Morgan's important contributions to the agency and social and economic planning in general. His aims were never base. Morgan's end at TVA paralleled his problems at Antioch. In both cases he felt others had failed to live up to his standards, and a deeply seated suspicion set in, causing him to lash out at his opponents. Eventually even he recognized that his own personality traits had not served him well. He preferred to think of his problem as a physical one—the brain damage excuse. Maybe it was. Who knows what forces drive people to irrationality? One can simply observe that during both the Antioch and the TVA fights he was clearly emotionally distraught. Furthermore, that he was often dogmatic, frequently narrow-minded, and moralistic to a fault cannot be denied.

That is not, however, the whole of Morgan's story. There is the equally established record of a man fiercely struggling to fulfill a vision. He was an early leader in the twentieth-century reform crusades, and in those several fights and more he achieved historical significance. Morgan is as important to the history of engineering as he is to that of education, Utopianism, eugenics, and conservation. He must be seen in the broad context of an age that allowed such diversity. Other students may find here some hints for further research, such as delving into the long argument with the Corps of Engineers over flood control, the operation of the League to Enforce Peace, the tradition of moral restraint, the moral basis of progressivism, or even Franklin Roosevelt as a personnel administrator. Morgan and his generation should provide continued interest for historians as we learn more about those early social scientists and socially minded engineers, about the reforming educators and the business community that often supported them, about the Utopian nature of the early planners, about the persistence of the idea of Utopia, and, on the negative side, about the paternalism of reformers and the basis for their racial views.

Morgan participated in all these aspects of his climate of opinion, and his writings can profitably be mined to broaden understanding of them. He ranks as a particular pioneer in education, social and economic planning, the study of Utopia, and eugenics. He was an avid participant, often with important roles, in the reform movements on behalf of peace, ecology, natural food, and planned communities. Altogether, he was a great reformer and a great moral conservative, and in understanding that combination one may well understand more about the progressive impulse that drove so many of his contemporaries.

That he never completely turned his vision into reality is evident from the record, but it is simply impossible not to express some admiration for the man who brought practical experience to the liberal arts; who built Norris, Tennessee, with all its idealism; who fought to save the ancient lands of the Seneca; and who crusaded on behalf of an impoverished village in remote India. It is equally impossible not to feel some sympathy for his failure to build that one Utopian model, out of all his attempts, that would prove to the world the possibility of life on a higher plane. It was the ideal community that was always his goal, and like New Harmony and Brook Farm before him, his Norris and Mitraniketan failed. Still, he pursued his dream with a remarkable relentlessness. Perhaps that refusal to admit defeat in the face of his failure is his most notable characteristic.

One last question: Is there any evidence that Morgan left a legacy? Yes, although it is faint. Norris Dam and the town of Norris still exist, and are well worth a stopover when passing through East Tennessee. In many ways Morgan's children continued his work. His daughter, Frances, married Landrum R. Bolling, who became president of Earlham College and chief executive of the Lilly Endowment, which supports higher education. His youngest son, Griscom, organized the intentional community (a term coined by him to replace *utopian society*) of "The Vale" outside Yellow Springs. He also continued the work of his father in Community Service, Inc. Ernest Morgan, son of Arthur Morgan and his first wife, founded the successful Antioch Bookplate Company. Ernest became a leader in calling for reform of burial styles, urging "simple burial," and he resided in another intentional community called Celo, near Burnsville, North Carolina. Arthur Morgan had arranged for the purchase of the Celo site in 1937 while at the TVA. There, Ernest's wife, Elizabeth, founded the Arthur E. Morgan School, in the tradition of progressive education, in 1963.[19] Probably the greatest contact the read-

19. Ernest Morgan, *A Manual of Simple Burial* (Burnsville, N.C.: The Celo Press, 1968); the story of the Arthur E. Morgan School is in Burton W. Gorman, *Education for Learning to Live Together* (Dubuque, Iowa: Wm. C. Brown Book Co., 1969). The latest information on the school can be found in a long article in the *Greensboro* (North Carolina) *News and Record*, May 18, 1986. The headline of a related article in the same issue claimed: "Arthur Morgan's visionary ideas live on in school and community."

er has with the Morgan leagacy is in the bookmarks made by the Antioch Bookplate Company, a proper Morganite small business in Yellow Springs. Virtually every bookstore has—usually near the checkout counter—a rack of these bookmarks, with their tassels and humorous, spiritual, and otherwise uplifting messages. Perhaps the reader will notice them somewhat differently in the future. Next time you see them, pause for a moment to remember their connection to the high ideals of Arthur Morgan, Utopian, of Antioch College in Yellow Springs in the 1920s, and of the town of Norris during the early years of the Tennessee Valley Authority.

Bibliographical Essay

For a look at Arthur Morgan and his problems at the Tennessee Valley Authority, two excellent sources are Thomas K. McCraw's *Morgan vs. Lilienthal: The Feud within the TVA* (Chicago: Loyola University Press, 1970) and *TVA and the Power Fight, 1933–1939* (New York: J. B. Lippincott Co., 1971). Not only does McCraw cover the intricacies of power policy and the several legal cases involving the TVA, but he examines the important manuscript collections, including the papers of George Fort Milton in the Library of Congress and of Harcourt A. Morgan in the University of Tennessee Library, Knoxville, Tennessee. Other significant archives are the papers of George W. Norris and Felix Frankfurter in the Library of Congress, while those most critical to McCraw, and to this present work, are the collections of Arthur E. Morgan, David E. Lilienthal, and Franklin D. Roosevelt.

Given the use of carbon paper, and even of photocopying machines, in the New Deal, these collections contain a fair amount of duplicaton, but each proved invaluable in a number of important instances. Morgan's papers are in the Olive Kettering Library, Antioch College, Yellow Springs, Ohio. Lilienthal's are in the Seeley G. Mudd Manuscript Library, Princeton University, Princeton, New Jersey; and Roosevelt's are in the Franklin D. Roosevelt Library, Hyde Park, New York. Other important documents are in the Tennessee Valley Authority's central files, at TVA headquarters in Knoxville, as well as in the TVA's technical library, also in Knoxville. Obviously, Morgan's papers at Antioch were the most crucial to this work. It appears that the Utopian rarely threw anything away, and his papers make it possible to trace the development of his thought, beginning with his early years. There are also a few Morgan papers, important to the Everglades episode, in the P. K. Yonge Library of Florida History, University of Florida Libraries, Gainesville, Florida. The Roosevelt Library is especially useful because it contains in addition to FDR's papers, those of some other important New Dealers, including Morris L. Cooke, Harry L. Hopkins, Louis B. Wehle, and Rexford G. Tugwell.

In terms of government documents that should be available in any large library, there are the TVA annual reports and the records of the several investigations involved in the Morgan story: U.S. Senate, *Everglades of Florida: Acts, Reports, and Other Papers, State and National, Relating to the Everglades of the State of Florida and their Reclamation* (Senate Document No. 82; 62nd Cong., 1st sess., 1911); U.S. House of Representatives, Committee on Expenditures in the Department of Agriculture, *Everglades of Florida, Hearings* (62nd Cong., 2nd sess., 1912); U.S. Congress, Joint Committee on the Investigation of the Tennessee Valley Authority, *Hearings, May 25–December 21, 1938* (Pursuant to Public Resolution No. 83. 14 parts; 75th Cong., 3rd sess., 1939); U.S. Congress, *Report, Together with the Minority Views of Mr. Davis, Mr. Jenkins, and Mr. Wolverton, and the Individual Views of Mr. Jenkins* (3 parts; 76th Cong., 1st sess., 1939); and U.S. President, *Removal of a Member of the Tennessee Valley Authority* (Senate Document no. 155; 75th Cong., 3rd sess., 1938). Except for the last, these hearings are important not so much for the testimony as for the documents entered into the record.

There are a number of older works on various aspects of the Tennessee Valley Authority that are well worth considering. Charles Herman Pritchett, *The Tennessee Valley Authority: A Study in Public Administration* (Chapel Hill: University of North Carolina Press, 1943) is such a study, as is Gordon R. Clapp, *TVA: An Approach to the Development of a Region* (Chicago: University of Chicago Press, 1955). Invaluable as a guide to understanding the long road to the creation of the TVA is Preston J. Hubbard's *Origins of the TVA: The Muscle Shoals Controversy, 1920–1932* (Nashville: Vanderbilt University Press, 1961; reprinted by Norton in 1968). Wilmon H. Droze, *High Dams and Slack Water: TVA Rebuilds a River* (Baton Rouge: Louisiana State University Press, 1965) examines the development of the Tennessee River for navigation, while Philip Selznick, *TVA and the Grass Roots: A Study in the Sociology of Formal Organization* (Berkeley: University of California Press, 1949), is a fascinating look at the agricultural program. The importance of Senator Norris to this entire story is included in Richard Lowitt's *George W. Norris: The Persistence of a Progressive, 1913–1933* (Urbana: University of Illinois Press, 1971) and *George W. Norris: The Triumph of a Progressive, 1933–1944* (Urbana: University of Illinois Press, 1978). Recent studies of the TVA are Marguerite Owen, *The Tennessee Valley Authority* (New York: Praeger Pubs., 1973), and the excellent work by Michael J. McDonald and John Muldowny, *TVA and the Dispossessed: The Resettlement of Population in the Norris Dam Area* (Knoxville: University of Tennessee Press, 1982). The latest broad look at the Authority is Erwin C. Hargrove and Paul K. Conkin (eds.), *TVA: Fifty Years of Grass-Roots Bureaucracy* (Urbana: University of Illinois Press, 1983). In terms of the general New Deal, an excellent survey is William E. Leuchtenburg, *Franklin D. Roosevelt and the New Deal, 1932–1940* (New York: Harper & Row, Pubs., 1963), while the best reference work is Otis L. Graham, Jr., and Meghan Robinson Wander (eds.), *Franklin D. Roosevelt, His Life and Times: An Encyclopedic View* (Boston: G. K. Hall & Co., 1985).

Harcourt A. Morgan has been largely neglected, except in Mouzon Peters, "The Story of Dr. Harcourt A. Morgan," book five of Louis D. Wallace (ed.), *Makers of Millions: Not for Themselves—But for You* (Nashville: Tennessee Department of Agriculture, 1951), and in Ellis F. Hartford, *Our Common Mooring* (Athens: University of Georgia Press, 1941). Lilienthal has received only slightly more attention. In addition to Willson Whitman, *David Lilienthal: Public Servant in a Power Age* (New York: Henry Holt and Co., 1948), it is best to turn to his own *The Journals of David E. Lilienthal* (3 vols.; New York: Harper and Row, 1964–1966); *TVA: Democracy on the March* (New York: Harper and Row Pubs., 1944); and *This I Do Believe* (New York: Harper and Brothers, 1949).

There are a number of studies on Arthur Morgan, all of them sympathetic. His wife Lucy Griscom Morgan produced the first: *Finding His World: The Story of Arthur E. Morgan* (Yellow Springs, Ohio: Kahoe and Co., 1928). Clarence J. Leuba, an Antioch psychologist, provided an interesting analysis in *A Road to Creativity, Arthur Morgan: Engineer, Educator, Administrator* (North Quincy, Mass.: Christopher Publishing House, 1971). Walter Kahoe contributed the most recent in *Arthur Morgan: A Biography and Memoir* (Moylan, Pa.: Whimsie Press, 1977). Also sympathetic were this writer's early works: Roy Talbert, Jr., "The Human Engineer: Arthur E. Morgan and the Launching of the Tennessee Valley Authority," M.A. thesis, Vanderbilt University, 1967; "Arthur E. Morgan's Ethical Code for the Tennessee Valley Authority," *East Tennessee Historical Society's Publications* (no. 40, 1968), 119–27; "Arthur E. Morgan's Social Philosophy and the Tennessee Valley Authority," *ibid.* (no. 41, 1969), 86–99; and "Beyond Pragmatism: The Story of Arthur E. Morgan," Ph.D. diss., Vanderbilt University, 1971.

Arthur Morgan was a prolific writer himself. His early engineering works include *A Preliminary Report on the St. Francis Valley Drainage Project in Northeastern Arkansas* (Washington: U.S. Government Printing Office, 1909); with S. H. McCrory, *Preliminary Report upon the Drainage of the Lands Overflowed by the North and Middle Forks of the Forked Deer River and the Rutherford Fork of the Obion River in Gibson County, Tennessee* (Nashville: 1910; available in the Morgan Papers); with S. H. McCrory and L. L. Hidinger, *A Preliminary Report on the Drainage of the Fifth Louisiana Levee District* (Washington: U.S. Government Printing Office, 1911); *Report on the St. Francis Valley Drainage Project in Northeastern Arkansas* (Washington: U.S. Government Printing Office, 1911); *Report of the Chief Engineer, Submitting a Plan for the Protection of the District from Flood Damage* (3 vols.; Dayton, Ohio: Miami Conservancy District, 1916); and *The Miami Valley and the 1913 Flood* (pt. 1 of the Miami Conservancy District's technical reports; Dayton: 1918; available in the Morgan Papers). Morgan's later works on engineering are *The Miami Conservancy District* (New York: McGraw Hill, 1951) and *Dams and Other Disasters: A Century of the Army Corps of Engineers in Civil Works* (Boston: Porter Sargent, 1971).

Morgan's works on Utopia are *Edward Bellamy* (New York: Columbia University Press, 1944); *The Philosophy of Edward Bellamy* (Morningside Heights, N.Y.: King's Crown Press, 1944); *Plagiarism in Utopia: A Study of the Continuity of the Utopian Tradition with Special Reference to Edward Bellamy's Looking Backward* (Yellow Springs, Ohio: published by the author, 1944, available in the Morgan Papers) and *Nowhere Was Somewhere: How History Makes Utopias and How Utopias Make History* (Chapel Hill: University of North Carolina Press, 1946). His works on education and community include *The Small Community, Foundation of Democratic Life: What It is and How to Achieve It* (New York: Harper and Brothers, 1942); *A Business of My Own* (Yellow Springs: Community Service, Inc., 1946); *The Rural University* (Sevagram, India: Hindustani Talimi Sangh, 1950); *The Community of the Future and the Future of Community* (Yellow Springs: Community Service, Inc., 1957); and *It Can Be Done in Education* (Yellow Springs: Community Service, Inc., 1962).

Although he never produced an autobiography, Morgan expressed his world view in a series of works: *My World* (Yellow Springs, Ohio: Kahoe and Co., 1928); *Purpose and Circumstance* (Yellow Springs: Kahoe and Co., 1928); *The Seed Man; or, Things in General* (Yellow Springs: Antioch Press, 1932); *The Long Road* (Washington: National Home Library Foundation, 1936; repr. by Community Service, Inc., Yellow Springs, 1962); and *Search for Purpose* (Yellow Springs: Antioch Press, 1955). *Observations* (Yellow Springs: Antioch Press, 1968) is composed of abstracts from his various writings, and *A Compendium of Antioch Notes* (Yellow Springs: Kahoe and Co., 1930) contains selections from *Antioch Notes*.

Morgan's last book was *The Making of the T.V.A.* (Buffalo, N.Y.: Prometheus Books, 1974). His other writings on the Tennessee Valley Authority date from the 1930s, when he wrote and spoke on it a great deal. Many of these were collected and bound in "Speeches and Remarks," two vols., and "Speeches and Writings," two vols., both in the TVA Technical Library, Knoxville, and also in the Morgan Papers at Antioch. He published a series on the TVA called "Bench-Marks in the

Tennessee Valley" in *Survey Graphic* 23 (January 1934), 5ff.; 23 (March 1934), 105ff.; 23 (May 1934), 233ff.; 23 (November 1934), 548ff.; 24 (March 1935), 112ff.; 24 (November 1935), 529ff.; 25 (April 1936), 236ff.; and 26 (February 1937), 73ff. Other important articles by Morgan on the TVA include "Planning in the Tennessee Valley," *Current History* 38 (September 1933), 663–68; "Tennessee Valley Authority," *Scientific Monthly* 38 (January 1934), 64–72; "Vitality and Formalism in Government," *Social Forces* 13 (October 1934), 1–6; "Next Four Years in the TVA," *New Republic* 89 (Jan. 6, 1936), 290–94; "Yardstick—and What Else?" *Saturday Evening Post* 210 (Aug. 7, 1937), 5–7, 77–81; and "Public Ownership of Power," *Atlantic Monthly* 160 (September 1937), 339–46. The *Atlantic Monthly* was an important outlet for Morgan well before the Tennessee Valley Authority: "Education: The Mastery of the Arts of Life," 121 (March 1918), 337–46; "New Light on Lincoln's Boyhood," 125 (February 1920), 208–18; "A Prospect," 129 (March 1922), 378–85; "What is College For?" 129 (May 1922), 642–50; "The Mississippi: Meeting a Mighty Problem," 140 (November 1927), 661–74; "Almus Pater: Antioch Introduces a Masculine Element into Higher Education," 143 (June 1929), 774–82.

Regarding progressivism, and Morgan in its context, the conservation mentality is surveyed in Samuel P. Hays, *Conservation and the Gospel of Efficiency: The Progressive Conservation Movement, 1890–1920* (Cambridge, Mass.: Harvard University Press, 1959), and in Michael James Lacey, "The Mysteries of Earth-Making Dissolve: A Study of Washington's Intellectual Community and the Origins of American Environmentalism in the Late Nineteenth Century," Ph.D. diss., George Washington University, 1979. Morgan is properly identified as a progressive engineer in Edwin T. Layton, Jr., *The Revolt of the Engineers: Social Responsibility and the American Engineering Profession* (Cleveland: The Press of Case Western Reserve University, 1971). Jean B. Quandt's *From the Small Town to the Great Community: The Social Thought of Progressive Intellectuals* (New Brunswick, N.J.: Rutgers University Press, 1970) discusses the importance of a sense of community, and what it meant to several progressives who were much like Morgan. Considerable attention is given to Morgan and another dominant theme in his thought in David E. Shi, *The Simple Life: Plain Living and High Thinking in American Culture* (New York: Oxford University Press, 1985).

Progressive education is illuminated in Lawrence A. Cremin, *The Transformation of the School: Progressivism in American Education, 1876–1957* (New York: Knopf, 1961), and in Patricia Albjerg Graham, *Progressive Education: From Arcady to Academe, a History of the Progressive Education*

Association, 1919–1955 (New York: Teachers College Press, 1967). Morgan's Moraine Park School is considered in Lloyd Marcus, "The Founding of American Private Progressive Schools, 1912–1921," senior honors thesis, Harvard College, 1948. The Arthur E. Morgan School in Celo, North Carolina, is described in Burton W. Gorman, *Education for Learning to Live Together* (Dubuque, Iowa: Wm. C. Brown Co., 1969). Also valuable is Harvard Forrest Vallance, "A History of Antioch College," Ph.D. diss., Ohio State University, 1936. Surveys of the eugenics movement include Mark H. Haller, *Eugenics: Hereditarian Attitudes in American Thought* (New Brunswick, N.J.: Rutgers University Press, 1963); Donald K. Pickens, *Eugenics and the Progressives* (Nashville: Vanderbilt University Press, 1968); and Daniel J. Kevles, *In the Name of Eugenics: Genetics and the Uses of Human Heredity* (New York: Alfred A. Knopf, 1985).

The tenuous link of progressivism to the New Deal is the topic of Otis L. Graham, Jr., in *An Encore for Reform: The Old Progressives and the New Deal* (New York: Oxford University Press, 1967). The story of public electricity proponent Morris L. Cooke is told in Kenneth E. Morris, *The Life and Times of a Happy Liberal: A Biography of Morris Llewellyn Cooke* (New York: Harper and Brothers, 1954), and in Jean Christie, *Morris Llewellyn Cooke: Progressive Engineer* (New York: Garland Pub., Inc., 1983). Judson King's memoir, *The Conservation Fight: From Theodore Roosevelt to the Tennessee Valley Authority* (Washington: Public Affairs Press, 1959) is also useful, as is D. Clayton Brown, *Electricity for Rural America: The Fight for the REA* (Westport, Conn.: Greenwood Press, 1980), and Joseph G. Knapp, *The Advance of American Cooperative Enterprise, 1920–1945* (Danville, Ill.: Interstate Printers & Publishing, Inc., 1973). Helpful examinations of Roosevelt prior to his presidency are Geoffrey C. Ward, *Before the Trumpet: Young Franklin Roosevelt, 1882–1905* (New York: Harper & Row, Pubs., 1985), and Bernard Bellush, *Franklin D. Roosevelt as Governor of New York* (New York: Columbia University Press, 1955). James M. Cox, *Journey Through My Years* (New York: Simon and Schuster, 1946), is the autobiography of the man who was governor of Ohio during the Miami Conservancy project and the apparent source of Arthur Morgan's nomination to head the TVA. Few New Dealers wrote about the TVA, but those who did, and then sparingly, include James A. Farley, *Behind the Ballots: The Personal History of a Politician* (New York: Harcourt, Brace and Co., 1938); Harold L. Ickes, *The Secret Diary of Harold L. Ickes* (3 vols.; New York: Simon and Schuster, 1953–1954); Francis Biddle, *In Brief Authority* (Garden City, N.Y.: Doubleday and Company, 1962); Donald Richberg, *My Hero: The Indiscreet Memoirs of an*

Eventful but Unheroic Life (New York: G. P. Putnam's Sons, 1954); and Louis B. Wehle, *Hidden Threads of History: Wilson Through Roosevelt* (New York: Macmillan Co., 1953).

Of the many contemporary articles on the TVA, two of the most interesting are Walter E. Myer's "learning unit for schools" in "The Tennessee Valley Looks to the Future," *National Education Association Journal* 23 (December 1934), 233–48, and the anonymous "TVA I: Work in the Valley," *Fortune* 11 (May 1935), 92–98ff. The fullest description of the Norris school is Glenn Kendall, "Experience in Developing a Community Program of Education," *Social Forces* 19 (October 1940), 48–51. Floyd W. Reeves described the adult education program in "T.V.A. Training," *Adult Education* 7 (January 1935), 48–52. A broader glimpse of Norris appears in Charles Stevenson, "A Contrast in 'Perfect' Towns," *Nation's Business* 25 (December 1937), 18–20, while an evaluation can be found in Larston D. Farrar, "Norris, Tennessee: An Abandoned Experiment," *Public Utilities Fortnightly* 40 (Nov. 20, 1947), 686–92. Norris may be compared to other New Deal communities described in Paul K. Conkin, *Tomorrow a New World: The New Deal Community Program* (Ithaca, N.Y.: Cornell University Press, 1959).

Index

DATE DUE